Quantum Macroeconomics

Quantum Macroeconomics presents a new paradigm in macroeconomic analysis initiated by Bernard Schmitt. It explains the historical origin, the analytical contents, and the actual relevance of this new paradigm, with respect to current major economic issues at national and international level. These issues concern both advanced and emerging market economies, referring to inflation, unemployment, financial instability, and economic crises.

In the first part of this volume, leading scholars explain the historical origin and analytical content of quantum macroeconomics. The second part explores its relevance with respect to the current major economic issues such as the sovereign debt crisis and European monetary union. The volume also features two previously unpublished papers by Bernard Schmitt. The main findings of this book concern the need to go beyond agents' behaviour to understand the structural origin of a variety of macroeconomic problems, notably, inflation, unemployment, financial instability, and economic crises. The originality that pervades all contributions is plain, when one considers the lack of any structural explanation of national and international economic disorders in the literature within the mainstream approach to economics.

This edited volume is of great interest to those who study macroeconomics, monetary economics, and money and banking.

Jean-Luc Bailly is Emeritus Associate Professor of Economics, University of Burgundy, Dijon, France.

Alvaro Cencini is Full Professor of Economics, University of Lugano, Switzerland.

Sergio Rossi is Full Professor of Economics, University of Fribourg, Switzerland.

Routledge Frontiers of Political Economy

For a full list of titles in this series please visit www.routledge.com/books/series/SE0345

209. Structural Analysis and the Process of Economic Development
Edited by Jonas Ljungberg

210. Economics and Power
A Marxist critique
Giulio Palermo

211. Neoliberalism and the Moral Economy of Fraud
Edited by David Whyte and Jörg Wiegratz

212. Theoretical Foundations of Macroeconomic Policy
Growth, productivity and public finance
Edited by Giovanni Di Bartolomeo and Enrico Saltari

213. Heterodox Islamic Economics
The emergence of an ethico-economic theory
Ishaq Bhatti and Masudul Alam Choudhury

214. Intimate Economies of Immigration Detention
Critical perspectives
Edited by Deirdre Conlon and Nancy Hiemstra

215. Qualitative Methods in Economics
Mirjana Radović-Marković and Beatrice Avolio Alecchi

216. Quantum Macroeconomics
The legacy of Bernard Schmitt
Edited by Jean-Luc Bailly, Alvaro Cencini and Sergio Rossi

217. Creative Research in Economics
Arnold Wentzel

Quantum Macroeconomics
The legacy of Bernard Schmitt

**Edited by Jean-Luc Bailly,
Alvaro Cencini and Sergio Rossi**

LONDON AND NEW YORK

First published 2017
by Routledge
2 Park Square, Milton Park, Abingdon, Oxon OX14 4RN

and by Routledge
711 Third Avenue, New York, NY 10017

Routledge is an imprint of the Taylor & Francis Group, an informa business

© 2017 selection and editorial matter, Jean-Luc Bailly, Alvaro Cencini and Sergio Rossi; individual chapters, the contributors

The right of Jean-Luc Bailly, Alvaro Cencini and Sergio Rossi to be identified as the authors of the editorial material, and of the authors for their individual chapters, has been asserted in accordance with sections 77 and 78 of the Copyright, Designs and Patents Act 1988.

All rights reserved. No part of this book may be reprinted or reproduced or utilised in any form or by any electronic, mechanical, or other means, now known or hereafter invented, including photocopying and recording, or in any information storage or retrieval system, without permission in writing from the publishers.

Trademark notice: Product or corporate names may be trademarks or registered trademarks, and are used only for identification and explanation without intent to infringe.

British Library Cataloguing in Publication Data
A catalogue record for this book is available from the British Library

Library of Congress Cataloging in Publication Data
Names: Bailly, J.-L. (Jean-Luc), editor. | Cencini, Alvaro, editor. | Rossi, Sergio, 1967- editor.
Title: Quantum macroeconomics : the legacy of Bernard Schmitt / edited by Jean-Luc Bailly, Alvaro Cencini and Sergio Rossi.
Description: Abingdon, Oxon ; New York, NY : Routledge, 2017.
Identifiers: LCCN 2016015198| ISBN 9781138186088 (hardback) | ISBN 9781315644059 (ebook)
Subjects: LCSH: Macroeconomics. | Money. | Quantum logic. | Schmitt, Bernard.
Classification: LCC HB172.5 .Q36 2017 | DDC 339--dc23
LC record available at https://lccn.loc.gov/2016015198

ISBN: 978-1-138-18608-8 (hbk)
ISBN: 978-1-315-64405-9 (ebk)

Typeset in Times New Roman
by Saxon Graphics Ltd, Derby

Printed and bound by CPI Group (UK) Ltd, Croydon, CR0 4YY

To the memory of Bernard Schmitt, our master and friend

Contents

List of figures	ix
List of tables	xi
Notes on contributors	xiii
Preface	xvii
Acknowledgements	xxix

**Introduction: the research work and scientific legacy of
Bernard Schmitt**   **1**
ALVARO CENCINI

**PART I
Analysing the domestic economy**   21

1   *La formation du pouvoir d'achat*: a historical perspective   23
CLAUDE GNOS

2   Absolute exchange and relative exchange   33
JEAN-LUC BAILLY

3   Inflation and unemployment   50
XAVIER BRADLEY

4   A macroeconomic analysis of unemployment   64
BERNARD SCHMITT

5   National banking reform   85
ALVARO CENCINI

viii *Contents*

PART II
Analysing the international economy 103

6 **From reparations to (net) interest payments on external debt: same script, different cast** 105
EDOARDO BERETTA

7 **Keynes's and Schumacher's plans and the failed attempt to understand international monetary relations** 122
NADIA F. PIFFARETTI

8 **European monetary union** 135
SERGIO ROSSI

9 **The sovereign debt crisis** 144
ALVARO CENCINI

10 **A one-country reform: the solution to the sovereign debt crisis** 158
BERNARD SCHMITT

Afterword: Bernard Schmitt and heterodox economics **173**
SERGIO ROSSI

Bibliography 181
Index 192

Figures

4.1	The production of the first two sectors	75
6.1	Net interest on external debt versus reparations: the previous-loan difference	107
6.2	The identity relation between commercial/financial imports and exports	117
6.3	The disequilibrium after servicing (net) interest on external debt (1)	118
6.4	The disequilibrium after servicing (net) interest on external debt (2)	118
6.5	Re-establishing the identity relation after the service of (net) interest on external debt (1)	119
6.6	Rc-establishing the identity relation after the service of (net) interest on external debt (2)	119
9.1	The two loans required to finance the real and monetary payments of A's net imports	150
10.1	A's production before and after the reform	170

Tables

5.1	The payment of wages as entered in Departments I and II	90
5.2	The evolution of loanable funds within period p_0	91
5.3	Bookkeeping entries at the end of period p_0	92
5.4	The investment of profit in the absence of Department III	94
5.5	The transfer of invested profit in Department III	95
5.6	The production of fixed-capital goods	96
6.1	The reimbursement of interest on external debt: the Brazilian case (billion US dollars)	114
6.2	Public debt *versus* external debt: the German case	120

Notes on contributors

Jean-Luc Bailly is Emeritus Associate Professor of Economics at the University of Burgundy in Dijon, France. He is a member of the Centre for Monetary and Financial Studies at the University of Burgundy and of the Research Laboratory in Monetary Economics at the University of Lugano, Switzerland. His research interests are in the area of monetary macroeconomics and history of economic thought. He has contributed several chapters to books and published papers in academic journals. Among his publications are: "Le modèle IS–LM en économie fermée" and "L'équilibre macroéconomique en économie ouverte", in M. Montoussé (ed.), *Macroéconomie* (Bréal, 2006), "La pensée économique de Keynes", in M. Montoussé (ed.), *Histoire de la pensée économique* (Bréal, 2008), "Consumption, investment and the investment multiplier", in C. Gnos and L.-P. Rochon (eds), *The Keynesian Multiplier* (Routledge, 2008), "Saving, firms' self-financing, and fixed-capital formation in the monetary circuit", in J.-F. Ponsot and S. Rossi (eds), *The Political Economy of Monetary Circuits: Tradition and Change in Post-Keynesian Economics* (Palgrave Macmillan, 2009), "From over-investment to households' over-indebtedness", *European Journal of Economic and Social Systems* (2010), "Labour, wages, and non-wage incomes", in C. Gnos and S. Rossi (eds), *Modern Monetary Macroeconomics: A New Paradigm for Economic Policy* (Edward Elgar, 2012).

Edoardo Beretta is Postdoctoral Researcher in the Faculty of Economics at the University of Lugano, Switzerland, and Adjunct Professor at Franklin University Switzerland. His interests lie in the fields of monetary macroeconomics, as he has analysed historical episodes like the German war debt problem, the ongoing debate on the international monetary order, and the effects of various exchange-rate regimes. Germany and the German economic literature are a significant source of inspiration for his research work. Recently, he has focused his attention on the euro area and on the analysis of contemporary economic policies, which also comprise minimum wages, payment methods, and the (reform of the) approach to work in the twenty-first century. His main research results have been published in international journals such as *Applied Economics Quarterly*, *Jahrbuch für die Ordnung von Wirtschaft und Gesellschaft, Kredit und Kapital* and *Spanish Journal of Economics and Finance*.

xiv *Contributors*

Xavier Bradley is Associate Professor of Economics at the University of Burgundy in Dijon, France. He is a member of the Centre for Monetary and Financial Studies at the University of Burgundy and of the Research Laboratory in Monetary Economics at the University of Lugano, Switzerland. His publications include: "From Keynes to the modern analysis of inflation", in M. Baranzini and A. Cencini (eds), *Inflation and Unemployment: Contributions to a New Macroeconomic Approach* (Routledge, 1996), "Taux d'intérêt et 'propriétés fondamentales' de la monnaie", in P. Piégay and L.-P. Rochon (eds), *Théories monétaires post Keynésiennes* (Economica, 2003), "Involuntary unemployment and investment", in L.-P. Rochon and S. Rossi (eds), *Modern Theories of Money: The Nature and Role of Money in Capitalist Economies* (Edward Elgar, 2003), "The investment multiplier and income saving", in C. Gnos and L.-P. Rochon (eds), *The Keynesian Multiplier* (Routledge, 2008).

Alvaro Cencini is Full Professor of Economics at the University of Lugano, Switzerland, where he holds the Chair of Monetary Economics. He is also the Director of the Research Laboratory in Monetary Economics at the Centre for Banking Studies in Lugano, and an external member of the Centre for Monetary and Financial Studies at the University of Burgundy in Dijon, France. He has a D.Phil. from the University of Fribourg and a Ph.D. from the London School of Economics. Among his main publications are: *Time and the Macroeconomic Analysis of Income* (Pinter Publishers and St. Martin's Press, 1984, reprinted 2013 by Bloomsbury), *Money, Income and Time* (Pinter Publishers, 1988, reprinted 2013 by Bloomsbury), *External Debt Servicing: A Vicious Circle* (Pinter Publishers, 1991, co-authored with Bernard Schmitt), *Monetary Theory, National and International* (Routledge, 1995, reprinted 1997), *Inflation and Unemployment: Contributions to a New Macroeconomic Approach* (Routledge 1996, co-edited with Mauro Baranzini), *Monetary Macroeconomics: A New Approach* (Routledge, 2001, reprinted 2014), *Macroeconomic Foundations of Macroeconomics* (Routledge 2005, reprinted 2007), *Economic and Financial Crises: A New Macroeconomic Analysis* (Palgrave Macmillan, 2015, co-authored with Sergio Rossi). He is also the author of several contributions to books and peer-reviewed journals.

Claude Gnos is Emeritus Associate Professor of Economics at the University of Burgundy in Dijon, France. He is the author of *L'euro* (Management et Société, 1998) and *Les grands auteurs en économie* (Management et Société, 2000), and co-editor, with Louis-Philippe Rochon, of *Post-Keynesian Principles of Economic Policy* (Edward Elgar, 2005), *The Keynesian Multiplier* (Routledge, 2008), *Monetary Policy and Financial Stability: A Post-Keynesian Agenda* (Edward Elgar, 2008), *Employment, Growth and Development: A Post-Keynesian Approach* (Edward Elgar, 2010) and *Credit, Money and Macroeconomic Policy* (Edward Elgar, 2011). He is also co-editor, with Sergio Rossi, of *Modern Monetary Macroeconomics* (Edward Elgar, 2012). He has also published a number of articles on monetary economics, circuit theory, and the history of economic thought in books and in refereed journals such as *Economie Appliquée, Economies et Sociétés, History of Economic Ideas, International Journal of Political Economy, Journal of Post Keynesian Economics, Revue d'Economie Politique, Review of Political Economy.*

Nadia F. Piffaretti is Senior Economist at the World Bank Group in Washington, DC. She has a D.Phil. (2000) from the University of Fribourg, Switzerland. She is a member of the Research Laboratory in Monetary Economics at the University of Lugano, Switzerland, and of the American Economic Association. Her research interests are in the area of macroeconomic systems, international systems, and post-conflict economic recovery. She held the position of Senior Country Economist for Zimbabwe at the World Bank, and has published peer-reviewed articles on monetary macroeconomics in *Review of Banks and Bank Systems, European Journal of Economic and Social Systems, International Journal of Humanities and Social Sciences,* and in the *World Bank Policy Research Working Papers.*

Sergio Rossi is Full Professor of Economics at the University of Fribourg, Switzerland, where he holds the Chair of Macroeconomics and Monetary Economics. He has a D.Phil. (1996) from the University of Fribourg and a Ph.D. (2000) from the University of London (University College). His publications include *Money and Inflation: A New Macroeconomic Analysis* (Edward Elgar, 2001, reprinted 2003), *Modern Theories of Money: The Nature and Role of Money in Capitalist Economies* (Edward Elgar, 2003, co-edited with Louis-Philippe Rochon), *Monetary and Exchange Rate Systems: A Global View of Financial Crises* (Edward Elgar, 2006, co-edited with Louis-Philippe Rochon), *Money and Payments in Theory and Practice* (Routledge, 2007), *Macroéconomie monétaire: théories et politiques* (Bruylant, LGDJ and Schulthess, 2008), *The Political Economy of Monetary Circuits: Tradition and Change in Post-Keynesian Economics* (Palgrave Macmillan, 2009, co-edited with Jean-François Ponsot), *Modern Monetary Macroeconomics* (Edward Elgar, 2012, co-edited with Claude Gnos), *Economic and Financial Crises: A New Macroeconomic Analysis* (Palgrave Macmillan, 2015, co-authored with Alvaro Cencini), and *The Encyclopedia of Central Banking* (Edward Elgar, 2015, co-edited with Louis-Philippe Rochon). He has also published many peer-reviewed articles on monetary macroeconomics in *L'Actualité Economique: Revue d'Analyse Economique, China–USA Business Review, European Journal of Economic and Social Systems, International Journal of Monetary Economics and Finance, International Journal of Pluralism and Economics Education, International Journal of Political Economy, International Journal of Trade and Global Markets, International Review of Applied Economics, Intervention: European Journal of Economics and Economic Policies, Investigación Económica, Journal of Asian Economics, Journal of Philosophical Economics, Journal of Post Keynesian Economics, Public Choice, Review of Keynesian Economics, Review of Political Economy,* xvi *Contributors*

Studi Economici, Studi e Note di Economia, and in the *Swiss Journal of Economics and Statistics*.

Bernard Schmitt was Emeritus Full Professor of Economics at the University of Fribourg, Switzerland, and at the University of Burgundy in Dijon, France, where he held the Chairs of Macroeconomics and Monetary Economics. He was also co-Director of the Research Laboratory in Monetary Economics at the Centre for Banking Studies in Lugano, Switzerland. He obtained a Ph.D. from the University of Paris-Panthéon-Sorbonne and was a member of the French National Centre for Scientific Research (CNRS) from 1984 to 1994. For his research work he was awarded a bronze medal and a silver medal by the CNRS in 1961 and in 1973. His publications include: *La formation du pouvoir d'achat* (Sirey, 1960), *Monnaie, salaires et profits* (Presses Universitaires de France, 1966), *L'analyse macroéconomique des revenus* (Dalloz, 1971), *Macroeconomic Theory: A Fundamental Revision* (Castella, 1972), *New Proposals for World Monetary Reform* (Castella, 1973), *Théorie unitaire de la monnaie, nationale et internationale* (Castella, 1975), *La monnaie européenne* (Presses Universitaires de France, 1977), *Inflation, chômage et malformations du capital* (Castella and Economica, 1984), *L'ECU et les souverainetés nationales en Europe* (Dunod, 1988), *External Debt Servicing: A Vicious Circle* (Pinter Publishers, 1991, co-authored with Alvaro Cencini). He also contributed to numerous books published by Blackwell, Edward Elgar, Macmillan, and Routledge.

Preface

Jean-Luc Bailly, Alvaro Cencini and Sergio Rossi

Born in Colmar (France) in 1929, Bernard Schmitt began his scientific career in 1954 when he became a member of the *Centre National de la Recherche Scientifique* (CNRS). Before completing his PhD in Paris, he spent a year in Cambridge (United Kingdom), working under the supervision of Dennis Robertson and Piero Sraffa. It was in the early 1950s that, reading Keynes's *General Theory*, Schmitt discovered his passion for macroeconomics and had his first intuition about the logical laws (identities) on which it rests. After that, he devoted the whole of his life to the development of a new analysis, known as 'quantum macroeconomics', which throws an entirely new light on the principles on which economic theory should be based. His lifelong work, for which he was awarded two medals by the CNRS, led to an astonishing number of manuscripts, the most important of which were published as books and articles, in both French and English, and some were translated into German, Spanish, Italian, and Portuguese. He was Full Professor at the University of Burgundy in Dijon (France) and at the University of Fribourg (Switzerland). His courses were the best example of his boundless dedication to scientific analysis, as well as of his capacity to galvanize students with the depth, intensity, and logical rigour of his thought.

This volume presents a new paradigm in macroeconomics initiated and developed by Schmitt in his long-lasting scientific career, which ended with his death on 26 March 2014. Paying grateful tribute to him, a selected number of authors working in this school of thought explain in this co-edited book the historical origin, the analytical content, and the actual relevance of this new paradigm with respect to the current major macroeconomic issues at national and international level. Their contributions were first presented in a research seminar, which took place at the University of Burgundy (France) on 20 June 2014 to commemorate the passing away of master and friend Bernard Schmitt. The objective of this book is to provide a survey, as well as a comprehensive understanding, of Schmitt's 'quantum macroeconomic approach', inviting readers to elaborate on it by reading the writings of Schmitt himself, whose relevance to addressing contemporary macroeconomic issues with a view to solving their major structural problems remains intact, as a perusal of this book will show. Several of Schmitt's writings are available in PDF form at www.quantum-macroeconomics.info/bibliography to download for free.

xviii *Jean-Luc Bailly, Alvaro Cencini and Sergio Rossi*

The volume starts with an introduction on Bernard Schmitt's research work and scientific legacy, where the reader is introduced to Schmitt's most relevant contributions to monetary macroeconomics. The writings chosen from among his numerous publications are those that best epitomize the main steps of Schmitt's investigation into the realm of macroeconomics, starting from his first analyses of money and its purchasing power up to his last analysis of countries' sovereign debt. While a central place is reserved for Schmitt's masterpieces – *Monnaie, salaires et profits* (1966a), *Théorie unitaire de la monnaie, nationale et internationale* (1975a), *Inflation, chômage et malformations du capital* (1984a), and *The formation of sovereign debt: diagnosis and remedy* (2014) – emphasis is also put on some of his less well-known contributions, the reading of which is nonetheless essential for a better understanding of his development of quantum macroeconomics. The aim of the introduction to this volume is to provide an overview of Schmitt's innovative work that may guide the reader along the path followed by the great French economist, and help the reader in the sometimes difficult task of remaining faithful to Schmitt's revolutionary message.

The contributed chapters forming this volume are structured into two parts. Part I deals with the quantum macroeconomic analysis of domestic economies. It represents both an essential step to understanding the workings of monetary economies of production and thus the origin of Schmitt's own analysis of the structural (instead of behavioural) factors of the two major macroeconomic disorders, namely inflation and unemployment, affecting any national economy. The first part ends, therefore, with a chapter presenting the reform advocated by Schmitt in order to dispose of both of these disorders eventually. Part II is the second step in Schmitt's quantum macroeconomic analysis, as it investigates in depth the structural problems of the international economy, which is the economic space that, in fact, exists between countries – hence a pure exchange economy, since all produced goods and services are the result of national economies. After addressing a number of issues at international level, this part ends with an analysis of the sovereign debt crisis and suggests an original way out of it, which each country will be able to put into practice itself – without the need to strive for an international agreement, as the latter remains utopian at the time of writing as well as for the foreseeable future.

In the first chapter, Claude Gnos explains that the analysis of money and the formation and spending of its purchasing power have been centre stage in Schmitt's work. As shown also by all other contributions gathered in this volume, Schmitt developed his thoughts on that topic and the approach to macroeconomics it involved all through his work, in connection with the examination of real-world issues like inflation, involuntary unemployment, the reform of the international monetary system, European integration, and the sovereign debt crisis. The first chapter focuses, therefore, on the former analysis, in order to put it in a historical perspective with regard to the development of Schmitt's original thinking and to the history of economic thought. To begin with, Gnos refers to Schmitt's (1960) first book, precisely entitled *La formation du pouvoir d'achat*. In the introduction to this book, Schmitt explained that he was puzzled by the equations that Keynes

Preface xix

(1936) introduced in *The General Theory*, namely (1) income = consumption + investment, and (2) saving = income − consumption. According to Schmitt, the concepts of consumption featuring in both these equations should not be confused. Otherwise, the two equations would contradict each other. This means then, as Schmitt argued, that the formation of national income should be clearly distinguished from its spending. Income, that is, the purchasing power of money, is formed in the payment of the remuneration of the factors producing consumption and investment goods (Equation 1), and spent on the goods thereby produced (Equation 2). This questioning of Keynes's equations by the founder of quantum macroeconomics has indeed been a starting point for a fundamental revision of macroeconomic theory. Further, Gnos examines the scope of this revision with respect to the standard interpretations of the Keynesian revolution. In particular, this revision shed new light on debates then prevailing about the relationship between saving and investment and about the relevance and meaning of Say's law. It also questioned the relevance of the Keynesian multiplier and of the theory of national income determination expounded in the writings of Keynesian authors like Samuelson. Gnos argues that the analogy usually made between price and income determination proves flawed. In the same way, the static and dynamic analyses of national income expounded at length in textbooks are invalidated and the principle of effective demand is reinterpreted. Elaborating on this, Gnos sets Schmitt's insights on money and its purchasing power in the context of the historical development of the theory of money. As a matter of fact, Schmitt committed himself to situate his own theory in relation to the history of monetary theorizing. He notably examined Ricardo's theory of money and the theories of the neoclassical school of thought. He pointed at the failures of all these economic theories. He notably overturned the quantity theory of money and was able to reject both the Keynesian flow analysis and the Walrasian analysis of the money stock. Schmitt was indeed convinced that it is because it was flawed that the classical theory of money prepared for the advent of the marginalist approach that, in turn, paved the way for a new conception of money and its purchasing power.

The second chapter, written by Jean-Luc Bailly, starts from a crucial point on which the vast majority of economists agree, namely the assumption that an economic transaction consists of a reciprocal transfer of wealth that agents would carry out between them in the marketplace. This is the main reason why these economists describe our economies as market-based systems, as if producing consisted of reciprocal transfers of goods and services. Indeed, they take it for granted, so that it does not merit any discussion, that economic activity is based on exchange of various endowments between individuals. In this hypothetical world, where everything is given and already distributed, exchanges are explicitly designed as being 'naturally' relative: they occur without the (need for) use of money. In the 1930s, rejecting these models of a 'real-exchange economy', which he criticized as being unrealistic, Keynes opened a new analytical way by suggesting developing 'a monetary theory of production' truly integrating money into economic activity. However, even though Keynes denies any relevance to the notion of relative exchange, he does not explicitly provide an alternative concept.

xx   *Jean-Luc Bailly, Alvaro Cencini and Sergio Rossi*

It is to Schmitt that we owe the discovery of the truly absolute nature of exchange in our wage economies. He shows indeed that production is a monetary phenomenon the result of which is the unity of physical output with its monetary form. In other words, output and income are the two faces of the same economic object. In his chapter, Bailly discusses first the meaning of the words 'exchange' and 'payment'. These two words are often used interchangeably to describe the transactions carried out in any kind of market. However, in his theoretical analysis of monetary emissions, Schmitt demonstrates that money is neither a commodity nor an asset. Money being an acknowledgement of debt issued by banks, it cannot be exchanged against physical products. It follows that payments do not consist of reciprocal transfers of commodities. The two words are not synonyms: a payment is not a relative exchange, because the payer does not transmit his income in payment, and the payee does not receive, therefore, the income spent by the payer. Referring to this analysis, Bailly explains that each producer, while he necessarily fits into the general division of labour and works to the needs of the community, first produces wealth for himself. As a logical result, all transactions in any markets are absolute exchanges. Although it partakes of generalized exchange, any payment concerns each income holder and is, therefore, immediately macroeconomic in nature. Hence, the introduction of the concept of absolute exchange in the theoretical corpus induces one to abandon methodological individualism and the idea that macroeconomic phenomena would be based on the behaviour of individuals carrying out relative exchanges.

Chapter 3, contributed by Xavier Bradley, elaborates on this. It explains that, as with all his studies of economic phenomena, Schmitt based his original analysis of inflation and unemployment on his ground-breaking conception of money and payments. In line with the great theories of unemployment, it is in the process of capital accumulation that Schmitt found the origin of inflation and unemployment. However, to identify truly structural causes, he departed from the tradition by discarding entirely any explanation based on individual or collective behaviour, for instance wrong expectations or rejection of market conditions. Schmitt also demonstrated that, contrary to the conventional view, inflation and unemployment are not polarized opposite disorders between which one would have to find the right blend; instead, he showed that they are two phases of the same process. To start with, Bradley presents the analysis of the process of capital accumulation developed by Schmitt. This study is founded on the circuit of incomes, more specifically the circuit of profits inserted into the primary circuit. With respect to the dysfunctions of modern economies, the key operation is the investment of profits: it is at this stage that, to use Schmitt expression, 'the malformation of capital' will take place. Because the nature of investment is not yet recognized, the accounting system does not currently allow for any specific recording of the payments involved in capital formation. Consequently, when profits are invested, their spending causes the fusion of two different circuits of incomes; in other words, the destruction of profits interferes with the formation of new incomes that then become defective. In the process, no direct payment will relate capital to households: in spite of the legal links to shareholders, capital then becomes

Preface xxi

autonomous; as a consequence, all ulterior payments involving this capital will by-pass households, specifically the owners of the firms. Further, Bradley shows that it is during the last phase of the capital cycle, that is to say, capital amortization, that the dysfunctional nature of accumulation will become apparent. Initially, amortization is carried out through a process of capital over-accumulation: for each unit of capital to be replaced, another unit of product must be newly invested. This is where inflation takes place: the units of income affected by the induced investment are effectively emptied of their content in the very process of their formation. Schmitt showed that this over-accumulation channel of amortization cannot be maintained indefinitely as such a process reduces the share of the incomes available for the formation of interest thereby provoking a fall in the profitability of capital. When this situation occurs, firms will lend their profits through the financial system, but this will imply abandoning the production of goods intended for induced investment and thereby causing (involuntary) unemployment. Bradley concludes with some preliminary considerations on the reform elaborated by Schmitt to prevent the recurrence of both inflation and unemployment, which is investigated in Chapter 5.

Before presenting the normative analysis developed by Schmitt, however, Chapter 4, derived from a manuscript written by Schmitt himself in 1998, offers a macroeconomic analysis of unemployment. In this chapter, Schmitt reconsiders the problem of unemployment through a macroeconomic analysis emphasizing the distinction into three sectors affecting national economies in today's capitalistic regime. This factual distinction is the result of the pathological lending by banks of the deposits formed following the investment of profits. Indeed, quantum macroeconomic analysis shows that, in the present system of fixed-capital accumulation, invested profits are still available on the financial market in the form of bank deposits originating from their expenditure (of profits) on the labour market. Although profit is a macroeconomic income derived from wages, today's economic systems are such that it is also added to them. The origin of the pathology leading to inflation and involuntary unemployment is to be found in the fact that profits – formed on the product market and spent on the labour market – are issued once again on the financial market and feed a banking loan granted to the set of households. More precisely, the emission taking place through the loan granted by banks to households is an emission of wages, because profit can but be derived from wages. The existence of sectors is explained by this macroeconomic loan in favour of households. The emission of profits on the financial market increases the amount of income households can spend and enables them to face the rise in value of produced goods and services caused by the transformation of the increase in the physical productivity of labour. The aim of this chapter is to clarify the terms of this new analysis, showing that the rise in income does not avoid the loss of fixed capital by income holders. Nor does it avoid all the consequences deriving from its appropriation by 'depersonalized' firms. If the production of wage-goods in the first sector, that of investment- and interest-goods in the second sector, and that of amortization-goods in the third sector do not directly give rise to unemployment, the constant growth of fixed capital and the need for its remuneration lead

xxii *Jean-Luc Bailly, Alvaro Cencini and Sergio Rossi*

unavoidably to it. The analysis that Schmitt advocates in this chapter converges with the one developed by him in *Inflation, chômage et malformations du capital* (Schmitt 1984a) in explaining unemployment by referring to the decreasing rate of profit imposed by the process of fixed-capital over-accumulation characterizing the actual economic regime worldwide. Yet, while the Schmitt 1984 analysis explains the pathological working of our economies in terms of value, the one offered here explains it in terms of prices, and emphasizes the role played by banks as financial intermediaries, thereby providing a further endorsement of the reform based on the distinction between three banking departments presented in the next chapter.

Written by Alvaro Cencini, the fifth chapter ends indeed the first part of this volume. It presents thereby the national banking reform advocated by Schmitt to eradicate both the problem of inflation and that of involuntary unemployment elicited thereby. The chapter aims at answering two questions. What are the principles of the banking reform required for the system of national payments to be monetarily neutral, that is to say, to avoid the formation of inflation and involuntary unemployment? And what are the mechanisms enabling their implementation? This chapter provides an answer to these two questions by referring to Schmitt's analysis and proposal advocated in his 1984 book on inflation and unemployment. In short, the changes that must be introduced in the way payments are entered into banks' ledgers are dictated by the bookkeeping nature of bank money and by the substantial, factual distinction between money, income, and capital. It is because monetary and financial circuits must be kept rigorously separated that an issue department needs to be distinct from a financial department in banks' books, and it is because an income transformed into fixed capital should no longer be available on the financial market that a third department, of fixed capital, has to be added to the first two departments within banks. The task of providing a reform capable to guarantee the orderly working of the system of national payments pertains to normative analysis. Yet, normative analysis itself is the natural outcome of a positive analysis determining the logical, macroeconomic laws at the core of any sound economic system. Normative analysis has then to establish the practical procedures allowing payments to be carried out in compliance with these logical laws. This is why, in his chapter, Cencini briefly reviews Schmitt's main tenets before presenting the key principles of his reform. Various numerical examples facilitate the understanding of the way different payments will have to be entered in the three departments of banks' bookkeeping. To be sure, Schmitt's quantum macroeconomic analysis has, among others, the merit of explaining how inflation and deflation may coexist at high levels. The simultaneous presence of both anomalies is due to a common cause; Schmitt succeeds in identifying it and in showing how it can be neutralized through a structural reform capable of avoiding the very formation of the pathology that actually generates it. The point of creating three distinct departments is, on the one hand, to keep the circuits of money and income separate and, on the other hand, to put an end to the emission of profits on the financial market as explained in Chapter 4. To date, profits invested in the production of new fixed-capital goods

Preface xxiii

give rise to an endless chain of bank deposits that, in their turn, feed additional loans granted by banks to households. These macroeconomic loans are the mark of the pathological distinction of the capitalist economic system into three sectors. The reform advocated by Schmitt, and presented by Cencini in the last chapter of Part 1, shows how the distinction between departments can, from the outset, neutralize that between sectors, thus avoiding the disorderly process of capital accumulation, which inevitably leads to inflation and unemployment.

The second part, focusing on international macroeconomic issues, opens with a chapter contributed by Edoardo Beretta. As he clearly shows, Schmitt's legacy of international monetary analysis is permeated by several years of study into (net) interest payments on external debt. This is actually an economic state of affairs (where interest due on external liabilities is greater than yields on foreign assets) which mostly affects Less and Least Developed Countries (LDCs), seriously endangering their economic well-being as nations. As a matter of fact, Schmitt amply demonstrated that the current non-system of international payments allows for interest to be paid by residents, and additionally by their nation as a whole; the baleful consequence being a supplementary loss of foreign reserves. Preposterous as it may seem, these countries are deprived of the same amount – not only in terms of domestic output transferred by residents to their creditors abroad, but also of external resources (stored in their country's foreign reserves) – leading to a double economic loss. Spurred by the gravity of this 'secondary burden', in his chapter Beretta traces its logic-analytical origins back to the Keynes–Ohlin–Rueff debate (1929) on German reparation payments. As a particular typology of external indebtedness, the process involving the German government suffered indeed from the same pathology. Although Keynes seemed well aware of the duplicitous economic loss sustained by the German people and their country as a whole, it has unquestionably been Schmitt's merit to have extended the analysis to (net) interest payments. The microeconomic is added on to the macroeconomic repayment of interest on external liabilities. If, on the one hand, residents must be sure to have a sufficient income (deriving from a production in their national economy), say $100\,x$, on the other hand, the transaction itself has to be carried out in a foreign currency. This amount (say $100\,y$), which is necessary to convert domestic income into externally accepted currencies, comes from exports – and to that extent deprives the country of a corresponding sum to feed imports. It therefore appears that net interest payments cause an equivalent payment deficit, that is, multiply the total economic loss by two. The proof of this (apparently absurd) 'secondary burden' is not easily graspable, as Beretta shows in his own chapter. Schmitt's ability to captivate his audience by explaining the same problem from different angles will nonetheless help clarify why this type of transaction (equally applicable to war reparation payments in the past) still weighs double on LDCs' shoulders. At that point, there will be even fewer excuses for continuing to avoid a structural reform of the international payments system, the ultimate cause of this detrimental state of affairs.

Nadia F. Piffaretti corroborates this novel analysis by investigating, in Chapter 7, both Keynes's and Schumacher's plans for world monetary reform. Indeed, while World War II was still raging, Keynes and Schumacher were part of a generation of economists that recognized early on the need to ground international relations on a new set of rules. Competing frameworks, and the new political imperatives of that time, finally led to the abandonment of the idea of a multilateral clearing union, leaving an unfinished agenda of international institutions that still reverberates today, as again a new multipolar world is taking shape and taking its very first uncertain steps. Indeed, the world still lacks an international system of monetary relations. However, while very much needed, Keynes and Schumacher's framework lacked internal coherence. Early on in his career, while striving to understand the nature of monetary payments, Schmitt turned his attention to international payments and to Keynes's writings. What he found was an attempt to set up a clearing of traded goods and services, based on a unit of account and the common agreement of how to deal with the balance. Schmitt's critique was scathing. In his view, this could not be what an 'international system' should be about. However, the Keynes Plan provided Schmitt the ground on which to test the international implications of his own maturing view on the meaning of domestic payments. Schmitt saw implications that Keynes had not suspected. If both authors diverged in considering solutions, it is because of their essentially diverging agendas: while Keynes was striving to find a solution to very practical problems in international payments, Schmitt was looking to understand the nature of payments and how they are to be carried out. Keynes's lack of interest in the theoretical nature of the problem hampered the search for a logical solution. He was looking for a mechanism to facilitate 'just trade'. Schmitt was looking instead to understand how international financial relations can be created and settled, and from that he built his critique. At times, he appeared irritated by the realization that finally Keynes had not abandoned the notion of monetary phenomena as separated from real flows. Keynes understood the importance of money and finance, but his framework remained unable to marry real and monetary phenomena in an integrated theory. In the end, Schmitt's approach proves a degree of superiority: it points to financial relations of different order than the ones within domestic monetary systems. Finally, this different order of financial relations led him down the path of exploring the double nature of net international payments: how is the debt of the '*maison France*' created and settled? That would ultimately be the question Schmitt started to pursue while studying the Keynes Plan. But if the question of an international monetary system remains unresolved, so are its analytical underpinnings. The real nature of international monetary relations is still veiled in mystery, as is clear in Schmitt's writings during his two last decades of work. The (neoclassical) dichotomic view of real goods and monetary flows still deeply hampers the fundamental understanding of the nature of international monetary and financial relations.

This issue is actually also at the core of the crisis that burst in 2009 across the European Monetary Union (EMU), as Sergio Rossi explains in Chapter 8. As he argues, Schmitt clearly foresaw the structural euro-area crisis as a result of his critical investigation of the conventional definition of money and the ensuing flawed conception of monetary union. To start with, Rossi presents Schmitt's

Preface xxv

critiques in this regard. He thereby points out that money is not a financial asset, that money's purchasing power does not depend on agents' confidence, that a payment is not a bilateral exchange, and that the balance of payments concerns the country as a whole. Rossi thus explains that monetary union does not imply the irrevocable fixing of the relevant currencies' exchange rates, that there is an essential distinction between a single currency and a common currency, and that the member countries of the European Union do not need a single currency, which is actually a factor of crisis. In light of this, Rossi then briefly recalls that in the Schmitt approach money is an 'asset–liability' whose purchasing power depends on production, and that each payment implies three parties (the payer, the payee, and the banking system as a go-between). He then explains that a national central bank should represent its country in the international monetary space, where a common (rather than a single) currency should be issued by a truly international settlement institution. If so, then the common European currency (such as the 'international euro') will not be used by residents for either their domestic or cross-border transactions, which they will settle using their own national currency thereby recovering their monetary sovereignty indeed. Between any member countries of the EMU, by contrast, payments will be settled using the international euro as an international vehicular currency that enables payments to be final at the international level. This contrasts with the situation at the time of writing in the so-called TARGET2 system, which does not imply payment finality at international level, because the national central banks involved thereby do not pay and are not paid finally when there is a transaction across that system. Rossi is thereby in a position to explain that today the European single currency area is neither a truly monetary union (because the euro is not actually a single European currency for its member countries) nor a factor of economic and financial stability and convergence across these countries. In fact, the monetary policy of the European Central Bank has been and is a factor of instability and crisis, because of its 'one-size-fits-all' stance as well as because of a lack of truly monetary integration as epitomized by the so-called problem of TARGET2 imbalances. Rossi's analysis shows thereby that a few countries, like Germany, did exploit these problems to benefit from the situation unduly, as the free movement of financial capital across the euro area has increased, rather than reduced, economic divergence across that area. The conclusion recalls Schmitt's critiques of the EMU and points out how his proposal for monetary integration is both urgent and appropriate to solve the euro-area crisis at the time of writing.

In Chapter 9, Alvaro Cencini takes this analysis a step further. The aim of his chapter is to introduce the reader to Schmitt's ground-breaking discovery of the pathological formation of countries' sovereign debts. In fact, contrary to what is usually believed, a country's sovereign debt is not the debt incurred by its State. To mix up public debt and sovereign debt is to forget that the State is a country's resident while, properly defined, a country is the set of all its residents. The country as a whole is the entity to which the sovereign debt refers, which means that the concept of sovereign debt is closely connected to (and strictly speaking synonymous with) that of external debt. Given the external net global (commercial

xxvi *Jean-Luc Bailly, Alvaro Cencini and Sergio Rossi*

and financial) purchases of a country's residents, the sovereign debt concerns therefore both the public and the private sectors and their foreign net purchases. Schmitt's insight consists in showing that sovereign debts form as the result of a duplication whereby a country whose net imports are financed by a foreign loan must pay twice its net foreign purchases, that is, once in real terms and once in monetary terms. The real payment implies the transfer abroad of part of the deficit country's future output, whereas the monetary payment implies the expenditure of a sum of foreign currency that the deficit country has to borrow from the rest of the world. In other words, the actual non-system of international payments is such that a deficit country has to run a sovereign or external debt to pay in foreign currency what has already been fully paid, in national income, by its residents. The payment carried out by the country's residents corresponds to a loss in domestic resources. The payment that weighs on the country itself is carried out in foreign currency and implies the incurring of an external or sovereign debt. As Cencini shows in his chapter, Schmitt provided several formal proofs of his claim, thereby establishing beyond dispute that countries' sovereign debts are of a pathological nature: their very existence is entirely unjustified and unjust, and so are the austerity measures imposed on the population of the countries on which they rest. The problem brought to the fore by Schmitt is indeed counterintuitive and of a macroeconomic nature, which explains why it has remained undetected so far and why it requires an open-minded approach and a serious effort to be properly understood. The proofs that Cencini has chosen to present in his chapter are relatively simple and are based on factual observation as well as on conceptual analysis. The pathological duplication giving rise to sovereign debts is the direct consequence of the lack of a true system of international payments providing countries, free of cost, with the vehicular currency they need to convey the real payments of their residents to their foreign creditors. Actually, the purchase of foreign currencies is the absurd, second payment indebted countries are subject to, and their external indebtedness is the result of this state of affairs.

The last chapter of this book was written by Bernard Schmitt shortly before his death. In it, Schmitt asks if a country can find a solution to the sovereign debt crisis. The answer is yes, and this chapter advocates a reform whose objective is to enable deficit countries to pay their net imports only once, without any negative consequence for their foreign creditors, who will be paid their due. The need for a reform depends on the fact that, in the present non-system of international payments, as Chapter 9 explained, net imports are paid by residents of deficit countries, in domestic money, as well as by their own countries, in foreign currency. Indeed, today external purchases are first paid in units of the national currency of the importing country: importers pay for all of their purchases as if they were carried out within their own national economy. However, all external payments are macroeconomic: it is the country as a whole that is required to pay the rest of the world, R, in foreign currencies. The problem of external debt crises cannot be offloaded on importing residents, even if they are members of the public sector. This 'crisis' is macroeconomic, because it is only the country considered as a whole that has to pay for its external debt. One of the main functions of the

Preface xxvii

reform is to avoid the very formation of sovereign debts, and prevent economies from sliding into a crisis. The macroeconomic payment occurs at the expense of the importing country, even though its residents have paid all their purchases. Logical consistency dictates that the 'macro-payment' does not get added to the 'micro-payment', but becomes its simple translation. This is one of the results expected of the reform Schmitt proposed. Another result is the gain in domestic currency obtained by the Bureau – the institution acting on behalf of the country itself and which will be paid by importers and credited by foreign lenders, while paying exporters (in domestic money) and foreign creditors (in foreign currency). All payments to the rest of the world, even to offset debits, will be carried out by the purchasers to the ultimate benefit of the Bureau, which will receive them in place of the foreign countries. After the reform, the Bureau will receive, as a net gain, the payment, in national currency, of the net imports carried out by the country's residents. Finally, the reform requires the Bureau's net gain to be invested in a new production, whose output would be acquired by the country itself (represented by the Bureau) since its very production. This investment of the Bureau's net gain will largely reduce unemployment and, together with the mechanism preventing the formation of the country's sovereign debt, is the main result of the new reform, whose implementation would put an end to the unjustified loss suffered today by countries forced to finance their net imports through a foreign loan.

The volume ends with a long postface, or afterword, which presents a structured and comprehensive survey of all the writings in the Schmitt school of thought as regards heterodox economics. It aims thereby at presenting the similarities and differences between quantum macroeconomics and other heterodox schools in economics at conceptual and methodological levels. It is also meant to offer a synthesis of these similarities and differences in the investigation of specific real-world issues from a quantum macroeconomics perspective, showing the originality of Schmitt's own thinking with regard to both orthodox and other heterodox schools of thought in economic analysis, with the hope of raising a sound interest in what is a very promising approach to understanding as well as solving the most dramatic economic issues of contemporary capitalism across the world.

Acknowledgements

Bernard Schmitt and his quantum macroeconomics have been a constant, privileged source of great inspiration for all contributors to this volume, which is humbly dedicated to him as a collective tribute to his research work. Remembering and honouring his ground-breaking scholarship, his humanity, as well as his tireless support, the contributors pay thus grateful homage to Schmitt, who passed away on 26 March 2014 at the age of 84. They are also very grateful to their undergraduate, graduate, and postgraduate students for their thought-provoking questions and comments on quantum macroeconomics. The co-editors wish also to thank Xavier Bradley for translating into English the original French version of Chapter 4, Jonathan Massonnet for carefully reading the whole typescript of this volume before its publication, Denise Converso–Grangier for her secretarial assistance, Lorna Hawes for her professional efficiency in copy-editing the whole book, as well as Laura Johnson and Andy Humphries at Routledge for their enthusiastic support for the publication of this book. The usual disclaimer applies.

Introduction
The research work and scientific legacy of Bernard Schmitt

Alvaro Cencini

Introduction

An entire volume would not be sufficient to properly introduce the reader to Bernard Schmitt's scientific bibliography. His texts are far too numerous and dense to give them the attention they deserve in the short space of a chapter. This is why we have been forced to make a choice and limit our presentation to some of his most relevant contributions to monetary macroeconomics. The reader is exhorted not to underestimate the texts that are mentioned just briefly in this concise overview.

The first building blocks of the new analysis: from 1959 to 1966

In an article published in 1959 titled "L'équilibre de la monnaie", Schmitt gives the flavour of a new analysis of money. But it is with the publication of his PhD thesis, *La formation du pouvoir d'achat* (1960), that he expounds on the insights he derived from his reading of Keynes's 1930 and 1936 volumes, *A Treatise on Money* and *The General Theory*.

In introducing his research method, Schmitt clarifies from the outset a distinction that is often ignored by economists, namely that between nominal and conceptual definitions. Nominal definitions are arbitrary and conventional, their usefulness being mainly that of providing "a univocal language enabling everyone to investigate the same objects" (Schmitt 1960: 27, our translation). On the other hand, conceptual definitions are the result of a process of scientific inquiry allowing for the understanding of the nature of things. This distinction has always been at the core of Schmitt's methodology, and he has consistently respected it throughout his life, avoiding any form of dogmatism and providing numerous logical proofs of his scientific claims.

In *La formation du pouvoir d'achat*, Schmitt (1960) lays down the basic concepts of a new approach to monetary macroeconomics. He starts his analysis from Keynes's equations, $Y = C + I$ and $S = I$, with the intent of establishing whether these equations are merely nominal, conventional, or the result of a deep insight into the nature of money and income. He thus asks the crucial question of whether the object of these equations is money or output. It is the answer to this

2   Alvaro Cencini

question that provides the main message of Schmitt's PhD dissertation and which allows him to support his claim that Keynes's equations are indeed identities and not, as still believed by most Keynesian economists, conditions of equilibrium.

In his first book, Schmitt advocates the thesis that income is the object of Keynes's equations, because they refer to the process of income formation, that is production, and to its final expenditure, namely consumption and investment. One key step in Schmitt's analysis of income formation is to consider the action through which money acquires a positive purchasing power over produced output, that is, what he calls *the investment of money*. A quotation shows the relevance of this new concept and its logical distinction with the traditional concept of investment as related to firms' purchase of investment goods: "*when one considers the investment that invades the whole production, one speaks of the investment of money, and not of the purchase of fixed-capital goods*" (ibid.: 59, our translation, italics in the original). In macroeconomics, the investment of money is the transaction through which income is formed, that is, through which money is invested with a positive purchasing power. Schmitt's idea is that money cannot be issued by banks already endowed with a positive value, but that it acquires it through its association with produced goods and services.

In his 1960 book, Schmitt's analysis of bank money is not yet fully developed, however he provides the key elements he will elaborate on in later publications. In particular, he points out that bank money is a mere collection of purely numerical units: "Money itself, a collection of pure units of account, is thus void of purchasing power" (ibid.: 64, our translation). Traditionally, money was and still is defined according to the functions it is believed to exert. The first of these functions is unanimously recognised to be that of a unit of account. Schmitt's claim is thus apparently the mere repetition of what is claimed by everybody. In reality, what is generally believed is that money is issued with a positive value, and that it is because it has a value that it can be used to express that of current output. This traditional vision can be summarised by stating that money is considered as a dimensional unit of account and is therefore assimilated to the category of dimensional standards used in classical physics. Schmitt breaks away from this conception that identifies money with a net asset, and claims that money as such is a purely numerical unit of account, a collection of numbers with no intrinsic purchasing power.

The investment of money is what gives money a positive value. Money's purchasing power is the result of a process of production, which, from a monetary viewpoint, coincides with the (instantaneous) payment of the factors of production. Schmitt cogently claims that this payment is the only one that does not require the expenditure of a positive purchasing power. Whereas payments taking place on goods and financial markets require the expenditures of a pre-existing income, it is through the payment of the factors of production that money is transformed into income, to wit, that it acquires a value. This clearly means that, when paying the factors they employ, firms do not spend a positive purchasing power and, therefore, do not purchase physical output, which is owned, in monetary form, by these very factors, who are *de facto* the initial holders of the totality of income.

Introduction   3

Formed by production, money's purchasing power is then exerted in the purchase of produced output. This final purchase is what economists call consumption, and Schmitt's analysis shows that if production is the event forming or creating money's purchasing power, consumption is the event destroying it. Money is thus invested with purchasing power by production and disinvested of it by consumption. This is one of the strongest messages conveyed by Schmitt's 1960 book. From it, the French economist derives the exact nature of Keynes's equation $Y = C + I$, and is able to provide a first proof of the fact that consumption cannot engender any multiplier effect: "Money's purchasing power is spent only once by society: it disappears when goods are purchased. *Purchases do not engender income*" (ibid.: 109, our translation, italics in the original). Schmitt's discovery that the Keynesian multiplier is always and necessarily equal to unity is just one of the revolutionary insights contained in *La formation du pouvoir d'achat*. In this extremely dense book, Schmitt provides also a first analysis showing that profits are logically included in the remuneration of the factors of production, and suggests an interpretation of Keynes's effective demand that is perfectly in line with the investment of money.

Some of the main ideas advanced in his 1960 book are further developed by Schmitt in his second volume, *Monnaie, salaires et profits*, published six years later. Here the French author goes deeper into the analysis of money, income and profit, and shows that his earlier concept of the investment of money is the only one compatible with the numerical nature of money.

In the first part of that volume, Schmitt (1966a) develops a critical analysis of mainstream economics, showing that in the neoclassical general equilibrium model, money is logically undetermined. The dichotomous vision of neoclassical economists – whereby the real and the monetary sectors are essentially distinct, with real variables playing the central role – entails the idea that the payment of the factors of production is identical to the purchase of their output. "So far as the remuneration of the factors of production is a purchase, it identifies itself with the final purchase of produced goods" (Schmitt 1966a: 35, our translation). This allows Schmitt to conclude that the neoclassical general equilibrium model describes a world where firms are mere intermediaries, producers and consumers being the only true actors in the economic play, where the only interacting forces are "the supply of productive services and the demand for products" (ibid.: 36, our translation). In this world, money is not essential and the only prices that matter are real, relative prices. The critical analysis of general equilibrium will be one of the topics to which Schmitt will repeatedly devote his attention, in the attempt to provide ever clearer proofs of the logical indeterminacy of relative prices.

In *Monnaie, salaires et profits*, the indeterminacy of money is the main argument advocated against neoclassical analysis. The homogeneity postulate – according to which real (relative) prices are invariant with respect to fluctuations in the quantity of money – does not allow for the integration between money and output, and leaves the former entirely undetermined. Once again, Schmitt's main argument rests on the conception of money's purchasing power, and on the logical

4   *Alvaro Cencini*

impossibility to explain its formation if money is merely added to the stock of products instead than being associated to or integrated with them.

It is in the second and third parts of his 1966 volume that Schmitt goes back to his analysis of money and its purchasing power, and that he gives it a form whose basic structure will remain essentially unaltered up to his death in 2014. By a rigorously logical analysis of banks' activity, Schmitt is able to show that commercial banks exert two distinct functions: they operate as financial intermediaries and as money creators. When acting as financial intermediaries, they lend to some clients what others have deposited. In this function, banks do not create what they lend, the object of their intermediation being an amount of already existing income deposited with them. "In its strict sense, the deposit is a sum deposited with a bank; it prepares a mediation, the transmission of deposits" (ibid.: 158, our translation). Things change when banks act as money purveyors. This time the deposit resulting from the creation of money is new and the beneficiaries of the money creation are both credited and debited at the same moment, while their bank is simultaneously a debtor and a creditor to them. It is through their spontaneous acknowledging of debt that banks can issue money, but it is only if it is integrated with produced output that money can acquire a positive purchasing power. The creation of money is that of a numerical form, of an a-dimensional mould necessary to provide a nominal support to physically heterogeneous goods. "Money creation fulfils this need: *to give current production its nominal support*" (ibid.: 169, our translation, italics in the original).

As shown by Schmitt in *Monnaie, salaires et profits*, money creation is neither an advance nor a purchase, both these transactions requiring the presence of an income, a purchasing power money cannot be intrinsically endowed with. A mere numerical form, money as such has no intrinsic value; it is issued by banks as an acknowledgment of debt and it is as a bank's acknowledgment of debt (a mere promise to pay) that it circulates. "The bank promises to pay: this is enough, the promise will never be fulfilled: until it is due, it will remain a debt and circulate as such as unique, actual and true money" (ibid.: 198, our translation). How is it, then, that monetary payments are final, to wit, that they can actually discharge debts? In other words, how can money be 'invested' with a positive purchasing power over produced output? It is in the third part of his 1966 volume that Schmitt provides a detailed answer to these questions and explains how a personal debt, that is the debt incurred by the bank with the economy, can become a real credit, that is a credit over real output.

What was generally described as the remuneration of the productive factors in *La formation du pouvoir d'achat*, is more precisely identified with the payment of wages in *Monnaie, salaires et profits*. Indeed, Schmitt claims that, as advocated by the Classics and later confirmed by Keynes, human labour is the sole macroeconomic factor of production. Being at the origin of economic value, labour is not itself a commodity and has no proper value. This means that the payment of wages is not a purchase; in other words, it does not require the expenditure of a positive purchasing power. The various microeconomic factors identified by mainstream economics pertain to the category of real goods, and

Introduction 5

their payment implies the expenditure of a pre-existing income. The payment of wages, on the contrary, leads to the very initial formation of income, because it is through this payment that money is associated with produced output and is formed into a new, positive income. Money is thus enriched with a positive purchasing power from the moment it is paid out by firms to workers. Banks credit wage earners with a deposit whose object is current output, which means that wage earners are initially the holders or the economic owners of produced output. "In our contemporaries economies, wage earners obtain, in monetary form, the totality of national income. Sole factor of production, labour is initially the only beneficiary of national product, because the whole of nominal wages (direct and indirect) gives the necessary power to purchase the whole of newly produced goods, consumption as well as investment goods" (Schmitt 1966a: 266, our translation).

It is in the third part of his 1966 book that Schmitt addresses the argument of the circulation of money and income, and introduces the law of the necessary equality between inflows and outflows. "The equality of inflow (flux) and outflow (reflux) is directly linked with the distinction between money and monetary incomes. Starting from firms, the inflow (flux) gives rise to income, transforming a right on banks into a right on products. Then the outflow (reflux) absorbs the income thus created: from a purchasing power, money becomes again a sum owed to the banking system" (1966a: 223, our translation). What Schmitt describes here is the successive steps through which money is transformed into income, invested with a positive purchasing power, and then recovers its initial form of pure nominal money after the final expenditure of income, that is, it is disinvested of its purchasing power. The circular flow of money is not yet described as an instantaneous flow as it will be in Schmitt's 1984 master work, *Inflation, chômage et malformations du capital*. Schmitt's intent in his 1966 volume is to show the logical distinction existing between money and income, and how the payment of wages and the final purchase of current output define the two complementary parts of a circular flow whereby money acquires (income creation) and loses (income destruction) a positive purchasing power. "Day after day, money is enriched with the *objective* power to purchase current goods. And, again daily, it is impoverished of its power, because, in final purchases, it becomes again what it was initially, simple money, purely personal credit, and this to the extent that nominal wealth is converted into real wealth" (1966a: 263, our translation).

Nominal wages are the measure of national income and wage earners are the initial holders of national output. Does this imply that wages are the only possible income, that profits are necessarily nil? Certainly not, as Schmitt explains in the last part of his 1966 book, profits may well be positive even if nominal wages define the totality of national income. This simply means that profits are derived from wages: they define that part of income that is transferred without counterpart from wage earners to firms. Whereas wages result from production, it is on the product market that profits are formed. By selling part of current output at a price greater than its cost of production, firms are able to supplant wage earners as income holders. Hence, "profits are positive incomes because they are incomes 'of substitution'" (ibid.: 288, our translation).

6 *Alvaro Cencini*

Nominal wages remain the correct measure of national income, even if part of the income initially owned by wage earners is successively transferred to firms as profit. The redistribution of income between real wages and profits does not alter the initial formation of national income, whose sole origin is the remuneration of labour.

In the last pages of *Monnaie, salaires et profits*, Schmitt sows the seeds for a future analysis of monetary disorders: inflation and deflation. If, as rigorously established in both his 1960 and his 1966 books, production creates the amount of income necessary and sufficient for the final purchase of current output – via the payment of wages – then it defines simultaneously a supply (output) and an equivalent demand (current income). The difficulty in dealing with monetary disorders is therefore that of explaining how it is possible for macroeconomic demand to be greater or lesser than macroeconomic supply while respecting their logical identity. It is only in 1984 that Schmitt will provide the complete solution to this conundrum, but before considering his fundamental contributions in this very prolific year, let us spend a few words on the volumes preceding and somehow preparing the 1984 research work.

From 1966 to 1984

Published in 1971, *L'analyse macroéconomique des revenus* is a volume in which Schmitt pursues his analysis of the macroeconomic formation of income. He does so by comparing his conception of the investment and disinvestment of money with that of the chain of incomes induced by consumption specific to the Keynesian multiplier. In particular, he shows that k (the Keynesian coefficient of multiplication) is always necessarily equal to one, which amounts to saying that once spent for the final purchase of current output, income is literally destroyed. The idea that consumption reproduces the income spent in the purchase of consumption goods is inconsistent with the nature of money and income, and leads to a vicious circle, where the formation of income is explained through its own expenditure. Having further proven that positive hoarding is logically impossible at the macroeconomic level, Schmitt shifts the emphasis from the multiplier to the multiplicand, and provides new evidence of the identity established by production between global supply and global demand. "These two magnitudes are linked to one another by a law as exact as those of physics. It is impossible to conceive an inequality between global supply and global demand" (Schmitt 1971a: 163, our translation).

Most of Schmitt's 1971 volume is devoted to a critical analysis of mainstream Keynesianism and to a new interpretation of Keynes's fundamental equations, of his concept of effective demand and of his definition of profit. The aim of the French author was to provide new arguments allowing him to develop further the monetary macroeconomic approach advocated in his previous volumes and to clearly differentiate it from the one followed by those mainstream economists who define themselves as faithful followers of Keynes. In this respect, the last pages of Schmitt's 1971 volume, devoted to a methodological note referring to the

Introduction 7

role of mathematical analysis in economics, are of particular interest. In these pages, Schmitt shows, through a critical investigation of the way Samuelson (1966) analyses the logical relationship between saving and investment, that mathematics is not the appropriate 'language' of economics, because "the specific object of economics is not that of the 'queen of sciences'" (Schmitt 1971a: 357, our translation).

In a paper titled "Vers une nouvelle théorie macro-économique?" published in 1972, Schmitt establishes the "*identity between the quantities supplied and demanded in each realised transaction*" (Schmitt 1972b: 141, our translation, italics in the original) starting from a critical appraisal of Keynes's volumes *The Treatise on Money* (1930) and *The General Theory* (1936).

In *Macroeconomic Theory: A Fundamental Revision*, also published in 1972, Schmitt presents to the English reader some of the main arguments advocated in his previous three French volumes, and corroborates his vision about the formation of income, the relationship between global supply and demand, the Keynesian multiplier, and the distinction between nominal and real money by a critical analysis of a selected number of Keynesian economists of the time, with the explicit intent "*of persuading economists to re-examine critically the whole corpus of modern macroeconomics*" (Schmitt 1972a: 7, italics in the original).

The following year, in a booklet titled *New Proposals for World Monetary Reform*, he made another attempt to persuade economists of the necessity of a new approach to macroeconomics. He did so by addressing the problem of international payments, and by proposing a reform of the international system of payments based on the idea that "the various national currencies must be expressed in terms of a general standard" (Schmitt 1973: 5), and that the reform must give the "possibility for all countries to accumulate net foreign reserves without weighing down official reserves in other countries" (ibid.: 5).

Unfortunately, economists' interest was already switching from Keynesian to new classical economics, and mathematical modelling was imposing itself together with the idea that macroeconomics has to be based on microeconomic foundations. Schmitt's message was of an entirely macroeconomic nature and instead than putting economic agents' behaviour at its core, it was based on objective relationships defining logical identities. It is therefore not surprising that with such conditions in place Schmitt's theory did not get the attention it deserved. Far from being discouraged by this lack of attention, Schmitt interpreted it as a sign that he had to step up his efforts in order to develop his analysis further and make it more encompassing. The first result of his renewed efforts was his 1975 volume *Théorie unitaire de la monnaie, nationale et internationale*.

What was to become Schmitt's most successful book – it was translated into German, Portuguese, and Italian – is of a particular relevance for at least two reasons: (1) it expands his analysis of money to the international field, and (2) it is at the origin of the so-called theory of the monetary circuit. In the introduction, Schmitt presents the key elements on which his theory of the circuit rests, that is, the numerical nature of bank money (an asset–liability) and the four laws deriving from it, namely:

8 *Alvaro Cencini*

1 The law of the numerical measurement of products and productive services by money.
2 The law stating that every purchase is financed by a sale and every sale finances a purchase.
3 The law of the necessary 'distance' between money's issuers and money's users.
4 The law of the numerical expression of national currencies by international money.

Money being an asset–liability, Schmitt's first law simply describes the fact that the monetary expressions of output and labour (the unique macroeconomic productive service) are merely numerical. "Money does not allow the expression of the value of real goods; it does not measure the extent of the economic value of goods. Money merely allows associating numbers to *count* real goods; in a word, to specify their number" (Schmitt 1975a: 15, our translation, italics in the original). Schmitt attributes the second law to Say and identifies it as the law of the circuit. If a circuit of money exists, it cannot be interrupted, because it is money itself that defines its own circuit through its circulation. "[T]here is an identity between the monetary circuit and the money that displaces itself in this circuit" (ibid.: 19, our translation). It thus follows that money must necessarily flow back to its point of departure, which implies that "money spent in purchases comes from the simultaneous sales of either the purchaser or the saver; reciprocally, money earned through sales is simultaneously spent in purchases of either the seller or the borrower" (ibid.: 19, our translation). Schmitt's third law states that no purchase can be financed by the spontaneous acknowledgment of debt of the purchaser. A 'distance' must separate the issuer of money from the user of money, a requirement that is fulfilled within every national monetary system, where economic agents use money issued by banks, and where banks are not allowed to finance their own purchases by money creation. The principle is simply that nobody pays by acknowledging his own debt, and it applies to every economic agent, and, therefore, also to countries, none of which can pay for its net purchases merely using its own national currency. A country's national currency is the acknowledgment of debt of its national banking system. Hence, in order to introduce a distance between the issuer of money and the user of money, it is necessary to "invent a superior agency whose goal is to issue the international means of payment without being itself involved in these payments" (ibid.: 23, our translation). Finally, the fourth law derives directly from the first and the third: an international or supranational currency cannot be issued as a net asset, and its role is essentially that of providing a numerical means to number or count national currencies.

Part I of Schmitt's 1975 volume is devoted to the analysis of national money and its circuit. He starts his investigation by observing that, logically and factually, not only the circulation, but also the circuit of money is instantaneous, because the circuit of money is co-extensive with (is defined by) its circulation. Schmitt is thus able to show that the nature of bank money is such that an interrupted circuit is a

Introduction 9

contradiction in terms. No net purchase can ever be financed by money, which is merely a numerical form with no positive value whatsoever. Purchases are financed by simultaneous and equal sales, and money acts as a numerical intermediary. As emphasised by Schmitt, the difficulty in properly understanding the circuit of money and its instantaneity lies in the widely diffused confusion between money and income. While money is created as an asset–liability by banks and instantaneously used in a circular flow that implies its immediate destruction, income is formed by production and its destruction takes place in a chronologically distinct point in time. It is therefore income and not money as such that is entered as a bank deposit in the financial department of banks.

Schmitt's second step is to introduce two identities whose co-existence establishes the condition of the very existence of the circuit. The first identity is that between the purchase of productive services by firms and their purchase of the output of these services. In a nutshell, this identity states that when firms remunerate their productive services they purchase current output. The second identity is that between the sale of current output and its purchase by firms. Less intuitive than the first, this identity is "necessary and sufficient for the establishment of the monetary circuit" (ibid.: 49, our translation). The necessary equality between firms' purchase and sale of produced output makes of firms a fundamental element of the circuit. This does not prevent them from being present also in a composite element, as holders of part of the income initially owned by wage earners. Indeed, firms can earn a positive profit or borrow from income holders. In both cases, they are part of a composite element in their quality of income holders.

In the second chapter of his 1975 book, Schmitt deals with the problem of monetary disorders and with that of reconciling the necessary compliance with the identity, which founds the circuit, and the possibility of firms selling current output for a greater (inflation) or a lesser (deflation) amount than they spend for its purchase. This apparently insoluble conundrum is not new. In fact, the identity founding the circuit is not substantially different from the identity established by production between global supply, Y, and global demand, $C + I$. Both these identities determine the logical framework of analysis and define the logical relationship necessary, as a referential mark as well as a conceptual interpretative key to explain inflation and deflation. Put it bluntly, it is because the value of firms' sales and purchases – or of Y and $C + I$ – can never differ that the numerical difference between them becomes meaningful. Hence, if firms sell for 110 money units a product that costs them 100 money units, that is, if global supply is numerically equal to 100 and global demand to 110, this means that a value of 100 wage units happens to be distributed on an increased number of money units: 110 instead of the initial 100 units paid to wage earners. Inflation is thus perfectly characterised as the pathology causing a decrease in the purchasing power (value) of each money unit. "Inflation is the decrease in value of the monetary unit" (ibid.: 67, our translation).

In the following chapter, Schmitt analyses the 'golden rule' followed by banks and shows that it is not up to the task of avoiding the risk of inflation caused by the still incomplete system of national payments. His considerations anticipated a

10   *Alvaro Cencini*

reform that would be completed in the years following the publication of his *Théorie unitaire de la monnaie.*

As previously observed, one of the aspects accounting for the relevance of Schmitt's 1975 volume is that in it he investigates the specific problems posed by international payments and provides a unified theory of national and international money. His 1975 analysis of international money is based on two theorems establishing: (1) "the formal impossibility of the direct definition of an international monetary circuit" (ibid.: 83, our translation), and (2) "the formal impossibility of an international monetary circuit based on national circuits" (ibid.: 86, our translation). From these two formal impossibilities, Schmitt derives the need for an international money issued by a supranational bank as an asset–liability, a pure numerical form whose function must be that of "financing sales–purchases and not net purchases" (ibid.: 94, our translation). As any other national currency, the international money can only define an instantaneous flow conveying reciprocal payments between countries. This implies that the international money can only be issued in a circular movement that entails its immediate destruction. Does this mean that every single country will have to equalise both its monetary and its financial transactions? Certainly not: Schmitt shows that, while each country's monetary balance of payments will be in equilibrium by the vehicular use of the new international money, the equilibrium of the financial balance of payments is by no means a necessity. Countries adopting the new system of international payments advocated by Schmitt will be free to export as much as they can and run a financial surplus.

What the new system sketched by Schmitt in the last chapter of his 1975 volume must achieve is the respect of the logical identity between each country's total purchases, both commercial and financial, and its total sales, commercial and financial. If this law is complied with, no international payment will have (international) money as its object, and no monetary disorder would arise. Unfortunately, this is not yet the case, and the pathologies denounced by Schmitt in 1975 are still affecting the present non-system of international payments. More specifically, it is still true that the payment of reserve currency countries' net purchases is at the origin of a duplication, which pathologically increases the capital available abroad, thus generating an inflationary process of an international character. What is wrong with the present non-system of international payments is the fact that the circuit of the currencies used as international means of payment is intertwined with the circuits of national currencies. The solution to this pathological state of affairs advocated by Schmitt "is very simple: it is necessary to prevent the international money from being used without replacing the national money; it would thus be possible to avoid that the same purchasing power be exerted twice, by the international money and, additionally, by the national currency" (ibid.: 104, our translation).

Between 1975 and 1984 Schmitt published five more books: *Génération de la monnaie des monnaies européennes*; *La pensée de Karl Marx, critique et synthèse* (Vol. I *La valeur*, Vol. II *La plus-value*); *La monnaie européenne*; and *L'or, le dollar et la monnaie supranationale.*

Introduction 11

The aim of *Génération de la monnaie des monnaies européennes* (1975b) is to show how it would have been possible to provide the European Union with a European currency issued by a European Monetary Fund without the need for European countries to give up their monetary sovereignty. According to Schmitt's proposal, the euro would have been issued as a nominal currency with no purchasing power and would have been used as a means of payments in a system where all transactions would have been made reciprocal, in conformity with the law of sales–purchases. The book considers also two possible scenarios concerning the working of the new European system of payments with respect to the rest of the world, and provides a critical analysis of the main plans of reform presented at the time.

The first volume of *La pensée de Karl Marx, critique et synthèse*, co-authored with Alvaro Cencini, was published in 1976. Devoted to a critical appraisal of the Marxian analysis of value, this volume was followed by a second addressing the question of Marx's surplus value. In both volumes, the authors provide the elements of a synthesis that allows one to overcome the weaknesses of Marx's analysis and to build a new labour theory of value consistent with a satisfactory explanation of profit (Cencini and Schmitt 1976; 1977).

The other two volumes authored by Schmitt in 1977 deal with the problem of the European currency, *La monnaie européenne*, and with the need to abandon the use of the US dollar as an international currency and to create a truly supranational currency, *L'or, le dollar et la monnaie supranationale*. In the former volume, Schmitt clarifies the nature of monetary payments, the nature and role of money within a national economy of production and in an international setting, the role of the European currency, and how the euro could be implemented (Schmitt 1977a). In the latter volume he widens his analysis to the world setting and, having shown that neither the use of gold nor of the US dollar are a valid alternative, advocates the creation of a supranational currency as a circular means of international payments (Schmitt 1977b).

Before considering Schmitt's pioneering intellectual production of 1984, it is worth mentioning his contributions to a collective volume, *Advances in Economic Theory*, edited by Mauro Baranzini in 1982: "Time as quantum" (Schmitt 1982) and "Wages and profits in a theory of emissions", the latter co-authored with Cencini (Schmitt and Cencini 1982). In these contributions, Schmitt introduces two of the main arguments he was to develop in his 1984 masterpiece on the pathologies affecting capitalism. The first concerns the concept of quantum time and represents up to now the most original concept of economic analysis, at least since Keynes. The second refers to the explanation of profit made possible by the discovery of quantum time. Let us consider both of them in the next section.

The year of 1984

Schmitt's 1984 volume *Inflation, chômage et malformations du capital* is undoubtedly one of the most important books ever written by the French economist. Its relevance is extraordinary, because it presents the principles of a

12   *Alvaro Cencini*

new macroeconomic analysis, the origin of which goes back to Schmitt's 1960 dissertation, in their most accomplished form. What is specifically relevant is the concept of quantum time, which provides the key to understanding the nature of production, the relationship between production and consumption, the circuit of income, the passage from income to capital, and the common origin of inflation and deflation. Let us try to give the gist of Schmitt's great 1984 volume by reference to this all-important concept.

Schmitt's new concept of quantum time derives entirely from his analysis of production, which, from an economic viewpoint, is an instantaneous event through which physical output is given a numerical form. Considered as a physical process of transformation, production takes time, say a month. But as an economic process whereby matter and energy are given a new utility form, production takes place in an instant. It is at the very moment when the physical process of transformation is finished that the new product (the new utility form) appears, and the use of money allows us to measure (to give a numerical expression to) it. In our modern economies, production is identified with the payment of wages. At the instant wages are paid, physical output is formed into an economic product and the chronological time during which matter and energy are transformed (the month) is issued as a quantum of time, that is an indivisible portion of continuous or chronological time.

Schmitt's ground-breaking discovery leads him to argue that "production quantises time; that is, *it takes hold in one go of a slice of continuous time*: the first result of production is therefore the definition of a quantum of time. The product is not laid in time; it *is* time" (Schmitt 1984a: 54, our translation, italics in the original). His second step is to show that, like production, every expenditure is also defined in quantum time: "as production, every expenditure is a wave-like operation, whose effect is to quantise a 'slice' of continuous time" (ibid.: 63, our translation). Hence, every expenditure is an instantaneous event defining a positive period of time issued as a quantum, to wit, every expenditure is a wave-like flow "*whose velocity is infinite in time*" (ibid.: 73, our translation, italics in the original), and which results in the (instantaneous) emission of a quantum of time.

The first expenditure to be analysed is the one defining production: the payment of wages. It is in the payment of wages that money is created, that the mere 'promise to pay' issued by banks finds its object and a positive income is formed. The second is consumption: the final purchase of produced output. If production were not at the origin of money, producers would immediately appropriate output. Production and consumption would take place at the same moment in time and would define the two complementary parts of a unique real emission. The presence of money allows for this real emission to be broken down in two half-emissions, each taking place at a different moment in chronological time. Thanks to money, an income is formed at, say, t_1 and spent at a successive point in time, t_2. The first half of the real emission takes place when wages are paid out to wage earners, and defines an *absolute exchange* through which physical output is transformed into a monetary product. The second half corresponds to the second absolute exchange, which takes place when income is spent in the final purchase of current output and

Introduction   13

income is thereby destroyed. Production and consumption are the two complementary parts of the real emission, and it is because money transforms each of them into an absolute exchange that they can be separate events in continuous time. Yet, production is an emission and an emission is a wave-like movement implying the simultaneity of a creation and destruction. This means that, being inscribed in quantum time, consumption is the necessary and simultaneous complement of production. How is it possible, then, to reconcile the apparently opposed requirements of production and consumption being both simultaneous and, at the same time, separate events?

The answer is provided by Schmitt's new concept of time. Even though they are separate events in continuous time, production and consumption are simultaneous in quantum time. This is so because both production and consumption define the same quantum of time. At the moment production takes place, a product is issued as a quantum of time corresponding to the period of continuous time during which matter and energy are transformed, say t_0–t_1. When consumption occurs, the same quantum of time, t_0–t_1, is issued again. The coincidence of the two half-emissions, production and consumption, is granted by their simultaneity in quantum time, that is by the fact that each of them refers to and defines the same product, to wit, the same quantum of time.

The usefulness of Schmitt's concept of quantum time is further corroborated by his analysis of profit. One of the greatest challenges posed by profits is the logical necessity of explaining with logical consistency both their formation and their expenditure. Authors from the past have provided either a theory of the formation of profits in real terms or in monetary terms, but nobody has been able to show how they can be positive both in real and in monetary terms. A satisfactory theory of profit must reconcile the logical identity between value and prices with the possibility of prices diverging from values. Once again, the task seems impossible. Yet, once again, the solution exists and is made possible by Schmitt's discovery of quantum time. His explanation of the way profits are formed is not different from that of the majority of economists: it is on the goods market that firms can derive as profit part of the income initially owned by wage earners, and the way they do it is by selling current output at a mark-up. Schmitt's original explanation concerns the expenditure of the profits formed on the product market. It is on the labour market that profits are spent, and they are spent in the purchase of part of worker's produced output. The simultaneity, in quantum time, of production and consumption is also the simultaneity of the formation and expenditure of profits. In other words, the expenditure of income on the product market (formation of profit) defines the same quantum of time as the one defined by the payment of wages (expenditure of profit): they coincide in quantum time. This leads Schmitt to argue that the formation of profits coincides retroactively with their expenditure: "[t]he formation of profits is an expenditures of wages; the expenditure of profits is a formation of wages" (ibid.: 141, our translation).

The simultaneity of the formation and expenditure of profits on the two markets makes it possible to reconcile the identity of value and prices with the fact that current output is sold at a mark-up. Indeed, once it is realised that "*[t]he price of*

14   Alvaro Cencini

wage goods is greater than their value only because it is inclusive of the price of non-wage goods" (ibid.: 142, our translation, italics in the original), it becomes clear that, from a macroeconomic viewpoint, no difference subsists between prices and values.

Schmitt's analysis of profit is a further example of the invalidation of the principle of the excluded middle, and a testimony of the fruitfulness of his quantum-time concept. Another application concerns the 'survival' of income in time and the formation of capital. Being the result of an emission, income cannot but be immediately destroyed. How can this unavoidable conclusion be compatible with the existence of a positive interval of time between the moment wages are paid and income is formed, and the moment they are spent and income is destroyed? Quantum macroeconomic analysis helps us to solve this conundrum. Indeed, the retroactivity allowed for by quantum time has the effect of reducing to zero (retroactively) the interval in continuous time, separating the instant wages are paid from the instant they are finally spent. Moreover, even in chronological time income does not survive the moment of its formation. If it is not immediately spent, income is saved and lent, a transaction that transforms it into capital. It is in the form of capital that income can be transferred from a point in continuous time to a successive one. As argued by Schmitt, the existence of capital implies that of a financial market and is possible only in the presence of banks: "*An economy without banks would be without any net capital*" (ibid.: 163, our translation, italics in the original). Saved by wage earners at the moment of its formation, income is lent by banks to firms, which, by investing it in the formation of a stock of produced goods, transform it into capital. At a later moment, when income holders (wage earners and whoever replaces them) decide to purchase the goods stocked by firms, capital is transformed back into income and spent on the market for produced goods and services. The first and simplest form taken up by capital is therefore that of capital-time.

The passage from capital-time to fixed capital is the subsequent step of Schmitt's analysis. It is through the investment of a firm's profit in the production of instrumental goods that income is transformed into fixed capital. Both capital-time and fixed capital result from saving, but while the former defines a reversible saving, the latter defines the formation of an irreversible or macroeconomic saving. To the extent that current income is saved in the form of profit and that profit is invested in the production of investment goods, it is transformed into fixed capital. The logical identity between macroeconomic saving and investment that Keynes had unsuccessfully tried to establish against the theory supported by some of his fellow economists is definitively proven correct by Schmitt's quantum analysis. Macroeconomic saving, that is, that part of current income that will never be consumed, is necessarily equal to that part of profit that is invested by firms, that is spent by them in the production (and final purchase) of investment goods. Profit is an income derived by firms through the sale of wage goods, and its investment transforms it into fixed capital.

Now, if the system of domestic payments complied with logic, the income invested by firms in the production of fixed-capital goods would no longer be

Introduction 15

available on the financial market. Invested to finance a new production, profit would be forever saved in the form of fixed capital. As shown by Schmitt, this is unfortunately not what happens today. Instead of being saved as fixed capital, invested profit is spent on the labour market, and fixed-capital goods are appropriated at the moment of their production by *disembodied* or *depersonalised* firms. The alienation of labour (and of its product) and its appropriation by what we could call 'pathological capital' is the mark of a disorder that inevitably leads to inflation and deflation. In a sequence of logical steps that leave no room for behavioural considerations, Schmitt shows first that the expenditure of profit on the labour market gives rise to what he calls 'empty money', because the wages paid to workers producing capital goods are deprived of their real content, which is appropriated by disembodied firms. Schmitt then establishes that the emission of empty money characterising the pathological formation of fixed capital occurs also when fixed capital is amortised owing to wear and tear. The production of new fixed-capital goods replacing those used up as means of production is at the origin of an empty money that, unlike the one generated when fixed capital is initially formed, cannot be filled up with consumption goods previously stocked with firms. Finally, Schmitt shows that, because of what he calls 'dual production', the process of fixed-capital amortisation entails a pathological increase of fixed capital and, at the same time, an inflationary decrease in money's purchasing power due to the emission of empty money: "to the extent of dual production, workers do not produce for income holders; they do not produce for persons: *they are enslaved to Capital*" (ibid.: 223, our translation, italics in the original).

In the subsequent pages Schmitt analyses the causes of unemployment and shows that the pathological process of capital accumulation is also at the origin of deflation, when the rate of profit no longer exceeds the market rate of interest. The difficulty in explaining inflation and deflation from a macroeconomic viewpoint lies in the fact that global supply and demand are the terms of an identity. To prove that global demand can be greater or lesser than global supply without denying their logical identity is to give another example of the non-validity of the principle of the excluded middle. Schmitt succeeds in his attempt thanks to his quantum analysis. The identity between global demand, D, and supply, Y, is imposed by the nature of money and income, by their quantum emission, while the numerical difference between D and Y is due to the fact that banks' double-entry bookkeeping does not comply with the logical law of quantum emissions. "The inflationary gaps that are present in our economies are all due to *empty emissions*, which, by definition, depose a 'money without product' in continuous time" (ibid.: 507, our translation, italics in the original).

Finally, Schmitt provides the key principles of a reform capable of eradicating the causes of inflation and unemployment. In a nutshell, they consist of introducing at the level of banks the distinction between three departments, namely, monetary, saving, and fixed-capital departments, which corresponds to the distinction between money, income, and fixed capital, respectively.

Schmitt's 1984 volume contains an impressive number of thought-provoking arguments on such topics as the distinction between micro- and macroeconomics,

16 *Alvaro Cencini*

that between relative and absolute exchanges, the measure in economics, the concept of hoarding, the rate of interest, and many others. It also provides a long synopsis where the French author reconsiders all the concepts introduced by the main text and develops them anew.

In this most prolific year, 1984, a second volume was published, wherein Schmitt analyses the problem of international payments with reference to the case of France and advocates a reform that would have allowed his country to avoid the pathologies inherent to the key-currencies regime. In *La France souveraine de sa monnaie*, Schmitt (1984b) explains how France could have obtained the true sovereignty of its currency while paying for the totality of its foreign purchases. Respecting the law of the identity between each country's sales and purchases is the key to the reform proposed by the French author, who shows that the "fusion of France's imports and exports in a unique movement (or circuit) is obtained through the intermediation of the foreign financial market" (Schmitt 1984b: 150, our translation), and that, thanks to the new absolute-exchange-rate regime, France's global balance-of-payments deficit would allow the French economy to "maintain the total benefit of its domestic incomes within the country; the incomes spent for the payment of excess imports being automatically invested [...] for the development and growth of France's industries" (ibid.: 294, our translation).

Based on the analysis previously developed in his 1975 and 1977 books, *La France souveraine de sa monnaie* delves further into the problem of international payments, and introduces two extremely important arguments to which Schmitt devoted the majority of his research in the last three decades of his life, namely the external debt servicing and the formation of a country's external debt.

Schmitt's third contribution of 1984 is a small book, *Les pays au regime du FMI* (1984c), where he shows that the actual system of international payments is at the origin of inflation in the case of both balanced and unbalanced commercial transactions. He locates the cause of this disorder in the use of national currencies as net assets. The last part of this dense little book is devoted to the double payment (in money as well as in kind) of interest on external debts. Together with *La France souveraine de sa monnaie*, *Les pays au regime du FMI* represents the end point of Schmitt's investigation on the use of a national currency as international money and the point of departure for a most innovative analysis that will lead finally to the discovery of the pathological nature of countries' sovereign debt.

The main achievements of the last three decades

Schmitt's main 1985 text is his introduction to the Italian translation of Ricardo's monetary writings. This 83-page long introduction is a masterpiece, an impressive novel interpretation of the thought of the economist that Schmitt always admired the most and considered the most logical economist ever. Although Keynes admittedly inspired his work, Schmitt found himself more akin to Ricardo, and his 1985 introduction is a tribute to the great classical author. Contrary to what mainstream economists maintain, Schmitt claims that Ricardo's monetary analysis is entirely at odds with the quantity theory of money, and at the origin of the modern theory of money emissions. Schmitt (1985a) investigates Ricardo's distinction between nominal and real money, the role of production in the formation of money's purchasing power, the vehicular function of money, the theory of value and prices, and concludes by advocating Ricardo's attempt to regulate banks' monetary emissions according to the necessary distinction between money and income.

A paper on "The process of formation of economics in relation to other sciences" published in 1986 shows the originality of Schmitt's quantum macroeconomic analysis with respect to that advocated by mainstream economics. By referring to money and production, Schmitt (1986) rejects the physico-mathematical approach introduced by Walras and his followers, and identifies the aim of economics as that of "discovering the laws of production and the distribution of 'exchange values' in nations and their relations. In this respect [economics] can be considered an exact science, though it is true that it is only teleologically so" (Schmitt 1986: 129).

Let us abandon the chronological order and present Schmitt's main contributions from 1988 to 2014 by distinguishing three central arguments to which he devoted his attention: the critique of neoclassical general equilibrium analysis; the analysis of unemployment; and the problem of external debt.

On relative prices

Schmitt's critique of neoclassical analysis concentrates mainly on Walras's attempt at determining relative prices and is contained in a series of published and unpublished papers spanning from 1996 to 2012. Among them are "A new paradigm for the determination of money prices" (Schmitt 1996b); "An internal critique of general equilibrium theory" (Schmitt and De Gottardi 2003); "Relative prices are undermined by a mathematical error" (Schmitt 2012a); and three unpublished texts distributed to his students at the University of Fribourg, Switzerland (Schmitt 1999a; 1999b; 1999c).

The core of Schmitt's critique rests on his proof of the logical indeterminacy of relative prices. What he shows in his papers is that Walras's attempt at determining prices through the direct exchange of goods on the product market is doomed to failure. Schmitt's first argument consists in proving that, given any number of goods brought to market, the number of independent equations that should allow for the determination of their relative prices is greater than the number of unknown, which makes the system of equations undetermined. This is so for two reasons: (1) Walras's law is but a mere tautology and can therefore not be used to reduce the number of independent equations of supply and demand; (2) extra equations must be added to those of supply and demand in order to equalise the prices determined by each equation.

Let us consider the simplest of cases, where two goods are present on the market. The first difficulty neoclassical analysis is confronted with is to reduce to one the number of equations equalising the supply of each good to its demand. That is precisely what Walras's law should allow for by establishing that the

18 *Alvaro Cencini*

demand for one good is necessarily equal to the supply of the other, and vice versa. Yet, as argued by Schmitt, this law is nothing other than the definition of exchange: it is true only when exchange takes place and prices are known. But the fact is that the number of independent equations has to be reduced before exchange takes place in order to prove that Walras's general equilibrium system can indeed determine (and not simply define) relative prices. Being valid only at equilibrium, Walras's law is a mere truism and cannot reduce the number of independent equations: the system is hopelessly over-determined. Moreover, as Schmitt argues, another equation must be added allowing for the equalisation of the numerical prices for the first and the second good "for there is no guarantee at all that an agreement could ever be reached as to an exchange, at any price level, between pens [first good] and razor-blades [second good]" (Schmitt 2012a: 20). Walras's system of relative prices is therefore twice over-determined, three independent equations being two too many for the determination of a single unknown (the relative price of one good in terms of the other).

Schmitt's second argument is that "one price in two is missing in the series of the prices of pens in terms of razor-blades and in the series of the prices of razor-blades in terms of pens" (ibid.: 32), so that relative prices are logically undermined by a mathematical error. Schmitt's proof rests on the fact that, according to neoclassical analysis, the price series of different goods (say pens and razor-blades) are linked together, the price of one good being necessarily expressed in terms of the other and vice versa. If, for example, in the search for equilibrium, the price of razor-blades is multiplied by two, the price of pens is simultaneously divided by two. This means that if the price of razor-blades (expressed in terms of pens used as *numéraire*) is increased from one to two, "then all the prices of pens included in the interval between a half and one are wiped off the map" (ibid.: 35), and if the price of pens (expressed in razor-blades, chosen as *numéraire*) is decreased from one to a half "then all the prices of razor-blades included in the interval between one and two are equally wiped off the map" (ibid.: 36). It thus becomes impossible to scan the whole set of real numbers in search of equilibrium prices. The mathematical error is not an error in the field of mathematics, but consists in the attempt to determine relative prices through a mathematical procedure: "a mathematical error of the first order is committed when mathematics is allowed to be polluted by an erroneous argument in economics" (ibid.: 28).

On external debt

Schmitt's first published contributions to the study of countries' external debt go back to 1984, when he advanced the idea that external debt servicing is at the origin of a pathology resulting in the double payment of net interest. From 1984 to 2012 he worked relentlessly to provide the clearest possible arguments showing why countries are subject to the double charge of their external debt servicing, and his published and unpublished texts are too numerous to cite all. Let us only mention *External Debt Servicing: A Vicious Circle* (Cencini and Schmitt 1991); *Projet de manuscript sur la dette extérieure* (Schmitt 1994–95); his four papers

Introduction 19

published in the series *Quaderni di ricerca* of the Research Laboratory in Monetary Economics (Schmitt 2000a; 2000b; 2004; 2005); *Le théorème de l'intérêt* (Schmitt 2007); and "Sovereign debt and interest payments" (Schmitt 2012c).

Starting from the payment of net interest on external debt carried out by less developed countries, Schmitt observes that interest payments are entered in their current account consistently with the balance-of-payments methodology, which means that they are 'fed' by part of the indebted countries' domestic resources. If net interest payments were entered in the financial account of indebted country A, they would be financed by the rest of the world, R. In reality, interest is paid by the indebted country itself, which does so through the unrequited transfer of an amount of its internal resources. Indeed, "[t]he value of A's current output is inclusive of the product added thanks to the use of a foreign capital in its domestic process of production" (Schmitt 2012c: 252). This means that a part of the indebted country's current output is owned from the moment of its production by (is due as interest to) the rest of the world. This explains why the payment of net interest implies that part of A's exports are transferred abroad without any counterpart: what Schmitt calls the 'real payment' of net interest reduces the amount of foreign currencies obtained by indebted countries in exchange for their exports of real goods.

If *IM* represents A's total imports (commercial and financial) and *EX* represents its total exports, the monetary payment of net interest, *in*, increases A's expenditures to $IM + in$. At the same time, the real payment of *in* reduces A's receipts from *EX* to $EX - in$. The total gap between A's expenditures and receipts is therefore equal to $2in$, and can be filled only through an external loan and a decrease in A's official reserves, each equal to *in*.

In his last four years Schmitt devoted all his energy to the study of the anomaly that is at the origin of the double charge of external debt servicing: the pathological formation of external debt itself. In his 2012 paper "Sovereign debt and interest payments", Schmitt applies the principle of 'double double-entry bookkeeping' and shows that when a country, A, borrows abroad a sum of foreign currency in order to re-finance its domestic economy, or to pay for its net total imports, it is subject to an outflow of foreign currency twice as high as the inflow (2012c). His argument is rigorous, but very abstract and hard to follow, and was soon to be superseded by one of Schmitt's most revolutionary and ground-breaking discovery: the illegitimacy of countries' sovereign debts. In his last text, published posthumously on the SSRN website in 2014, Schmitt shows that sovereign debts, that is, debts affecting countries *vis-à-vis* the rest of the world, are the pathological result of a non-system of international payments where indebted countries are forced to pay twice their net global imports (of commercial and financial goods). Consider the case of an indebted country A. The first payment is made by A's residents and implies a loss of A's domestic resources; the second payment, of a macroeconomic nature, weighs on the country itself, defined as the set of its residents, and consists in the purchase of the foreign currency necessary to pay foreign exporters. Having already been fully paid by A's residents, A's net imports

20   *Alvaro Cencini*

should not require any additional payment. Yet, this in not so, because A's creditors require to be paid in foreign currency and because foreign currencies are wrongly considered as if they were net assets. Country A is therefore forced to purchase a means of payment that should be provided free of cost by a system of international payments that is still to come.

As shown by Schmitt, in today non-system net imports are paid both in real and, additionally, in monetary terms. The real payment is a transfer of domestic resources, which are the very object of the sum borrowed abroad by A's residents to finance their net purchases: *"foreign currencies borrowed to pay for net imports have as their object real goods to be exported in a future period"* (Schmitt 2014: 37, italics in the original). The monetary payment is the payment of the foreign currency necessary to pay R's exporters. All in all, country A and its residents pay twice their net imports, the second payment being *"carried out in favour of a 'financial bubble'"* (ibid.: 40, italics in the original). In the first part of his 2014 paper, Schmitt gives various proofs of the double charge of foreign debts and the pathological nature of sovereign debts. These proofs confirm that, far from having benefitted from 'free lunches', indebted countries have suffered, and still suffer, from an illegitimate spoliation that drastically reduces their chances to develop their economy.

In the second part of his 2014 paper, Schmitt advocates the principle of a reform that would allow each country to avoid incurring a sovereign debt while earning, as a net profit, the amount paid by its residents, denominated in domestic currency, to finance their net imports. Today, the amount of domestic currency paid by A's residents is lost and recovered only through a foreign loan that adds to the one incurred by A to obtain the amount of foreign currency needed to pay R's residents (which defines A's sovereign debt). Tomorrow, the amount of domestic currency paid by A's residents would be earned by their country (more precisely by A's Sovereign Bureau), and no sovereign debt would affect country A.

Directing the interested reader to Chapter 10 of this volume, let us merely note that A's foreign creditors will be fully paid, and hope that Schmitt's legacy will soon find a concrete outcome, since the order introduced by the reform will benefit deficit and surplus countries alike.

Part I

Analysing the domestic economy

1 *La formation du pouvoir d'achat*

A historical perspective

Claude Gnos

Introduction

The analysis of money and the formation and spending of its purchasing power were centre stage in Schmitt's work. As this volume attests, Schmitt developed his thoughts on this topic and on the approach to macroeconomics it involved throughout his work, in connection with the examination of current issues such as inflation, unemployment, the reform of the international monetary system, European integration, and the sovereign debt crisis. This chapter focuses on the former analysis, with a view to putting it in a historical perspective with reference both to the development of the author's own thinking and to the history of economic thought.

The next section mainly refers to Schmitt's first book, entitled *La formation du pouvoir d'achat* (1960), which was a revised version of his PhD dissertation he defended in 1958 in Paris. In this book, Schmitt emphasised, with reference to Keynes's *General Theory* (1936), the need for a clear distinction between the formation and spending of income. This distinction has been a starting point for a fundamental revision of macroeconomic theory. The third section aims at examining the scope of this revision with respect to the standard interpretations of the Keynesian revolution. The fourth section sets Schmitt's insights on money and its purchasing power in the context of the historical development of the theory of money. The fifth section concludes the chapter.

Formation and spending of income: the nature and role of money at issue

In the introduction to *La formation du pouvoir d'achat,* Schmitt (1960) explained that he was puzzled by the equations Keynes (1936: 63) introduced in *The General Theory*, namely:

$$\text{income} = \text{value of output} = \text{consumption} + \text{investment}$$
$$\text{saving} = \text{income} - \text{consumption}$$

According to Schmitt, who attached paramount importance to compliance with logical thinking, the concepts of consumption featuring in these two equations

24   *Claude Gnos*

should not be confused, otherwise the equations would contradict each other. This means, he argued, that the formation of the national income should be clearly distinguished from its spending. Income, that is the purchasing power earned by households, is formed in the payment defining the remuneration of the factors producing consumption and investment goods, it is spent on the consumption goods produced, and saved for the remainder.

Reviewing the economic literature relating to Keynes's equations, Schmitt observed that most writers, despite the diversity of approaches, share the same postulate, that is the idea that national income results from purchases of produced goods (Schmitt 1960: 49). Very few of them have the intuition that the payment of the production factors may fall into a somewhat different category. Yet, the contradictory nature of this postulate should be obvious. In so far as national income is supposed to result from its spending, neither its formation nor its spending can be explained logically: according to this assumption, in order for income to be formed and spent, it should first be spent (and formed beforehand). This is clearly illogical. To understand why leading economists may have overlooked this contradiction, we may assume that they are entangled in the usual representation by which economic transactions are mere exchanges, goods and money being supposed to circulate in opposite directions, passing continuously from hand to hand. That is precisely the representation Schmitt undertook to dismiss while arguing for an in-depth review of the nature and role of money in the economy.

The critical issue is whether the purchasing power of money pre-exists or not to the payment of the wage bills of the production factors. In the first case, firms would pass an income they own or borrow, that is, pre-existent purchasing power, to the factors. The factors would thus earn a purchasing power that the firms would loose; it would be a zero-sum game for the economy as a whole. Moreover, supposed to be pre-existent, income would be left unexplained. Therefore, to account for the formation of the community's income, we have to consider the second case. Actually, firms do not have to transfer any purchasing power to the factors. It is enough that they ask banks to pay out money units that will form the monetary cost of the production they undertake. To repay the bank loan and make good the production cost, firms will have to sell the produced goods to the factors (see Schmitt 1960: 64–5).

In this way, we have the confirmation that a monetary income is formed whose objects are the goods being produced. This income is net for the economy as a whole. It should be noticed that the expression 'factors of production' indicates workers exclusively. As a matter of fact, from a macroeconomic viewpoint, the cost of intermediate and capital goods *in fine* reduces to the wage bills paid by those firms that produce these goods. When purchasing these goods, firms spend formed incomes. This does not mean, of course, that capital goods are not physically productive: labour solely could not produce the diversity and variety of goods currently supplied in markets. Simply, in so far as we are dealing with the monetary dimension of output and income, the payment of wage bills alone is relevant.

La formation du pouvoir d'achat   25

Schmitt insisted that when created or, to use a more appropriate word, *issued* by banks, money units are just "pure units of account" (Schmitt 1960: 64, our translation). As he confirmed in further writings, these units of account or numbers derive their purchasing power from production:

> What the bank does on behalf of its customers is merely to lend a numerical form to their payments. What one may term the 'substance' of the payments is entirely provided by the national economy, whose production of physical goods and intangible services, for consumption and investment, is cast into 'bank numbers'. The national economy *integrates* its physical output into the issued bank numbers (their envelope).
>
> (Schmitt 2012b: 73)

Paid out in wages, nominal money units thereby monetise output and thus acquire a purchasing power. Referring to Adam Smith's distinction between 'real' and 'nominal' money, we may say that, according to Schmitt's analysis, 'nominal money' turns therefore into 'real money'.

The usual expression 'economic value' needs thus to be revisited. Neither money nor physical objects have a value on their own. Value is a relationship: it denotes the fact that goods are integrated into a given amount of units of account, which, by the same token, transform the heterogeneous physical output into a homogenous economic magnitude. To insist on this feature of the monetary economy of production, Schmitt opposes what he terms 'absolute' exchanges – produced goods are changed into a monetary magnitude – to the usual notion of relative exchanges (see next chapter).

The fact that firms successively spend money on production costs and get it back when selling the goods produced induced Schmitt and some other writers – especially Barrère (1979) and Parguez (1975) in France, Graziani (1990) in Italy, Lavoie (1984), Seccareccia (1996) and Rochon (1999) in Canada – to put the focus on the concept of the monetary circuit that, although usually unsung, underpinned many approaches in the history of the economic thought (see Gnos, 2006). However, Schmitt fundamentally stood apart from his colleagues who viewed the circuit as a flow of money that is offset, after a given time interval, by a backflow. With reference to double-entry bookkeeping, he came to the conclusion that the flow and the backflow of money are simultaneous events:

> Since wages are paid in bank money, they are paid by credit–debit transactions, not by simple credits. This is absolutely certain, because every person who is credited by a bank is, in the same moment of circular flow, debited by the same bank for exactly the same amount. Money wages' life span is thus reduced to an instant.
>
> (Schmitt 2012b: 79)

The payment of wage bills actually defines an instantaneous circuit that is at odds with the usual conception developed by other schools of thought. "The emission

26 *Claude Gnos*

of wages is a monetary circuit as rigorously defined, for the reason that the [money units] issued in the payment 'start' from the issuing bank and are immediately recovered by it, at the same instant" (Schmitt 2012b: 81).

The fact that banks instantaneously recover the money wages they issue on behalf of firms does not mean, however, that production factors obtain a zero sum of wages. They actually obtain bank deposits, that is, financial assets or, in Schmitt's words, "financial wages". As he pointed out, "[t]he debit attached to the credit of wage earners has a necessary and univocal significance: *money wages are replaced by an equivalent sum of financial wages*" (Schmitt 2012b: 79, italics in the original).

What is the object of bank deposits? We noted that money wages are a form incorporating the goods produced. Credited with money wages, workers obtain simultaneously the form and its content. The banks instantaneously recovering the form (the money units), what is left to wage earners is bank deposits, that is, the content in a new form: "In each instantaneous circuit a part of national output is deposited with banks. What can be found in banks is not a deposit of money, but a deposit of produced output" (Schmitt 2012b: 82).

Depositing the output with banks, wage earners save it until they consume it. As we just noted, deposits are financial assets, that is, claims on banks whose object is the current output. Of course, banks are not net debtors to wage earners: to every entry made on the liabilities side of a bank's balance sheet corresponds an equivalent entry on the assets side of it. Thus, workers' claims on banks are balanced by claims of banks on firms. *In fine*, workers are creditors of firms through banks. Banks owe nothing to workers; it is firms that owe the output to them. In order to consume the goods produced, wage earners will ask banks to proceed to payments on their behalf. Then, like they do in every payment they operate, banks will issue a number of money units that they will immediately recover. As a result, workers' deposits and the corresponding debt of the firms will decrease accordingly. It should be noted that firms do not necessarily borrow money from banks in order to pay out wages: they currently draw on bank deposits they own. Nevertheless, the analysis does not change: firms become, so to say, indebted to themselves since they have to replenish the deposits they spent on wages. The payment of wage bills by firms generates workers' bank deposits that are cancelled when wage earners and their dependents spend them on the goods produced.

The fact that workers' bank deposits incorporate all the goods currently produced does not mean that workers will obtain them in full when spending their bank deposits. Firms also earn incomes, that is, profits they will either redistribute in interest and dividends or spend on their own in order to invest in capital goods.

If so, then how are profits formed? Consistent with his plea for a clear-cut distinction between the formation and the spending of incomes, Schmitt denied the argument that profits resulting from sale proceeds would be additional to factors' income: this argument amounts to an assumption that part of the income of the community as a whole could result from purchases. In fact, "profits are transferred incomes" (Schmitt 1960: 83, our translation). When paying, say, 100 money units (mu) for goods whose factor cost is 50 mu, workers and their dependents spend an income of 50 mu and transfer the additional part to the firms that, literally, take their original place and then own the corresponding bank deposits. Schmitt suggested that this analysis also accounts for the payment of bank charges, that is, charges bank borrowers have to pay for in addition to the repayment of their loan. Indeed, how can borrowers as a whole repay 1200 mu when they only got 1000 mu from banks? "We suggest that the paradox is resolved once we conceive of the existence of income transfers: charges are paid out of borrowers' purchasing power" (Schmitt 1960: 102, our translation).

Banks never recover more money units than the amount of money units they issue (1000 mu in the above example). What they obtain, in the form of charges paid by borrowers, is part of the borrowers' income transferred to them, which they or their dependents will spend on goods produced. Then, through their sales, firms recover the total amount of money units they spent on factor cost and are able to pay back their loans (1000 mu).

A fundamental revision of macroeconomic theory

The distinction between the formation and spending of income entails a fundamental revision of macroeconomic theory that Schmitt developed ever since his first book. He notably questioned Keynes's multiplier theory. According to Keynes (1936: 113–15), as we know, any autonomous increment in investment (DI) would induce an increment of current income (DY) equal to k times the increment in investment:

$$DY = k \times DI$$

Schmitt's conclusion is clear: "The purchasing power of money can be spent only once: it cancels when goods are purchased. Purchases do not generate incomes" (Schmitt 1960: 109, our translation). This means that, contrary to the common interpretation of Keynes's multiplier, there is no possible chain by which the spending of incomes, albeit on investment goods, would generate incomes over space and time.

However, Schmitt developed an original interpretation of the multiplier. He argued that "Keynes's multiplier theory implies a revolutionary definition of autonomous expenditures. They must be financed out of money and not out of money income" (Schmitt 1972a: 125). This is an argument that Schmitt developed in two books, *L'analyse macroéconomique des revenus* and *Macroeconomic Theory: A Fundamental Revision*, published in 1971 and 1972 respectively. This argument was first introduced in his 1960 book, where Schmitt proposed a clear-cut distinction between the formation and the spending of income, and depicted income formation as the association, in the payment of wage bills, of pure money units issued by banks and produced goods. As a consequence, he then argued, "the multiplier is always equal to one over time and space" (Schmitt 1960: 109, our translation). The formation of a given amount of income allows the expenditure of the same amount of income on goods, no more and no less.

28   *Claude Gnos*

In his 1960 book, Schmitt endorsed Keynes's rejection of Say's law according to which supply creates its own demand, "meaning by this in some significant, but not clearly defined, sense that the whole of the costs of production must necessarily be spent in the aggregate, directly or indirectly, on purchasing the product" (Keynes 1936: 18). Schmitt admitted that part of the current money income may be left unspent, that is to say, hoarded. Therefore, the equality $S = I$ that Keynes induced from his income equations would be an equilibrium condition: "the economy is in balance provided that the purchasing power that is not spent in the current period be invested, capitalised" (Schmitt 1960: 71, our translation). In his further books, however, Schmitt argued that the way output is integrated in money units allows for a renewed interpretation of Say's law, which, far from denying the possible existence of unemployment, would contrariwise condition its occurrence. The argument is a follows. Physical output is integrated in a sum of money units that forms factors' income. This income defines a purchasing power that is sufficient to allow income holders (including profit, rent, and interest holders) to purchase the whole output. However, the spending of this income is also necessary, whatever may be the behaviour of income holders:

> If the public – including profit holders – refrain from spending all their available incomes on final purchases, firms will incur a loss which can only be compensated by 'forced' purchases at the firms' expense of the goods that nobody wants to buy. In such a case identity $Y=C+I$ diminishes profits. In order to avoid a loss, firms curtail employment.
>
> (Schmitt 1972a: 196)

In this view, Say's law means the identity between supply (Y) and demand ($C+I$), part of the latter possibly being 'forced' at the expense of firms. Schmitt emphasised that this identity holds with respect to realised quantities, that is, the income actually formed in the economy. As a consequence, the determination of national income and its variations cannot result from the adjustment between Y and $C+I$ depicted in usual macroeconomic textbooks: "Identity $Y = C+I$ only means that each and every output must finally be bought and paid for by somebody. From this 'tautology' we can derive no consequence whatever concerning the dynamic variation in national income" (Schmitt 1972a: 186).

Schmitt (1972a: 190) insisted that "identity $Y = C+I$ is thus verified during any interval of time, however short or long". This observation notably induces a strict divergence between income and price determination:

> In price theory, we can adjust supply and demand. No logical error is involved, for identity $s = d$ only holds instantaneously, when transactions actually take place. At any other time, the two factors of demand and supply are separate and they can thus be weighted against each other.
>
> (Schmitt 1972a: 190)

La formation du pouvoir d'achat   29

With regard to income determination, Schmitt pointed out that when firms have to make decisions about the variety and quantity of goods they are going to produce, supply and demand are only virtual and may be subject to adjustments. Firms will not produce goods they expect income holders not to buy. That is the core argument of Keynes's principle of effective demand as exhibited in *The General Theory*. In his further writings (from 1984 onward) Schmitt deepened his analysis and showed that unemployment is not, fundamentally, due to consumers' behaviour, but to the way the process of capital accumulation is managed by banks and the financial system. According to this view, contrary to Keynes's argument, demand deficiency has nothing to do with income holders' propensity to consume. It is generated by capital's malformation (see Chapters 3 and 4 in this volume). In this way, Schmitt deepened our understanding of macroeconomics: the latter is definitively autonomous with respect to microeconomics. Macroeconomics is concerned with laws and features such as the identity of output and income, and the instantaneous flow and backflow of the money units issued by banks, both of which underpin the economic system. These laws are key to understanding both the orderly functioning of the economic system and its flaws like inflation and unemployment.

Schmitt's considerations about the time dimension of economic magnitudes led him, in his further books, especially in *Inflation, chômage et malformations du capital* (Schmitt 1984a), to formulate what he termed 'quantum macroeconomics'. Although the physical process of production takes time, the transformation of output from physical objects into 'real money' units is instantaneous. Consequently, from the economic viewpoint, production itself is instantaneous. It is the process through which the physical output is changed into income and thus becomes a homogeneous economic magnitude. By the same token, the time period during which matter and energy are made into physical goods is instantaneously transformed into a quantum of time, that is, an indivisible interval of time. This view is in sharp contrast to the mainstream approach by which production is considered as a function of continuous or discontinuous time.

The reference to the history of monetary theory

As evidenced by his first book, Schmitt essentially found inspiration in Keynes's theory. According to him, the distinction between the formation and the spending of income was the true foundation for Keynes's theory (see Schmitt 1960: 77). In support of his argument he notably recalled that Keynes had the intuition thereof in his *Treatise on Money*, when he proposed to renew the monetary theory, as the following passage attests:

> I propose therefore, to break away from the traditional method of setting out from the total quantity of money irrespective of the purposes on which it is employed, and to start instead – for reasons which will become clear as we proceed – with the flow of the community's earnings or money income, and with its twofold division (1) into the parts which have been *earned* by the

30   *Claude Gnos*

production of consumption goods and of investment goods respectively, and (2) into the parts which are *expended* on consumption goods and on savings respectively.

(Keynes 1930/1971: 121)

We noticed that the analysis of the nature of money is central to Schmitt's approach to macroeconomics. He highlighted the fact that money is a pure unit of account that banks simultaneously debit and credit to their clients' accounts. That is the foundation of his account of the formation and spending of national income. In his writings, Schmitt committed himself to setting his theory against the history of monetary theory. He notably examined Ricardo's theory of money and the theories of the neoclassical school. He pointed out the failures of these theories. He was convinced that because it was flawed the classical theory of money prepared for the advent of the marginalist approach that, in its turn, paved the way for a new conception of money and its purchasing power (see Schmitt 1960: 115). The reference to the history of economic thought, he argued, allows for a better understanding of what is at issue.

In the first instance, Schmitt (1960) examined the Ricardian theory of money, which was, he argued, the most coherent approach compared to the approaches of the other classical writers. He noticed that two main features characterise classical monetary thought: money is a commodity among others, and it is not consumed by income holders. Consequently, money has a value on its own (an intrinsic value) just like any commodity and may circulate in the form of debt instruments (paper money).

Ricardo (1821/1951) was a proponent of the labour theory of value: the labour spent on the production of goods was deemed appropriate to determine their exchange value. Therefore, in this view, the purchasing power of the money unit (in terms of goods) is proportional to the relative value of the money unit and goods. Production is the source of the goods available in markets and the source of their value. The role of money is to ensure the circulation of produced goods from producers to consumers. It is, in the words of Smith (1776/1970: 385), "the great wheel of circulation". Not being a consumer good, commodity-money may be replaced by convertible paper money, provided the latter is not issued in excess compared to the goods available, hence Ricardo's search for an economical and secure currency (Ricardo 1816/1951).

However, Ricardo's approach was trapped in an impasse. He could not conceive of an invariable unit of measure since the value of money, just as the value of other commodities, was likely to vary over space and time. Moreover, the varying lapses of time necessary to produce and bring goods to markets disrupted the theory of labour-value.

Later on, Schmitt continued to examine the conundrums of the classical theory of value in two books, co-authored with Cencini, on Marx's theory (Cencini and Schmitt 1976; 1977). In this way, he intended to confirm the need and relevance of the renewed conception of money and its purchasing power that he was promoting, as well as the theory of income distribution this conception displays.

La formation du pouvoir d'achat 31

The idea that value is a dimension or substance intrinsically attached to goods and money exchanging for each other had proved to be irrelevant.

To the same end, Schmitt also reviewed the neoclassical theory of money. He praised the marginalist school for dismissing the concept of intrinsic value incorporated in goods and money. However, he criticised it because, this feature notwithstanding, it retained the notion that value is a subjective dimension of goods, as a result of the utility economic agents expect to draw from consuming them. In this view, money that can in no way be consumed derives its value from the value of the goods it allows the purchaser to obtain. So far so good, but how is the purchasing power of money determined? Schmitt (1960) shows that the neoclassical theory is at a loss to give a relevant answer. This theory is entangled in a dichotomy between real quantities and money: it assumes that real economic quantities and prices may be determined without any consideration for money that is thus left undetermined. In *Monnaie, salaires et profits*, Schmitt (1966a) examines at length the attempt by Patinkin (1965) to challenge this dichotomy with the introduction of the so-called 'real balance effect' of changes in the money supply. Schmitt showed that the dichotomy cannot be overcome in this way: when real variables are determined independently of the quantity of money, as they are supposed to be in the neoclassical system, an increase in the quantity of money cannot but decrease the purchasing power of each money unit; it does not affect the purchasing power of the quantity of money as a whole. The purchasing power of money balances fundamentally remains unchanged. "The real value of money balances is thus determined whatever the level of money prices and it is always well-balanced by definition" (Schmitt 1966a: 81, our translation). There is no real balance effect and the dichotomy is confirmed.

Schmitt praised Walras's theory for its attempt to measure goods by pure numbers. However, he criticised it, because, to do so, Walras (1926) argued that a pure number may be attached to a commodity he named '*numéraire*', in terms of which the (relative) value of other commodities would be expressed. On this basis, relative prices and hence numerical prices would be determined through the resolution of the usual system of supply and demand equations. The trouble is that expressing values in numerical terms does not leave the number of independent equations of supply and demand unchanged. Schmitt (2012a: 21) showed that "the solution is hopelessly over-determined". He thus found confirmation of the relevance of his own analytical view, according to which the wage unit, rather than a pure number attached to a '*numéraire*', is the actual standard of value in economics, and confirmation of the need for a renewed approach to the way goods and money get integrated in the real world.

Conclusion

Bernard Schmitt used to say to his entourage that his research work had been motivated by an idea that literally grabbed him when he was examining Keynes's income equations. From then, he had no option but to deepen this idea and to endeavour to make it duly recognised by the scientific community. This idea, as

32 *Claude Gnos*

explained above, was the need to clearly distinguish the formation of national income, that is to say, the formation of money's purchasing power, from its spending. Should not this simple idea have been familiar to economists?

The brief historical perspective outlined in this chapter shows that this idea was more complex to develop than one may think at first. It specifically questions the representation of the economy that both classical and neoclassical writers favoured throughout their research work, that is, the general idea that monetary production economies may be conceived of as exchange economies where goods and money circulate in opposite directions. It also questions the age-old definition of money as a commodity or an asset, which complements this representation. Truly, the new definition of money has the disadvantage of looking at odds with common sense. "Admittedly, the proposition that money is but a number defies common sense" (Schmitt 2012a: 36). Last but not least, Schmitt's insights with respect to the formation of money's purchasing power challenge the usual conception of the determination of national income, and introduce the concept of quantum macroeconomics that dismisses the usual macroeconomic approaches defined in terms of static or dynamic analysis.

2 Absolute exchange and relative exchange

Jean-Luc Bailly

Introduction

Bernard Schmitt demonstrates scientifically in his quantum theory of money and production that payments hinge on *absolute exchanges* and not, as the vast majority of economists believe, on relative exchanges, which at rock bottom would be barter. In this, he continues along the path Keynes opens up in asserting that the principles governing our economies are not the principles of a *real-exchange economy*. Keynes contests the representations by which economic relations are supposedly articulated upon reciprocal transfers of goods and money among autonomous individuals: "The theory which I desiderate would deal, in contradistinction to this, with an economy in which money plays a part of its own and affects motives and decisions and is, in short, one of the operative factors in the situation" (Keynes 1933/1973: 408). However, although he radically dismisses the idea that economic activity is based on relative exchanges, Keynes fails to give any explicit indications about the nature of the exchanges we engage in daily. It is only with the works of Bernard Schmitt that it has come to be understood that the economic circuit is not tantamount to a space in which money and goods cross paths as they move around.

Methodological individualism sets itself the assumption that economic activity rests on the exchange of 'initial endowments' among separate individuals who meet up on markets. Economists infer from this archetype that microeconomics underpins macroeconomics. Production itself supposedly consists of reciprocal transfers of pre-existing wealth that is conserved in exchanges.[1] In this way microeconomics – the analysis of individual behaviour on markets – is supposedly the 'natural' foundation of economic analysis and macroeconomics a derived field, the purpose of which is the study of aggregate forms of individual behaviour.

In the next section I take the proponents of methodological individualism quite literally and scrutinise the economic activity of an autonomous individual. The aim is to showcase the principle that any worker forms an equivalence relation between his output and his consumption when he issues the proceeds of his labour on himself. Relying on the works of Bernard Schmitt, I shall endeavour to show that money is included in its real emission. Thereafter, it will be possible to understand that, in our generalised wage-earning economies, although firms and

34 *Jean-Luc Bailly*

the banking system stand between producers and their physical output, the principle of the equivalence of production and consumption on each producer taken individually remains entirely relevant. As production and consumption are determined mutually, it follows that, although workers are paid in bank money, they are not separated from their output and accordingly all exchanges on the various markets are absolute exchanges by nature.

The absolute exchange of the isolated worker

Bernard Schmitt shows in his quantum theory of production that *it is in the nature of money to be endogenous*. In other words, money is not integrated into the real world in the way that an object formed outside of the economic process might be. The theory of emissions gives us to understand that money is immediately a component of the real world.

> From the moment labour appeared, money was present within the emission. This idea runs counter to the most widespread opinion that monetary exchange is concluded between two 'partners'. In point of fact, the worker performs a perfect exchange all on his own.
>
> (Schmitt 1984a: 340–41, our translation)

The autonomous producer's real emission

Any isolated producer immediately consumes his own output as soon as his work takes on a material form liable to satisfy his wants. "The produce of labour constitutes the natural recompense or wages of labour. In that original state of things, which precedes both the appropriation of land and the accumulation of stock, the whole produce of labour belongs to the labourer" (Smith 1776/1904: I.8.1–I.8.2). Although the worker has no prospect of exchanging with others, even so he does evaluate things since he compares the exertion he puts into producing his output and the satisfaction he derives from consuming it. To discuss this, I propose like many economists to use Daniel Defoe's *Robinson Crusoe*,[2] which was first published in 1719. The only thing that has real value for Crusoe is what he consumes: "But all I could make use of was all that was valuable: I had enough to eat and supply my wants, and what was all the rest to me?" (Defoe 1719/1920: 170). The purpose of his production is consumption. If he does not consume, the fruit of his labour is lost. "[I]f I sowed more corn than I could eat, it must be spoiled" (p. 170). Spoiled wheat is worthless to Crusoe. It is as if it did not exist and therefore had not been produced.[3]

> In a word, the nature and experience of things dictated to me, upon just reflection, that all the good things of this world are not farther good to us than they are for our use; and that, whatever we may heap up to give others, we enjoy just as much as we can use, and no more.
>
> (Defoe 1719/1920: 170)[4]

Absolute exchange and relative exchange   35

So, it is consumption that validates production.

Having failed to dig a canal, Crusoe reflects on the episode: "This grieved me heartily; and now I saw, though too late, the folly of beginning a work before we count the cost, and before we judge rightly of our own strength to go through with it" (Defoe 1719/1920: 169). If it fails to contribute to satisfaction, labour is lost; the effort has vanished without any equivalent return for the worker's benefit. Despite the effort expended, Crusoe's work is not encapsulated in any useful form; he has toiled in vain; he has produced nothing.

Schmitt (1984a: 58, italics in the original, our translation) explains that "*[p] roduction is a wave motion*". In other words, it is because the labour is completed in a particular useful form at a given instant that it is productive from the instant when the manufacture of the desired object was undertaken. This means that Crusoe's activity could not be termed production unless he had completed his canal and used it to satisfy his needs. The productive character of labour is grasped all at once, retroactively, as of its completion, and not over the course of the activity unfolding. The useful character of labour flows from the completion of the project that motivated the producer, and not from its performance and its qualities. Because it ends in the creation of a form utility, so "*[a]ll production is completed at an instant of continuous time*" (Schmitt 1984a: 57, italics in the original, our translation). He goes on: "Production only comes into existence upon its completion [...] because it is the coming together of a plan and its accomplishment" (Schmitt 1984a: 58, our translation). As output does not exist until it is achieved, it can be said that "*work quantises time*" (p. 59, italics in the original, our translation), and so, as each output is a quantum of time, it is from the outset a magnitude. In this way, production relates to finite and *unitary* durations, and it can be measured at the very instant that it is accomplished in the completion of the producer's plan. The canal is not finished; the digging of a hole in the ground is not production, because Crusoe does not fulfil his plan.

Generally, it can be said that carrying out work can be called production, not just with respect to the creation of utility forms, but also with respect to their use. Hayek (1931/1967: 36) wrote: "The term production I shall always use in its widest possible sense, that is to say, all processes necessary to bring goods into the hands of the consumer."

Crusoe consumes the output to which he gives rise forthwith. The product is converted into use value immediately, and that conversion marks the end of the process of appropriation in which Crusoe has engaged. It is because he finally has the output at his disposal that his work is meaningful. The process of appropriation is a unitary one. Production and consumption are organically related, and no production is to be observed without consumption and no consumption without production. "Reduced to their essence, production and consumption are defined one by the other" (Dieterlen 1964: 119, our translation). In other words, consumption cannot be determined outside of its relation with production, and production cannot be determined outside of its relation with consumption.

Production and consumption are connected by a relation of equivalence. However, this equivalence does not arise from any adjustment between supply

36   *Jean-Luc Bailly*

and demand. Being alone on his island, Crusoe does not exchange with anyone but himself. He is identically both supplier and demander of his output. It follows from this that the relation between production and consumption is an *identity* quantitatively defining and delimiting Crusoe's economic activity.

As production and consumption are not two separate activities in time, we can say that Crusoe *converts* his efforts and the exertion his work causes him into satisfaction and enjoyment of his output. Through his work, he effects real emissions consisting in the "creation–destruction of the 'economic form' of matter. Before work, matter is entirely 'natural'; work transforms matter into use value" (Schmitt 1984a: 340, our translation).

Crusoe's economic activity is composed of a twofold *conversion*: (1) the conversion of matter into a useful form; (2) the conversion of that useful form into a use value. In other words, the full process of production and consumption hinges on *absolute exchanges*. Crusoe exchanges with himself when he converts, through his labour, matter into output and also when he changes his output into satisfaction. The relation between his production and consumption is not a relative one. The one is not compared with the other. It is immediately an equivalence that defines Crusoe's production and consumption.

In that it is an emission, Crusoe's revenue is not imaginary or of the mind. It is real or *effective* so to speak. Income does not originate from the use of goods and services, as Fisher (1906) claims. It results from the full production–consumption movement. Although it is instantaneous, Crusoe's income is net, both in its formation and its destruction. In its formation, it consists in the attribution of a new utility form to matter. In its destruction, it consists in the conversion of a utility form into a use value. We can say that Crusoe makes emissions in that he shapes matter into useful forms (production), which prove useful because matter (consumption) comes out of them for enjoyment.

Money in Crusoe's real emission

It might still be thought that the question of equivalence can be handled by sticking to the logic of analyses in terms of relative exchanges, that is, by *relating* effort to satisfaction or vice versa. For there to be a relative determination, the two things present would need to have some form of cardinal measurement. However, this is not the case. There is no homogeneous measurement unit for effort or for work generally.[5] Nor does satisfaction have any homogeneous measurement unit. So a quantity of satisfaction cannot be compared against a quantity of labour. Ultimately, no reciprocal relationship of objective determination can be established between labour and satisfaction. Accordingly, the equation connecting production and consumption cannot be expressed either in units of effort or in units of satisfaction, nor even in the relation between them. This means that Crusoe does not engage in relative exchanges with himself.

Having recovered money from the ship, Crusoe might use it to materialise the measurement of his activity. But this 'exogenous' money is of no use to him. "I had [...] a parcel of money, as well gold as silver [...]. Alas! there the sorry,

Absolute exchange and relative exchange 37

useless stuff lay; I had no more manner of business for it" (Defoe 1719/1920: 171). These pieces of gold and silver are alien to his activity and can at no time be integrated into his economy as money. The gold and silver are not involved in his production or consumption, and they have no bearing on the process capable of determining any aspect of his life on his island.

To measure things means escaping from the physical or mental conditions of production and consumption. The *relation* between production and consumption is objective by nature. This becomes clear when Friday settles on the island. There arises at this point a new overall relation that takes account of his existence; both his contribution to production and his consumption, in short, his own equivalence. However, no market relationship is established between Friday and Crusoe. So, they have no need to homogenise their respective production–consumption, and accordingly they do not create any monetary *signs*.

As said above, each output is the object of production and consumption, it is the identity between them and, at the same time, it marks the existence of a relation of equivalence between the producer's production and consumption. It can be thought, then, that by measuring the output we will obtain the measurement of the equivalence. It is certain that equivalence cannot be measured in units of utility; utility does not have a unit of measurement.

Let it be repeated, what is to be measured here is neither the output itself, nor production or consumption separately, but the production–consumption relation. Schmitt (1984a: 340, emphases added, our translation) asserts that, "[a]s soon as labour appeared, money was present within the emission. *What is money if not the equivalence between production and consumption?*" Later he adds that "money was for ever present in people's labour, *within real emission*" (p. 341, italics in the original). To understand money in its real emission, we must go back to the question of Crusoe's emission.

Relying on the dictionary definition that to produce is "to bring into existence (what does not yet exist)",[6] in a word to create, we can say that in truth what Crusoe *creates* is strictly an equivalence, and only equivalence, of his production and his consumption. This equation is not the outcome of matching numbers against physical outputs obtained. Crusoe does not issue numbers on himself and, moreover, "[i]t is superfluous for the equivalence to be exerted through an object that is inscribed in time" (Schmitt 1984a: 340, our translation), and this, more especially as what is produced is consumed immediately.

We have argued that production–consumption is a wave and particle phenomenon of creation–destruction. In making things Crusoe expends energy, but that expenditure, that energy *debit* is reflected by a gain, because it is converted into an output that goes to his *credit*. His efforts *pay off* so to speak. However, that is not the purpose of production. The process is accomplished in consumption, in other words the moment the output is converted into use value, which is reflected by its destruction. In accounting terms, Crusoe is *debited* by the output in its utility form, while he is *credited* with use values from which he derives some satisfaction. No matter what the nature of the output and the unit in which it is physically measured, this law invariably holds for any producer taken individually.

38   *Jean-Luc Bailly*

For as much as money is "a balance sheet operation" (Minsky (1986) cited by Wray (1990: 267)), we can say that Crusoe issues his own money, without there being any need for him to issue numbers or to use objects apart from what he produces, since he does not exchange with anyone.

As money is "inside the real emission", if Crusoe produces 20 kg of bread and wants to keep a balance sheet of his activity, he will write 20 kg as his *assets*. But as the bread is immediately converted into use value, since it is in that that the process is accomplished, he chalks up 20 kg to his *liabilities* by the same token. He does so because, in view of his plan to consume 20 kg of bread, he *owes* himself the 20 kg of bread that he *delivers* to himself. Being part of the real emission, it cannot exist outside of the actual emission of the 20 kg of bread; in other words, neither before nor after the completion of the plan. As money is the *equivalence* of what is produced and consumed, if we draw up Crusoe's balance sheet, it can be seen that what is produced is listed in his *assets*, but, given that he consumes his output immediately, that output is also listed in his *liabilities*. In short, the money emitted by Crusoe, the equivalence of his production and consumption, is an asset–liability. Indeed, "[b]y definition money is an asset and identically a liability, in other words an *asset–liability*" (Schmitt 1975: 13, italics in the original, our translation). Money is zero wealth, and therefore neither a net claim nor a net debt.

Although he benefits from an income that he consumes forthwith, Crusoe has neither created nor destroyed any matter. Lavoisier's law has been observed. So has Say's law; because he is supplier–demander on himself, his demand cannot differ from his supply and vice versa. As an isolated worker, Crusoe exchanges on himself and with himself. He converts his work into satisfaction, that is, he does not barter with himself, since he does not transfer satisfaction against work; his right hand is not in a barter relationship with his left hand. His labour is not determined with respect to his satisfaction nor is his satisfaction determined with respect to his labour. The production–consumption relation is instantaneous. It arises from *conversions* and not from *transfers*; the two terms are not determined with respect to one another. In other words, as an economic agent, Crusoe engages in absolute exchanges and in absolute exchanges only.

However, money is indeed present, in the identity between assets and liabilities. This means that money is not introduced or 'integrated' into the real emission from which it is supposedly initially absent; it is not an additional or exogenous object; it is always part of accomplished production plans. So, if Crusoe joins in relations with others as a producer, he will be an issuer of money confronted with other issuers of money, and accordingly we can say that the conditions are right for the production–consumption of the various producers to be expressed in a common numerical unit. For this, each individual money must be converted into the money that has currency in the economic space under consideration. So, the output of each must be monetised "a second time",[7] as a contribution to the formation of national income.

This is what we shall now examine from the perspective of generalised wage-earner economies as we know them today.

Absolute exchange as a principle of economics

From the moment his activity becomes part of the general division of labour and he therefore establishes market relations with others, each producer is subject to the disjunction of his production and consumption in continuous time. It may then be asked whether that does not call into question the principle of absolute exchange that we came up with above.

When they reason on the basis of 'primitive man' as we did with Crusoe, economists see him as a spatiotemporal producer–consumer unit. When they consider man in society, they represent him as two separate entities: supplier on the one hand and demander on the other. The analyses are then developed as if being in a position to have at his disposal goods and services manufactured by others might alter the nature of the activity of each individual producer. The generally held idea is that exchanges occur for the reason that individuals have surpluses available that they do not consume. Adam Smith (1776/1904: I.4.1) wrote that:

> [w]hen the division of labour has been once thoroughly established, it is but a very small part of a man's wants which the produce of his own labour can supply. He supplies the far greater part of them by exchanging that surplus part of the produce of his own labour, which is over and above his own consumption, for such parts of the produce of other men's labour as he has occasion for.

So, because of the division of labour, there would seem to be a sort of fragmentation of beings who, in becoming economic agents, supposedly are net suppliers or net demanders and no longer identically supplier–demanders. Whereas for the isolated primitive man, production and consumption form a unity, for civilised man, production and consumption apparently define physically separate spaces. The conceptual infrastructure of microeconomics stands as proof of this. In this framework, there are constructed on the one side production functions that contain no information about consumption, and on the other side consumption functions that know nothing of production. So, the supposedly rational economic agent is apparently schizophrenic: when he produces, he is unaware that he is a consumer, and when he consumes, he has forgotten that he has produced. This wholly unrealistic approach nurtures the "fable of barter" (Servet 1988; 2012) that is the representation of markets that do not exist:

> Markets aren't real. They are mathematical models, created by imagining a self-contained world where everyone has exactly the same motivation and the same knowledge and is engaging in the same type of self-interested calculating exchange. Economists are aware that reality is always more complicated; but they are also aware that to come up with a mathematical model, one always has to make the world into a bit of a cartoon.

(Graeber 2011: 114–15)[8]

40   *Jean-Luc Bailly*

In these models, individuals are supposed to engage in relative exchanges, since it is accepted that if someone has a good made by someone else, it means that he himself has given over a good or money for an equivalent value. Markets are supposedly places of transfers, and payments are not final operations but transmissions of wealth after which each agent is as rich as before the exchange. So, in a relative-exchange economy, one could not observe either creation or destruction of any objective income. It is from this absence of net income that there arises the conception of the economic agent as being formed of two separate entities: consumer and producer. But such a hypothesis is never confirmed.

Our economies are organised on the basis of production units (firms) grouping production factors (workers) who receive monetary income (wages). Whether the firm is a one-man operation or whether it brings together a number of workers makes no difference at bottom. Each worker, in direct or indirect collaboration with others, seeks to satisfy his consumer needs and it is indeed with a view to accomplishing this plan that firms operate. That wage-earners' activity is part of aggregate production relations does not call into question in any way the identity of production and consumption.

> Human effort and human consumption are the ultimate matters from which alone economic transactions are capable of deriving any significance; and all other forms of expenditure only acquire importance from their having some relationship, sooner or later, to the effort of producers or to the expenditure of consumers.
>
> (Keynes 1930/1971: 120–21)

More often than not, wage earners do not wish to obtain the utilities they form but those made by others. Even so, when gathered in various production units, they all contribute more or less directly, depending on the sector in which they are active, to the production of consumable goods and services.

However, wage-earning implies that the real emission of workers is split into two semi-emissions, in other words, production and consumption are separate in continuous time. This distancing arises because wage earners do not have direct access to the physical form of their output because of two intermediations: the intermediation of firms and the intermediation of the system of payments.[9]

Firms, as production units, are first of all intermediaries between workers and workers themselves. Workers form and deposit products in firms and subsequently buy that output. Given that firms make available to workers the equipment and materials with which they form utilities, it is logical enough that workers leave these materials in the hands of firms. However, it is the workers who create the utility forms, that is why they are paid, as production factors of useful output. Of course, their employers cannot pay them with the material forms. The forms and materials cannot be dissociated, so workers are not paid in kind but in money.

> The *numéraire* dimension of output cannot appear unless the act itself is [...] a double wave operation; in other words, to obtain a *numéraire* output, the

Absolute exchange and relative exchange 41

worker must produce 'twice in one go', first for the firm (where the output in its time dimension is deposited) and then for himself (in the form of the output in its number dimension).

(Schmitt 1984a: 62, our translation)

What characterises wage earners is not solely the creation of output in two different forms – a utility form specific to the material characteristics of production and a numerical form – but also the fact that these two forms are first deposited in two separate places; one in firms and the other in the wage-earners' holdings.

Although he leaves the physical form of his output on deposit with the firm that employs him, the wage earner does not lose possession of what he has produced for all that. He receives money for it, in other words the wages by which he has the power to purchase that same output, but also any other issued in the same currency area. As can be seen, the payment of wages is not a relative exchange: no mutual transfer of goods can be observed between firms and workers. However, at this instant, an equivalence is established between money and output.

The correspondence between money and output must be understood for what it is. It is not a relationship between values, because money is devoid of any positive value, however we define positive value. The terms of the correspondence are output on the one side and money on the other, and not the value of output and the value of money. The monetary value of output is not the relation between the value of money and the value of output but the straightforward monetary measurement of output: the relationship alone is a value or equivalence, the terms of the relation being purely physical.

(Schmitt 1975a: 31–2, our translation)

It results from this equivalence that each worker obtains the purchasing power that is necessary and sufficient to procure his own output.

The equivalence relation that we observed for Crusoe remains true for wage earners. In the very context of his theory of exploitation, Marx wrote that

When I produce a commodity, the precondition is that, if that my product has a use value, it does not for me […], it is not for my livelihood (in the broadest sense), but immediate exchange value; it becomes livelihood after taking, in money, the form of general social product, that can now be realized in any qualitatively different form of work of others. Hence, producing for society, each member, in turn, works for me in another sphere, *I produce for myself.*

(Marx 1858/1972: 214, emphasis added, our translation)

This means that the question of the *nature* of economic exchanges is not subordinate to the question of distribution.[10] The essential principle of the equivalence between production and consumption on each producer is not called into question by the division of labour and the generalisation of wage-earning. Each wage earner receives his own output, but because of the interposition of

42   Jean-Luc Bailly

firms and money, "instead of changing his output into immediate consumption, he changes his real production into monetary production" (Schmitt 1984a: 342, our translation). In other words, his income consists of the units of money he receives and not of the objects he personally manufactured.

If we pursue the reasoning from the idea that everybody works for himself, it is logical to think that the money one receives from his employer gives the objective and social measure of the equivalence between his production and consumption. The point is that each wage earner accomplishes a plan and, foremost, for himself, he seeks to transform the efforts he provides into personal satisfaction. It is in the payment of wages that his individual evaluation of his production–consumption is converted into an undifferentiated economic magnitude. Besides, conflict may arise over the discrepancy between personal measures and measures made because of wage agreements, but it is the amount of the wages paid that prevails economically.

Unlike Crusoe, who gives himself the use values immediately, the wage earner receives money and so his consumption is postponed. Even so, he obtains in money what he has produced with regard to his position in the general division of labour. Although he receives the social measure of his exertion, his efforts, his skills, and so on, the wage earner does not sell anything to the firm that employs him: he deposits physical output and receives the same output in money. Accordingly, from his point of view, the payment of wages is an absolute exchange in that it is the conversion of his work into monetary income. In other words, "money is the *object* of production" (Wray 2010: 4), but it is also in the same way the object of consumption, since it is in spending the money at his disposal that the wage earner converts his income into use values. In fact, in our monetary economies, the complete production–consumption emission is split into two semi-emissions. The first semi-emission takes place on the market of producer services (production), and the second semi-emission on the market of products (consumption). The two semi-emissions are of the same nature and the same magnitude, but opposite directions.

Exchange on the producer services market

On the producer services markets, workers sell nothing to firms, who buy nothing from them. On these markets, transactions are not intended for transferring pre-existing wealth, but for emitting output and the corresponding wages. Through the intermediation of banks, wage earners convert the physical output of their labour into monetary income, while firms receive as deposits the product resulting from the productive activity of the workers they employ. The transaction consists therefore in firms receiving the output in physical form and giving over that same output to workers, but in numerical form. The exchange is absolute, on the side of both workers and firms. "In the same transaction, the firm both gives and receives the same object: it is indeed an absolute exchange" (Schmitt 1984a: 347, our translation).

In as much as money is a form, it does not originate from a fund supposedly constituted prior to production. Schmitt (1984a: 95–6, italics in the original, our translation) shows that

Absolute exchange and relative exchange 43

[w]ages do not originate in any spending by firms but in labour alone, the expenditure, the effort of wage earners. Labour is an expenditure and it is the only expenditure that yields income. This means that the emission of wages is based on a real emission: the worker emits his own output; but instead of receiving it directly in kind, he obtains it *first* in form of money.

To pay workers, firms mobilise banks that then issue money, which is both positive and negative. "In creating wages, the bank acquires a claim on the firm (the 'payer') and a debt towards the worker (the 'payee'). It follows that the operation does not produce any net claim on banks" (Schmitt 1984a: 413, our translation). In paying wages, firms transfer nothing to banks and banks transfer nothing to them. Indeed, banks write down to their assets the amount of monetary credit they have granted to firms. Firms have therefore formed a monetary debt backed by the output that workers have deposited in their hands. But, given that the debt is not fuelled by any prior monetary fund, we can speak of 'negative money' in which the output is (provisionally) 'absorbed' (see Schmitt 1984a).

On the other side, banks do not transfer anything to wage earners. They merely, so to speak, receive the wage-earners' deposits in their own money, that is, they credit the wage-earners' current accounts. In the case in point, on this side, money is 'positive', since it measures a claim, that of workers on firms which have given a commitment, by paying them, to deliver to them, on the markets, the output they hold in stock. In short, the subject-matter of the claim is not money but output. It can be seen that, in their function as issuers of money, banks are pure intermediaries between firms and wage earners. Banks make payments at the request of each of the others.[11] It is certain that while bank intermediation is essential nowadays, it does not influence in any way the nature of exchanges between workers and firms. "It is indeed evident, that money is nothing but the representation of labour and commodities, and serves only as a method of rating or estimating them" (Hume 1742: II.III.6).

What wage earners produce and obtain immediately is money; but this is *real* money because it bears output. "Just as the real flow [the physical output] is in reality changed into a monetary flow (in issuing wages), output is absorbed by money. The exact representation is that of money, as a pure form, including output, which is the body of money" (Schmitt 1984a: 460, our translation). The wage units that workers receive may therefore be defined as units of money in which physical output is incorporated. So, it can be said that each worker receives an envelope in which is inscribed output, which is materially deposited in the firm that pays him. In the operation, the worker does not sell anything to the firm, which does not buy anything from him in paying him. No mutual transfer of goods between wage earner and firm is to be observed, which means that each wage unit issued is a net creation for the economy as a whole; it is *macroeconomic*.

Each worker is, as Crusoe was, the bearer of an individual consumption plan that motivates his production. These Crusoes who work together do not issue any concrete nominal form of their 'own money', but, being wage earners, through the firms that employ them, they mobilise the banking system in its dual monetary and

44   *Jean-Luc Bailly*

financial function.[12] They give rise to a nominal issue of socially accepted units of money. This issuing is in a sense a 'repetition' of their individual emissions (Schmitt 1984a: 98), which, transposed into the collective space by banks, will enable workers to obtain use values they have not themselves produced. Whether the money paid to wage earners is materialised by a good or not matters little; it exists objectively as a numerical form of the production–consumption equivalence that workers produce. "Money is not a thing, it is a social relation. […] this relation is a link and as such […] corresponds to a definite mode of production neither more nor less than does individual exchange" (Marx 1847/1965: 34–5). When he yields to the firm that employs him the utility form to which he has given rise, the worker is not dispossessed of what he has produced, since he obtains in the form of money what he has really emitted. However, as the money is bank money, wages are immediately deposited in the bank; it follows that, not being finally consumed immediately, output exists in the form of two separate deposits, one within firms in physical form and the other in the form of savings in bank accounts.

It is still possible today to see some likeness between Crusoe and a wage earner, since the wage earner, whatever sector he is engaged in, increases by himself the national income by the amount of his own wage. Unlike Crusoe, however, as the wage earner develops his activity in a relation with others, his output must be put into numbers and measured in money external to his real emission. It is by this means that each producer can purchase goods and services on the product market that are not the goods and services that give rise to the issue of money he has available to him. As shown in the following section, payments on product markets are the reverse image (as in a mirror) of payments on producer services markets and pertain themselves to the category of absolute exchanges.

Exchange on the product market

Generally, payments on product markets are conceived as reciprocal transfers of money against products. The purchaser is supposed to hand over money to the seller who transfers the product to him in exchange, with money being supposed to replace the product in the seller's assets and reciprocally the product is supposed to replace the money in the purchaser's assets. In this way, the transaction is thought of as barter, with exchanges on the products market being dyadic, of the nature of relative exchanges and ultimately detached from production. "Every man thus lives by exchanging, or becomes in some measure a merchant, and the society itself grows to be what is properly a commercial society" (Smith 1776/1904: I.4.1). Besides, this is the way that the economic circuit is usually represented in terms of monetary circulation from one agent to another. If this were true, the general principle that would prevail would be that presented in particular by Joan Robinson (1937: 14, emphasis added): "income is the product of expenditure as well as the source of expenditure. Men earn their incomes *by supplying each other's demands.* One man's expenditure provides other men's incomes, and one man's income is derived from other men's expenditure." But such an approach is wanting in that it conflates the formation and the spending of

Absolute exchange and relative exchange   45

income, which means that in reality they are not explained. They are supposedly magnitudes that are never created because, being always passed on, they are never destroyed. There would be no beginning or end to economic activity.

The second half-emission

We have seen that income is created in production when wages are paid, with consumption being the accomplishment of the economic process. It would be quite illogical to envisage that it might be reflected by the creation of new income. Besides, there is no reason to think that the relation of workers with output, the production–consumption equivalence determined in the payment of wages, is modified in the period that precedes the spending of wages on the product market. When deposited with the bank, income is dormant in some sense, saved, while waiting to be 'reactivated', that is, to be finally spent in the purchase of products. Neither the money envelope nor its contents are changed for so long as no product is purchased.

In actual fact, any payment on the product market is reflected by a twofold (monetary and physical) movement, of the same nature but in the opposite direction to that observed on the producer services market. The formation of wages is a semi-emission during which workers emit on themselves their own output putting it into the monetary envelope they receive; it is production. The spending of wages is the complementary semi-emission. Wage earners re-emit on themselves their own output, but this time releasing it from the monetary mould. As happens on the producer services market, payments on the product market are intermediated by firms and banks. This means that when they go to the markets to consume, workers–demanders do not find themselves dealing with other workers–suppliers of production, but with firms. The interposition of firms and banks has as its consequence that transactions on the product market do not consist in mutual transfers of goods or money among workers.

To pay the firm that sells him a product, each income holder mobilises his bank so that it debits his deposit account. As the income deposited has been saved, the bank must therefore recreate the money that was initially deposited. Now, as the purchase is made from firms in which physical products are stored, the money is re-issued negatively on the side of wage earners, with their accounts being debited, and positively on the side of the firms selling, with their monetary debt, formed with respect to banks in the payment of wage earners, then being cancelled. The upshot of this is that, money being finally destroyed, the income spent is itself irredeemably destroyed in consumer spending.

In the operation, no reciprocal transfer can be observed between firms and income holders. Income holders have destroyed their monetary deposits, written down to banks' liabilities, and in exchange they obtain the use values they made. Now, bank deposits were nothing other than the monetary form of that same output. This means that income holders set about a conversion: they transform their monetary assets into use values. On the firms' side, the stocks of output corresponded to a monetary debt (negative money) recorded in banks' assets. At

46 *Jean-Luc Bailly*

the same time, as firms see their stocks of products diminish, they also see their monetary debt decline by an equivalent amount. On this side too, the exchange is absolute, with firms converting their assets in products into cancelled debt.

As pure intermediaries banks are not stakeholders in the real transaction. They merely record things numerically. On their side, no movement of money is to be observed. They destroy positive money, the claims of income holders recorded in their liabilities and in the same movement they destroy the negative money by cancelling the claim on firms, which they had written in their assets. In payments on product markets, no money unit is passed on in the operation. Having been recreated, money units are destroyed immediately by simple accounting techniques.

The exchange of money against output is not relative but absolute. The payment is not a transfer but the conversion of one and the same thing from one form into another. Moreover, what is converted is not conserved but destroyed, which marks the completion of the economic process. Voided of its content, money is destroyed definitively at the same time as the output to which it corresponded is consumed.

We have stated here the general principle. However, because of the division of labour and because producers give rise to utility forms that they do not use themselves, it may still be asked whether individuals do not transfer output among themselves via firms and banks. The question is whether inter-individual relative exchanges (and therefore microeconomic exchanges) are not to be observed, which it is true would be masked or framed by absolute exchanges, but that would nevertheless be the essence of economic activity. Thus, for example, the post-Keynesian circuit theorist Graziani writes that finally it is relative exchanges that decide everything since the real purchasing power of economic agents depends on relative prices: "Since agents are not granted credit on the same footing, the system of relative prices reflects the way in which purchasing power has been granted to different agents" (Graziani 2003: 26).[13]

The products are not exchanged between them

It is true that, generally because of the division of labour, workers do not consume the physical output that they have brought into being. Let us consider two workers, A and B, who are respectively employed in two firms, F1 and F2, one producing good x and the other producing good y. Let us further suppose that A wants to buy good y, and B wants to buy good x. In actual fact, payments are not dyadic but, as Hicks (1967: 11) observed, triadic. Any payment on the products market[14] brings together an income holder, a firm, and the banking system, now unified by a central bank.

As the two firms are in the same monetary space, the money issued on the two workers is homogeneous, which means that the money paid to A, employee of F1, may be spent with F2. Similarly, money paid to B issued on F2 may be spent with F1. From the outset we can say, to use the term employed by Schmitt, that the money units issued by the two firms are 'interchangeable', in the same way that two $100 bank notes can be. But that does not mean that the incomes they

Absolute exchange and relative exchange 47

correspond to are interchangeable. To wit, that the income earned in F1 can be spent in F2 and the income formed in F2 spent in F1. In actual fact, this is impossible.

As the two outputs are expressed in the same unit of money, if good x corresponds to the issuing of 100 units of money and good y corresponds to 100 units of money, then goods x and y are equivalent. The producer of good x can procure good y, and the producer of good y can purchase good x. Therefore, plainly on the product market we can observe each of the two workers purchasing the use value made by the other. But, can it be said, even so, that there is a reciprocal transfer (of income) between the two workers, or, in other words, are we dealing with a relative exchange of goods x and y?

In the textbooks, things are presented *as if* A spent his income with F2 to buy good y and *as if* B purchased good x by paying F1 with his income formed in F2. Everything would be therefore *as if* the incomes were transferred. F1 supposedly receives in payment the income formed in F2, and F2 receives the income formed in F1. So through the intermediary of money, A and B supposedly barter their income at the same time as their output; in point of fact, things cannot happen that way.

The wages issued in F1 are spent on the output issued in F1, good x, and the wages issued in F2 are spent in purchasing the output of F2, good y. This means no transfer of income is to be observed in payments.

When A becomes a purchaser of good y, produced by B, the money he received in F1 substitutes[15] for that F2 paid to B. When A buys good y, his account is debited, and the money he spends enables F2 to cancel its money debt (negative money) with the banking system and in the same way as if it were B who had come to purchase his own output. On the other side, when B purchases good x, he allows F1 to cancel its monetary debt. There is actually a substitution between the two monies issued, but not a substitution of incomes. In actual practice, the scriptural monies are substituted in the relations between banks, in particular, in the compensation operations and those related to them.

As all the monies of the different banks are defined in terms of the central bank money, it is as if A and B were exchanging $100 bills that they received respectively from F1 and F2 as their wages. If A buys good y with the bill that B has just given him, that means that the money issued by B is indeed spent in the purchase of the corresponding output formed in F2, namely good y. On A's side, things are the same; he has issued good x, and the banknote he gives B enables B to purchase good x. So the money issued in F1 can be used to purchase the output formed in F1, and the money issued in F2 can be used to purchase the output formed in F2. In fact, it can be said that the central bank has issued an envelope of $200 in which goods x and y are accommodated, and, so, any agent holding the envelope or part of the envelope can procure goods x or y indifferently, knowing that goods x and y are, respectively, in firms F1 and F2 and are not transferred from one to the other when the income holders purchase them. Never mind what the use values consumed by A and B are, what they produced is consumed there where they produced it and in the form in which they produced it.

48   *Jean-Luc Bailly*

In such payment, no reciprocal economic (monetary) transfer is observed between the various participants, as the exchange of bank notes is not an economic transfer.[16] On the product markets as on the producer services market, payments consist in absolute exchanges. The general law is that everyone consumes their own output, even when they derive satisfaction from use values other than those they themselves have made, because each himself has produced the monetary form of output deposited in the firms that paid him. "Even after the intervention of money, the circuit is simply the creation–destruction, by human labour, of the utility form of matter" (Schmitt 1984a: 346, our translation). Each income can only ultimately be spent there where it was produced; this is the deep reality of the economic circuit.

Conclusion

This chapter has endeavoured to explain the concept of absolute exchange and we have not dealt with the question of distribution and, in particular, of the formation of profits. This is because analysis of the formation of non-wage income flows from the analysis of production. Thanks to the quantum theory of production, it can be understood that because of the absolute character of exchanges, all income necessarily originates in human labour and therefore, in our economies, in wages. Of course, it is not because they initially receive all of their production that wage earners will ultimately have at their disposal all of the output: through their interposition, firms have the ability to capture a fraction of the output formed within them. But again, it will be a question of absolute exchanges.

Any payment is a macroeconomic operation that does not consist in transfers of wealth from payer to payee but in the creation–destruction of economic magnitudes. So, each wage unit paid, like each unit of money spent in purchasing products, alters the level of available national income. Inasmuch as macroeconomics is the study of relations among economic magnitudes, it is therefore not the outcome of the aggregation of individual forms of behaviour. The quantum theory of production confirms Arrow's (1951) impossibility theorem and, through the concept of absolute exchange, demonstrates that it is pointless looking to hit upon economic laws that supposedly arise from the psychology of individuals. It therefore follows a strict scientific definition of macroeconomics, which excludes any possibility of the real existence of microeconomics that would function on the articulation of relative exchanges, which, in truth, cannot be observed in the form in which they are presented in economics textbooks. This is why the markets as described in the books are unseen; they simply do not exist. However, the circuit is not an abstract intellectual construct, but rather the phenomenon that constitutes the basis of economic activity.

Of course, the principle of the identity of production and consumption does not in any way restrict each individual's freedom of action. Like the law of gravity in physics, for example, it only marks out the bounds within which individuals may act as economic agents. Economics is a specific area of human activity and not everything is economics, and it is not in behaviour that explanations for economic crises should be sought, but in the logic of the equivalence relation between production and consumption.

Notes

1 On the principle of conservation in economics, see for example Mirowski (1991).
2 No intention to be flippant should be read into this, but it should be seen as the choice of a reference that is implicitly shared by a good many economists.
3 Manufacture and production must not be confused.
4 In the opening pages of his *Principles*, Ricardo (1821/1951: 11) writes that "[i]f a commodity were in no way useful – in other words, if it could in no way contribute to our gratification – it would be destitute of exchangeable value... whatever quantity of labour might be necessary to procure it."
5 Marx's vain efforts to reduce complex labour to simple labour units are familiar enough (see Marx 1847/1965).
6 "Faire exister (ce qui n'existe pas encore)" (Petit Robert 1979: 1537).
7 "Money is already present within emissions and must be present a second time 'between' [producers'] outputs" (Schmitt 1984a: 341, our translation).
8 By other ways, based on logical analysis, Schmitt (2012a: 24) shows that "[n]either relative exchange nor relative prices are to be found in the real world."
9 For simplicity, the term bank is used here to refer to this system.
10 This is why we do not deal at all with this question here, no more than that of prices for that matter.
11 For analytical elaboration see Rossi (2009b).
12 For analytical elaboration see Gnos and Schmitt (1990).
13 See Cencini (2005, 2012) for more specific criticism of this approach.
14 This is also true for financial markets, which we do not discuss here.
15 This is because monies are interchangeable.
16 Besides, it is strictly pointless.

3 Inflation and unemployment

Xavier Bradley

Introduction

Bernard Schmitt's work is quite distinctive in that it applies logic in all its rigour and is situated at a high degree of abstraction. However, he never considered abstraction as a pure academic exercise but viewed it, on the contrary, as a necessity to understand the true origins of the dysfunctions affecting modern economies. Instead of the common belief that it suffices to gather data and 'let them speak', Schmitt insisted on the necessity of starting with defining with precision the nature of economic magnitudes and then analysing economic operations in order to detect the real cause of the troubles. This way of proceeding has an obvious cost: it requires patience and accepting a precise step-by-step analysis instead of jumping to conclusions.

In this perspective, the analysis of inflation and unemployment has to start with money and payments. Apart from the obvious reason that inflation is an 'illness' that affects money, unemployment is a characteristic of monetary economies of production. Building on his ground-breaking conception of money and payments, it is in the process of capital accumulation, in line with the great theories of unemployment, that Schmitt identified the origin of inflation and unemployment. However, to discover truly structural causes, he departed from the tradition by discarding entirely any explanation based on individual or collective behaviour, such as errors of expectation, rejection of market conditions, and market imperfections. Schmitt also demonstrated that, contrary to the conventional view, inflation and unemployment are not polarized opposite disorders between which we would have to find the right mix; instead, he showed that actually they are two phases of the same pathological process.

The next section of this chapter will start with a description of the process of capital accumulation developed by Schmitt. The reader will then have a broad sketch of the mechanisms at work and see where we are heading to, without having yet to explore the details of the analysis. We will thus point out the basic concepts and operations that are needed to prepare an in-depth analysis of the dysfunctions that plague our economies. In the third section, we investigate first the over-accumulation consequence of amortization that is responsible for inflation and then the causes of unemployment and over-indebtedness. The chapter ends with some considerations on the reforms elaborated by Bernard Schmitt to prevent the recurrence of inflation and unemployment.

The accumulation process

Schmitt's analysis weaved together, in a coherent set, elements that were viewed separately by other economists; he was able to do this thanks to his new conception of money and especially the circuit of incomes.

In order to focus on the key features that cause inflation and unemployment, let us begin this section with a brief outline of the process without explaining it.

A description of the accumulation process

Inflation and unemployment are usually considered either as two polar opposites in the economic conjuncture or, in the orthodox perspective, as the opposite fluctuations away from the 'natural trend' of the economy. The originality of Schmitt's approach[1] is that he identifies inflation and unemployment as the two phases of the same dysfunction. In his view, the key problem of the capitalist economic system is the process of capital accumulation, starting with the current conditions under which investment is carried out.

The chronology of events is the following. First, investment is carried out by firms; this is the key operation as far as the origin of the dysfunctions is concerned. However, at this stage there are no immediate, obvious negative effects: capital is just accumulated in the firms. The second stage is when capital is used in a production process. This involves a loss of value that has to be compensated through amortization. This is precisely where the dysfunctions have a patent effect on the economy. Owing to, as Schmitt put it, the *malformation* of capital that took place in the investment operation, amortization cannot be carried out directly as a simple exchange where, to get access to the goods, consumers would just have to compensate the loss of value in the stock of capital.

Under current conditions, amortization can only be finalized indirectly once an intermediary operation has been carried out. More specifically, if direct amortization were possible, firms would directly obtain *gross* profits in order to finance the replacement of the obsolete capital; under current conditions, firms will first obtain *net* profits and it is the spending of these net profits that will enable them to form gross profits. It is the circuit, formation and spending, of net profits that constitutes the intermediary operation; the latter's nature will depend on how net profits are spent and this is what will determine the existence of inflation and (involuntary) unemployment.

During a first phase, amortization will be conditioned on carrying out an equivalent amount of new net investment, an *over-accumulation* of capital. This feature of the early phase in the amortization process explains why an economy that goes on a path of steady investment will rapidly see an acceleration of the process with very high rates of growth once it enters the phase of amortizing the initial stock of capital. It is in this phase that inflation develops in the economy, because consumers will not only pay for the amortization of capital, this being just a sort of exchange for accessing goods in a larger number or in an improved quality, but they will also have to pay for the same amount of new net investment.

52   *Xavier Bradley*

However, the inflationary phase of amortization through capital over-accumulation cannot last indefinitely, precisely because it 'preys' or 'feeds' on current incomes. In other words, over-investment requires that there is a sufficient base of incomes to allow it to proceed. Moreover, this condition also concerns the remuneration of capital, which means that, as the over-accumulation process develops, there will be more and more pressure on the share of earnings attributed to interest. Consequently, capital yields will start falling, which in turn will push shareholders and firms' owners to look for alternative sources of remuneration; precisely, a more profitable one will be to invest profits in the financial system. That corresponds to the financialization process so characteristic of the late stages of an economic boom, and this is when the amortization process enters a new phase, one accompanied by involuntary unemployment. Lending profits through the financial system, instead of investing them in the (over) accumulation of capital, enables the finding of higher gains including interest paid by borrowing households and capital gains on financial markets.

It might seem that this channel is a solution to the over-accumulation crisis. This is not at all the case, because it causes a net loss of economic activity. The choice is between producing (and this will necessarily correspond to an over-investment), producing profit goods in the form of consumption goods (which leads to deflation), and not producing but spending on financial markets; the latter will therefore be accompanied by unemployment. Being caused by the structure of the accumulation process, it is truly an involuntary unemployment.

However, could sacrificing full employment be a way to avoid an economic crisis? The answer is negative. The financial channel implies for households a situation of over-indebtedness that cannot be sustained for long: there will come a time when no household is able to borrow anymore. And even before reaching this stage, there will probably be more and more borrowers defaulting on the payment of their interests. This is compounded by the fact that unemployment increases and therefore reaches more households, thereby reducing further the number of those able to meet their financial commitments as well as those with the capacity to obtain new loans. A financial crisis will therefore begin. It will be accompanied by a production crisis, given that production will be reduced, and by the unavoidable increase in unemployment.

The basis of the analysis: a renewal of key economic concepts

We need now to substantiate the process that has just been described, and for this we have to explain the meaning of each operation and how they link together.

The circuit of incomes: a fundamental tool for understanding money and payments

To understand the structural dysfunctions in modern monetary economies we have first to examine the nature of payments.

Inflation and unemployment 53

Payments are flows. The traditional approach to stocks and flows is to view the latter as stocks in motion; this implies that stocks come first in any economic process. The necessary consequence of that approach is that stocks are a given in the economy, and only the motion of stocks will bring any change.

Schmitt (1984a) showed that this is based on a false analogy between economic magnitudes and those of the physical world. Producing is not to be confused with manufacturing. This amounts to saying that economics is not dealing with material transformations.[2] But then what is the nature of economic magnitudes? If we are considering production as a creation, then a destruction must logically follow; consequently, that is precisely what consumption, the symmetrical opposite of production, is all about. As production is not the manufacturing of goods, consumption is not the physical use of these goods. To identify the true nature of these operations, the easiest way is to start with consumption. To consume goods means to withdraw them from the economic community: goods that were available are no longer so.[3] Going back to the initial operation, we thereby understand that production brings the goods into the economic community, makes them available to the members of the community. What is produced is that 'availability', to wit, the ability of the community to take possession of the goods. In other words, to produce is to create the power on the goods and this power will be used once the goods are consumed, that is, appropriated by members of the community. In this perspective, only labour can produce.[4]

We have two complementary operations: production and consumption; however, we know that in monetary economies income holders do not purchase goods as soon as they are paid. A positive period of time usually elapses between receiving an income and finally buying goods. Does it mean then that incomes are suspended in time until being used up in consumption? The approach that conceives of production as making goods available enables us to understand that a key feature of flows is their instantaneity. Indeed, as soon as goods are available in the economy, they must necessarily be located somewhere, and therefore they must necessarily be appropriated (either temporarily or definitively) by certain economic agents. The appropriation is final in the case of consumption, because the goods will no longer be available to anyone, but it is only temporary when the goods are stocked in a firm. The financing of the stock precisely indicates that the firm borrows to obtain the rights to detain the goods temporarily. To put it differently, incomes are not suspended over time, because goods cannot stand-by unappropriated.[5]

The complete cycle of incomes is therefore composed of two instantaneous circuits, one of creation/temporary destruction and the other of re-creation/final destruction,[6] separated by a positive period of relations between stocks, real and financial. Once completed, the whole process constitutes a production/consumption cycle.

A question of time

Mainstream economists are torn between two different approaches to economic phenomena: either they emphasize logical relations, therefore using the tool of

54 *Xavier Bradley*

general equilibrium, or they claim to follow a more realistic approach by using sequence analysis. In the first case, the logical precision is obtained at the expense of excluding the passing of time. In the second case, the time period is necessarily arbitrary, and complex relations like feedback cannot be included in the analysis.

The circuit approach used by Schmitt enables the combination of the instantaneity of flows with the passing of time corresponding to the existence of stocks. However, Schmitt (1984a) emphasized that production encapsulates a time quantum.[7] In other words, although production has an instantaneous result, it does take time to be carried out. At the instant of payment, it is as if the whole 'preparation' period were 'covered' in one moment (Schmitt 1984a: 55–6). This is crucial concerning the nature of economic magnitudes but also for a clear understanding of how payments are articulated, especially in relation to the formation of profits.

The two 'markets' and the circuit of profits

How can there be profits in a circuit of incomes? This question is especially crucial in view of the instantaneity of the circuits. Indeed, if production and final consumption were completed instantaneously, there would be no room for profits. We know, however, that final consumption does not take place at the instant of production, if a stock of goods is constituted. The first instantaneous circuit corresponds to what Schmitt (1984a) calls the "producing services market", because this is where production occurs. The second instantaneous circuit is the "goods market", where final consumption takes place.[8] Concerning profits, we know that firms' earnings require an amount of sales in excess of the firms' expenditures. This implies that profits are formed in the final consumption transactions or, in other words, on the goods market. Given the logic of circuits, the consequence is that profits are necessarily spent on the producing services market. This makes sense, because it means that the initial operation of income formation is reinterpreted or, to put it differently, the incomes are redirected towards beneficiaries other than the initial wage earners.

Let us concentrate for the moment on profits that will be distributed to shareholders. It might appear strange to claim that profits are spent on the producing services market, given that the firm pays dividends to its shareholders and that the latter will spend their dividends on the goods market. The answer to this is that profits are indeed spent on the producing services market, because this is how the initial formation of incomes will be redirected towards the owners of the firm. The result of this circuit is that part of the goods stocked within the firm now become the property of its owners.[9] In normal circumstances, dividends are not paid in kind. This only means that the owners will not get the actual goods captured by the firm, but instead will obtain the proceeds from selling these goods and then will buy something else. In other words, an exchange is added on to the basic profit circuit.

One essential lesson can be drawn from the study of profits: the latter's circuit is embedded into the basic wage-income circuit. This has very important

Inflation and unemployment 55

consequences with regard to the limit of the amount of profits that can be 'captured' from the pool of wages. The formation of profits is not an empty payment, precisely because it is linked with a wage circuit. Namely, the profit circuit has to be nested into a wage circuit and this implies that profits can never exceed wages. Consequently, profits cannot get beyond half of the total incomes in the economy. This characteristic plays a vital role in the amortization process, because it is the reason why dividend-profits will have to compete with net profits in the over-accumulation mechanism.

Another key feature to emphasize at this juncture is the distinction between pure transfers and profits. Transfers mean that an income is spent by one agent instead of another one; it is just a change of identity. By contrast, profits are incomes that are redirected within the production/consumption circuit. This is again a crucial element in the amortization process, as it explains the shift from over-accumulation to over-indebtedness.

A new definition of investment

We noted that investment is the key operation in the pathological process that leads to inflation and unemployment. In order to fully understand why investment is responsible for these dysfunctions, we need to discard the usual view defining investment as the purchasing of equipment by firms. The latter definition is imprecise: given that the same piece of goods could be purchased either by households or firms, this is obviously not a good criterion. But the main point is that a purchase carried out by a firm on the goods market defines the purchase of wage goods and cannot be identified with an investment.

Investment has to be defined as the spending of profits. Now, is it not the case that some (or even most) investments are carried out through loans instead of being auto-financed? In fact, if a firm borrows to finance an investment, it is only advancing future profits, precisely those profits that will allow the firm to repay the loan in the future. Once this is done, then everything will be as if the investment had been financed with profits right from the start.

Being the spending of profits, investment is necessarily carried out on the producing services market, because this is where all profits are spent. However, the purpose here is not to redirect incomes as was the case with dividends. Consequently, instead of being spent 'backwards', profits will be spent 'forward', that is, on a new production. For this reason, the goods just produced will become capital accumulated in the firm.

> Profits are invested in a very original operation; they buy labour. [...] Now labour becomes a merchandise; it is bought by the transformation of new profits. [...] By buying the activity of workers, firms buy in the same movement the product of this activity, the real goods [...]. The goods bought through the purchase of the workers' activity are defined as fixed capital.
>
> (Schmitt 1984a: 204, our translation)

56 *Xavier Bradley*

Obviously most firms do not produce their own equipment, so that the actual investment on the producing services market will be followed by the sale, to consumers, of the capitalized goods. The proceeds of this transaction will then be used to buy equipment manufactured elsewhere. This pattern explains why the transaction on the goods market (the purchase of equipment to another firm) is confused with the real investment operation that has already taken place on the producing services market.

But then, in what way is it pathological that invested profit should be spent on a new production? The dysfunction is that the mixing of two income circuits, the profit circuit and the circuit of new incomes, will result in an empty emission[10] or, in other words, will empty of its content the result of the emission. The operation is only identifiable with the concept of income circuit, because it happens in instantaneous payments and cannot be directly detected when only considering the stocks either preceding or following the investment. The very originality of investment explains that the payments system is not specifically designed to deal with it, and this is the reason why currently investments lead to the malformation of capital. If profits are spent 'forward' on a new production, as is the case for investment, the effect will be to empty the new incomes of their content in favour of the firm.

Now, if we only consider the question of the content, that is, the access to available goods, investment does not seem to have negative consequences. In actual fact, the factors of production whose wages are affected by the investment will still get access to goods present in the economy, these being the goods that had been captured when profits were initially formed (ibid.: 190). From this point of view, the whole operation will appear to be just an exchange of goods. This is precisely the reason why the pathology is not apparent at this stage. However, a pathology takes place in the investment process because, in bank accounts, all payment operations are treated in an identical way. Consequently, the debit corresponding to the payment of new wages will be directly imputed to the credit position corresponding to the profits. The spending of profits creates a sort of loop, on the producing services market, from which the firms' owners are excluded.[11] Unlike dividend-profits that entail an ulterior actual payment to shareholders, investment-profits are spent in a payment that does not involve the owners either on the spot or later. It is true that the investment programme has to be endorsed by the firm's owners, at least formally, but this concerns the decision to invest and not the actual payments. Although the firm's owners retain the legal property of the capital accumulated through investment, they are not part of the payments related to this stock. The consequence is that the firm, which should only be an intermediary, becomes the final destination of the payments. It means that the firm becomes a sort of black hole that absorbs some incomes now lost to households.

The amortization process explained

Let us now use the concepts just examined in order to analyse more thoroughly the consequences of pathological investment on the mechanism of capital amortization.

Over-accumulation and inflation

A new approach to inflation

Whatever the sophistication of the 'model', the conventional view of inflation is still basically that of 'too much money chasing too few goods'. If that were the reality, inflation would then be the end result of individual and/or collective behaviour of economic agents, including institutions like the government and banks (both commercial and central). Having inspired monetary policy for ages, this conception has failed to prevent inflation from reappearing regularly. Each time monetary authorities think they now have mastered the art of central banking and policy mix, troubles come back in some unexpected way. At the bottom of it all, the key problem is the dichotomic view that separates money on one side from 'real' products on the other. All the efforts to control behaviour stumble on the fact that it is impossible to predict the optimum behaviour. Therefore, we have either strict controls that stifle economic growth by preventing economic agents from freely expressing themselves, or we have a laxity that leads to wide fluctuations in the level of economic activity.

As explained in the previous chapters, Schmitt followed a completely different perspective. Amortization reproduces the initial investment. It is therefore dependent on the conditions of that operation. The fact that the dysfunctions become effective only at the stage of amortization, while the original cause is situated at the level of the initial investment, makes it particularly difficult to identify the cause of the process, and therefore makes it all the more difficult to find a solution.

Amortization is a very complex process, because in its basic form it involves the stock of capital losing value together with a compensation through an equivalent investment. As observed by Schmitt (1984a), amortization is at the same time a reproduction, whereby fixed capital is restored to its initial value, and a new production of investment goods.

Firms as intermediaries

Payments are ultimately made between 'final' agents and only pass (or rather should only pass) through intermediary agents, that is, banks and firms. This is straightforward in the case of banks, because there are always two non-bank economic agents involved in payments carried out by banks (here we are not considering banks in their capacity as firms that produce services but only as account keepers). It does not seem so clear cut with firms: is it not the case that the payment of wages to employees originates from firms, which therefore seem to be the starting point and not just an intermediary? To start with, let us consider the symmetrical operation of selling goods. It is clear that if the sales are in excess of the production costs, the profits belong to the owner of the firm. To that extent, the firm is only an intermediary. If we consider now the other part of the sales, then we see that the firm does not 'earn' anything for itself either, because the sales only compensate the costs. With this in mind, we can understand that the initial

58   Xavier Bradley

operation, the payment of wages, is in actual fact an absolute exchange where, through the bank and the firm, the employees receive their own product in a monetary form. This means that even in the payment of wages, ultimately firms are only intermediaries while the factors of production are exchanging with themselves.

Now, the problem with the current conditions of the accumulation process and the amortization of capital is precisely that firms are not confined into being intermediaries (either acting on behalf of the owners or as intermediaries between the wages-earners and their product). The loop mentioned above is the consequence of the firms' owners being by-passed in the payments related to capital accumulation. In a sense, the payments will stop at the firms instead of being extended to their owners, and this creates a dysfunction in the economic system: the circuit of invested profits, formation and spending, is completed at the level of the firm.

It is true that the firm's owners retain the ownership of the assets of the company (and we can include among the owners those who have advanced profits by lending to the firm). However, the problem is not related to the stock of capital, and therefore to its legal ownership, but rather to the payments regarding capital. To put it differently, it is not by looking at financial relations and at stocks of goods that we can identify the dysfunctions, but rather by focusing on incomes and production.

When the stock of capital is used in the production process, it undergoes amortization, that is, a replacement process. It is precisely in these payments that the 'loop' can take place, and, notably, that two payments may collide in the firm.

Amortization and inflation

The heart of the mechanism is the amortization of capital. In the current accounting and financial system, amortization cannot be carried out through one direct transaction, that is, through the capture of gross profits that would be directly spent to replace obsolete or worn-out fixed capital. What is then the lengthy amortization channel that includes the intermediary stages required by the ill-formed capital?

The process is the following:

1   The capture of profits that should be gross profits but actually prove to be net profits.
2   The necessary intermediary operation of spending these net profits.
3   The return of funds as revenues in order to form profits that are now gross profits.
4   The spending of gross profits to complete the amortization process.

Why is it that an intermediary operation is required in the current conditions of amortization? The reason is that it is not possible to carry out a direct exchange between the owners of the firm and the consumers in order to amortize capital (owners' side) and to gain full access to the improved/augmented goods (consumers' side). In other words, we cannot have initially an exchange between households. This is because with any payment related to accumulated capital, the firm is no longer just acting on behalf of its owners.[12] Consumers spend the incomes that will feed the formation of profits; unfortunately, instead of gross profits (a case of a direct amortization), the profits will be net. In the case of direct amortization, capital would be instrumental in the production process, and profits would be gross. This is so, because consumers would gain full access to the goods, that is, they would lose some incomes (profit formation) but they would gain augmented goods (therefore only gross profits). As the value cannot be released directly, the expenditures from consumers can only generate net profits. The necessary formation of a net profit means that the set of firms finances part of its production out of this profit. What Schmitt's concept of dual production conveys is precisely the fact that the production of amortization goods necessarily entails an equal production of new investment goods that, adding to the fixed capital already accumulated, defines an over-accumulation. Amortization restores fixed capital to its original value, while the investment of the net profit increases its value for the same amount. The over-investment, or over-accumulation, takes place, as usual, by spending profits on the producing services market, thereby affecting new incomes. The latter are emptied of their content but will be spent by consumers together with the other incomes and, in that way, gross profits will be formed.

Here we have a truly inflationary process, because households as a whole, that is to say, including all categories, lose the content of the incomes affected by over-accumulation. This content is somehow sucked into the black hole formed by the loop on the firms; the purchasing power of the incomes vanishes completely.[13]

It is precisely this over-accumulation phase that explains the 'economic miracle', characterized by very high rates of growth of the gross domestic product, experienced by certain countries. However, this phase cannot last indefinitely, because the problem of remunerating capital will sooner or later become prominent: the profits constituting the earnings of capital cannot be formed unless there is a large-enough basis of wages to feed it. To capture one unit of wages in profit, the operation has to take place within the formation/spending circuit of another unit of wages, the latter being spent to the benefit of wage earners. In other words, the profit circuit works inside (is nested in) a wage circuit.

Over-indebtedness and unemployment

Amortization and the financial market

With each new round of amortization, the over-accumulation process will represent a higher proportion of the wage base, thereby reducing the share that can feed capital earnings. The rate of profits, that is, of earnings, will start to fall. This will push the firms' owners or lenders to look for alternative returns for their funds, to wit, returns that would not be affected by the falling rate of profit. This is the moment when the financialization phase starts:[14] from that time on, the

60   Xavier Bradley

intermediary operation required to carry out the amortization of capital will be a financial detour. Instead of being invested in the production of capital-goods, profits (net profits that is) will be invested on financial markets, where the funds will be lent to consumers thereby feeding the formation of gross profits.

Financialization prevents rates of return on capital from falling, because, through this channel, capital is remunerated with transferred incomes instead of profits coming from a nested circuit. In other words, if households borrow money, they will pay interests by transferring part of their wages directly to the lender. That kind of remuneration is therefore not directly in competition with the formation of net profits. In addition, intervening on financial markets may allow capital gains, which are also transfers.

Although it prevents, for a while, a fall in the rate of return on capital, the financialization channel has dramatic consequences: it causes involuntary unemployment.

A truly involuntary unemployment

We know that the amortization process starts necessarily with the formation of net profits, and that the spending of these profits will condition the formation of gross profits. The key operation here is how net profits are spent. If it is in a production, then this necessarily becomes a production of capital-goods (or of consumption goods, which generates deflation), that is, an over-investment. But if the financial channel is chosen, the production of capital-goods is abandoned and no other production can replace it: the corresponding labour force will stay unemployed.[15] It is not a question of the material characteristics of the goods but whether or not the goods are acquired on the producing services market, that is, right at the stage of production rather than on the goods market at the stage of consumption. If there is a production available and of the same amount as the net profits, then the latter will be spent on this production, and this will result in an over-accumulation. The only other way to spend the net profits is to lend them through the financial system (markets and banks) but, for this to be achieved, there must not be any production available to profit spending. Therefore, there must be a net loss of production. Any kind of production would act as a sort of magnet to the net profits, and inevitably attract them on the producing services market. The only way to avoid this is to abandon an equivalent amount of production in order to close that path to the profits.

Now, is this unemployment really of an involuntary kind? The question has to be raised, because it seems that a decision is made, namely to renounce over-investing in favour of financial operations. We saw that decisions are indeed part of the process. However, managers and owners do not really have a choice, once over-accumulation causes a fall in the rate of profit: the rational option is to choose the financial channel. This is so because the rate of profit has to be compared with the market rate of interest, and once the former falls below the latter the economic system reaches a situation where capital accumulation must necessarily be reduced. Even if the 'capitalists' accepted a reduction in the rate of their profits, the pressure of over-accumulation would continue to build-up and cause a further decrease in the profit rate. Ultimately, if the firms' owners were to sacrifice completely their remuneration, the amortization process would reach the limit of one third of the activity and become impossible to pursue. Firms would prefer to develop their activities in order to increase the volume of profits. To renounce producing is therefore only a defensive move, albeit one that only postpones the inevitable. Whatever the decisions taken, they will sooner or later lead to unemployment. The latter is therefore truly structural and involuntary.

In addition to causing unemployment, the financial channel gives only a temporary reprieve from the falling rate of profit. In each following period, there will be a need for new financial operations in order to carry out the amortizations. This implies increasing indebtedness on the part of households (Schmitt 1984a: 238). We have here the structural explanation of the trend observed at the end of business cycles, when the financial system lends more and more to categories that are not truly creditworthy. This process will lead to an open crisis when borrowers can no longer afford to pay the interest on their loans. At this point, the financial channel will close owing to the ever increasing number of failures. The precise features of the financialization channel will change with each new crisis: new financial instruments will be used, different financial institutions will play the leading role. Nevertheless, the financialization process will always close the cycle of amortization.

Making investment innocuous by reforming payments

Inflation and unemployment are structural dysfunctions of monetary economies of production. How then could it be possible to avoid them and make the economic system work more smoothly? The origin of the troubles is situated in the payments. It is therefore at this level that a reform must be applied. The key point is to avoid the mixing of circuits, that is, the 'fusion' between spending profits and paying new wages.

Schmitt (1984a) explained that the only way is to filter payments within the banking system, because this is where payments are carried out. The very first stage is to isolate payments related to production in order to prevent any interference with the creation of new incomes. This requires setting up a specific banking department of emission that would issue the new incomes. This is what Schmitt (1984a) called the 'first department'. A necessary corollary is the creation of a department that would deal with deposits resulting from the instantaneous spending of incomes. As we explained earlier, new incomes are temporarily spent to form savings, and this is what the 'second department' would have to manage.

This kind of reform is not unheard of: we have the example of the Ricardian reform of the Bank of England or, to stay at the level of commercial banks, the separation between commercial banks and investment banks introduced by the Glass–Steagall Act in 1933, and similar systems adopted in Europe after the Second World War. However, one important difference is that the reform advocated by Schmitt (1984a) would go to the heart of banking operations with a precise criterion, in contrast with past and current experiences in separation

62 *Xavier Bradley*

systems that were or are always imprecise and always missing the key point of isolating production payments. In addition, according to Schmitt (1984a), a two-department system is not enough to make payments completely pathology free. A 'third department' is necessary to isolate investment and contain capital (Schmitt 1984a: 321–2). Firms' profits would be debited from the second department, that of savings or loanable funds, and credited into the third department, that of capital.[16] Of course, any payment of dividends would be debited from the third department, but now investment would no longer impact on new production payments. The same sort of firewall would automatically apply to amortization.

Conclusion

The analysis of the dysfunctions occurring in the economic system has to start with the study of payments, and the tool for this study is the circuit of incomes. On this basis, it becomes possible to have a precise definition of investment, which then proves to be the key operation from where all the troubles originate. Once the fundamental concepts are firmly established and the crucial operations correctly understood, we can observe that inflation and unemployment are two phases of the same amortization process of malformed capital. The only way to prevent any malformation of capital is to elaborate an adequate accounting system that would isolate payments related to the accumulation or maintenance of capital. The task ahead is to develop such a precise system of payments that would filtrate flows and avoid the mixing up of different income circuits.

Notes

1   The main published work by Bernard Schmitt on the subject is his 1984 book entitled *Inflation, chômage et malformations du capital* (Schmitt, 1984a).
2   As Schmitt (1984a: 90, our translation) noted, "it is easy to imagine that the product is in the nature of physical matter [...]. However, we must not confuse human production with the creation of the universe. Let us not forget the truism according to which human-beings cannot produce a single amount of physical matter." He further pointed out that "[i]t would be a mistake to view production as an addition of matter and the product as an 'added matter'" (ibid.: 92, our translation).
3   As Schmitt (1984a: 90, our translation) cogently argued, "[t]he appropriation of the product is precisely its destruction as a product and its denaturation into a utility or value in use".
4   "Taken lightly, production may be identified to all sorts of actions: even the wind is a factor of production. But, taken seriously, production is a solemn operation: in the dictionary it means a creation. And we cannot see how the wind might produce anything. Human labour can do it and, outside theology, humans are the only being able to create, to 'create-destroy'" (Schmitt 1984a: 80, our translation).
5   As Schmitt (1984a: 158, our translation) explained in this respect, "[a]s soon as incomes are born, they are loaned by their holders until the time of their withdrawal. This is to say that incomes are instantaneously transformed into savings or, identically, into a capital." He further pointed out that "[a]ny income holder is instantaneously transformed into a securities purchaser; symmetrically, the firms are instantaneously transformed into sellers of securities: they owe the incomes created at the bank" (ibid.: 159, our translation).

Inflation and unemployment 63

6 "The sale of stocks reproduces an old income instead of concerning a new income" (Schmitt 1984a: 161, our translation).

7 In Schmitt's own words (1984a: 54, our translation), "[p]roduction quantifies time; that is to say it captures at once a block of continuous time."

8 "Incomes are created on producing services market [and] destroyed on the goods market" (Schmitt 1984a: 156, our translation).

9 "The formation of non-wage incomes in the spending of wages is an operation that is started first on the goods market, by a (positive) difference between prices and costs of production of 'wage-goods'; but the same operation – formation of non-wage incomes – is simultaneously happening on the producing services markets, non-wage goods being retroactively withdrawn from workers since the emission of wages" (Schmitt 1984a: 124, our translation).

10 "The emission is empty precisely because it projects the product into money but withdraws it at once, in the same movement" (Schmitt 1984a: 190, our translation).

11 As Schmitt (1984a: 190, our translation) explained, "the empty emission defined by net investment has heavy consequences; capital slips away from income holders and this 'expropriation' will cause malignant emissions."

12 "If at the moment of its formation, each piece of fixed capital were appropriated within the whole set of income holders, the amortization of fixed capital would boil down to indirect purchases such as the fabric bought through the purchase of the suit: amortization goods would reach households in the same way as the original piece of capital. In reality, we know that firms, as a whole, constitute a barrier; investment goods are blocked within the firms, so are amortization goods; to enable them to eventually reach households – the production of amortization goods has to be duplicated" (Schmitt 1984a: 221, our translation).

13 "The emission of profit goods, dual production of amortization goods, is irrevocably empty. It has to be deemed irrevocable because, unlike with the empty emission corresponding to net investment, the empty emission induced by the production of amortization goods results in a money whose emptiness is not at all compensated; this time no saved wage-goods are ready to fill in the emptiness. The workers employed to produce the profit goods receive definitively empty wages, the spending of which can bring absolutely nothing to income holders, whoever they are" (Schmitt 1984a: 223, our translation).

14 Here we shall not consider another possibility, namely that of investing profits in the production of consumption goods. Therefore, we shall leave aside Schmitt's explanation of deflation. On this issue, see Schmitt (1984a: 236–9).

15 "Unable to find a sufficient remuneration for the whole new capital, firms will partially abandon its production and thereby reduce national production [...]. Unemployment is setting up" (Schmitt 1984a: 237, our translation).

16 "If the profit of [a firm] were carried by the second department, it would constitute an amount of *savings still available*. But, it is illogical that it should be so because profits result from a final spending *already* carried out; the wages spent in the formation of profits must not constitute monetary savings still available on the financial market: if the wages transformed into profits are not withdrawn from the financial market (represented by the second department), they constitute loanable funds that will feed a second amount of final expenditures. The borrowers will spend incomes already spent by households in the formation of profits. The second expenditure of the (same) incomes is an empty emission, at the root of the disorder, inflation and unemployment" (Schmitt 1984a: 323, our translation, italics in the original).

4 A macroeconomic analysis of unemployment

Bernard Schmitt

Introduction

The analysis of unemployment presented in the volume devoted to the pathologies of capital accumulation (Schmitt, 1984a) was carried out in value terms and by distinguishing between three periods corresponding, respectively, to the formation of profits, their investment, and the amortization of fixed capital. The analysis proposed in this chapter concerns the same problem, but it is carried out in terms of prices and the distinction between periods is replaced by that between sectors, corresponding to the production of wage-goods, profit-goods, and amortization-goods respectively. Both analyses lead to the same result and to the same solution. The advantage of the analysis advocated here is that it accounts for an increase in value of produced output due to the increase in the physical productivity of labour made possible by the presence of fixed capital. Labour alone remains the only macroeconomic factor of production, and wage units remain the unique measurement unit of produced output. Yet, value may consistently be brought at the level of prices.

Once more the core of the analysis is represented by money and its vehicular nature, and by the need to explain how profit can be derived from wages. But this time the challenge is to explain how profit can nevertheless increase, in value terms, the monetary expression of produced output. The next step is to show that, in the present capitalistic regime, the amount of income is pathologically increased to enable the purchase of an output whose value is greater than the amount of wages. A macroeconomic loan granted by banks to households and made possible by the deposit of profits is the crucial transaction characterizing the capitalistic process of capital accumulation. To explain the origin of unemployment, however, it is necessary to include amortization into the analysis. This is done by showing that the macroeconomic loan granted by banks, which corresponds to the financial emission of profits, takes place also with respect to amortization, and determines the distinction of the economy into three sectors. The chapter ends with some essential remarks concerning the reform required to overcome unemployment.

About money and income

Economists are not aware that money is issued in a creation-destruction operation rather than through net creations; they believe that money comes out of banks through an *ex nihilo* creation; they therefore do not abide by Lavoisier's principle, which is a much more fundamental mistake than any mathematical error; because of this, the whole conception of political economy is then irrevocably jeopardized. It is precisely because the bank that monetizes the product of the nation issues a sum of money, for instance 1,000 euros, in a *creation-destruction* that the issued money replaces the real product in the assets of the production factors; the destruction of money implies the formation of an equivalent amount deposited in the bank, deposits whose object is precisely the product of the nation. The economists still 'reason' as if money were moving in only one direction, whereas each monetary movement is an instantaneous perfect circle. Even money as defined in perennial deposits follows, in all its movements, *creation-destruction* operations. The 1,000 units of money launched by the bank will form a full circle in an instant thereby coming back to their starting point; again, it is the reflux of money (the second half-circle) that replaces the real product by a certain amount deposited in the bank; it all comes as if the product were deposited in the bank, acting as an intermediary, and therefore were taken out of any property in the national economy: the ownership of the new product is initially expressed exclusively in the form of bank deposits, therefore in the form of money units.

It is easy to understand that the product of the nation is a sum of wage units when these units constitute the (monetary or numerical) form of this product from the moment of the formation of the macroeconomic income until the moment of its spending in the final purchases.

In the view of mainstream economists, wage units are just money units used as wages; in reality, they are much more than that because they constitute the definition of the real product, temporarily neutralized inside money, in the bank deposits. As the product is 'pressed' into money, a form that carries it for a while, the wage units replace it, so that the wage unit is not just the measure of the product, it is the very identity or definition of the product until later when the bank deposits are withdrawn and spent on the markets, the product thereby finally recovering its physical definition.

What about incomes other than wages?

If the wage unit were not defining the unit of product, it could not measure non-wage incomes. A profit unit would then be required to measure profits. The problem would not yet be solved because of the need for a common scale between wage and profit units. We would then fall back into a problem for which no solution has been found for more than 200 years. But the wage unit is the very definition of the product unit, *a macroeconomic unit of the national product, whatever its division between wages and profits.* It is certain therefore that the wage unit measures profits as well as wages. The in-depth analysis of profits

66 *Bernard Schmitt*

requires that they should be explained as wages. Indeed, if wages and profits were distinct incomes, it would not be possible for the wage unit to be the measure of profits, and not just that of wages.

It is the distinction between physical productivity and value productivity that makes possible a unified explanation of wages and profits.

An essential distinction: physical productivity and productivity defined in value units

Let us consider, for example, the production of 100 shirts in an economy without any capital and a production of 600 shirts in an economy that employs capital. Physical production is multiplied by six thanks to the use of capital (machines); in reality, the multiplying coefficient is much higher; a vast number of goods could not be produced at all without any capital; it might be more accurate probably to consider 6,000 or 60,000 shirts. In our example, the 500 shirts added on are the product of the capital employed. Or, so it seems in a simple, simplistic, reasoning: without any capital, labour alone will produce 100 shirts, bringing on capital results in 500 more shirts, which are 'therefore' the product of capital as a factor of production. This is obviously incorrect, because it is human labour aided by the machine that produces the 600 shirts; it is impossible to distinguish in the global product what originates from labour and what originates from capital.

However, a much deeper and conclusive argument establishes without any doubt that capital is not a factor of production. It is the fact that the use of capital multiplies the physical efficiency of labour. Let us consider the problem at its fundamental level: what is precisely the operation that introduces the new product into the money units in a national economy using capital equipment? It is exactly the same as in the 'rude state of society' (devoid of any capital): the emission of wages and it alone. Even in an economy benefiting from the presence of capital (all sorts of equipment), the workers obtain, in their wages, the *whole national product*.

The readers know well the importance of the distinction between production and distribution. Production comes first and thereafter the product is distributed among the households and among households and firms. At the production stage, the product only exists as a whole. When the physical production is transformed into a creation of money, national product is still undifferentiated; it will be divided into wages and profits only *subsequently*. Economists have long been accustomed to distinguish operations carried out on the producing-services market from those carried out on the goods market. A positive chronological difference separates these operations because the macroeconomic income has first to be formed; only afterwards can it be distributed and spent.

A key problem to reflect on is to determine through what operation capital is remunerated. Income capital is made up by the interest but, then, how is interest formed? It originates from profits. And the profit of companies taken as a whole can only be formed on the goods market in the final sales. It could be indeed that a company fails to 'earn' an income that would have been distributed in interest;

A macroeconomic analysis of unemployment   67

in such a case, the company is unable to sell its product at a price higher than the wage bill. We can see here that interest is a secondary, derived income, the only primary incomes being wages. We understand that it would be illogical to locate the formation of profits on the producing-services market, where only one category of income is created, undivided, namely the total amount of wages. The fund of all types of profits, redistributed and finally gained by the firms as a whole, is defined by the wages.

The solution to an age-old problem is therefore at hand: for more than two centuries, theoreticians have dithered about whether profits have to be added on to wages; usually they have answered positively. For example, Smith's view considered that the income of the nation is made up by adding wages, profits and rents. According to Ricardo, profit also adds up to wages. For Marx, the key division of the national product is between wages and profits (surplus value). Walras is the exception: to him there cannot be any profit at the equilibrium level, because exchanges logically take place between equivalent items; therefore, profits are cancelled out, but that does not mean that profits are drawn from wages. It is only much later and only in a dim way, in Keynes's work, that one starts to discern another entirely new explanation: profit is positive although it is entirely financed by wages. This is the beginning of the correct explanation, profit being 'hidden' in the wages.

A national economy that produces 1,000 units of wages during the period has at its disposal a domestic product that is exactly equal to 1,000 units of wages. If, in this economy, profits amount also to 1,000 units, then the macroeconomic product amounts in total to 2,000 units of wages. This result is puzzling on two accounts:

- How is it possible that 1,000 units of wages should change into 2,000 units of wages?
- How is it possible that wages should be the unique unit of measure while the amount of profit is equal to that of wages?

Let us sum up the explanations needed to answer these questions.

Labour has become more efficient thanks to the use of real capital, that is, equipment. In our example, labour is now six times more efficient. If profit were nil, the increase in the physical productivity of labour would be entirely translated into a reduction in the unit price, item by item, of the national product: instead of being sold for 10 units of money, a shirt would now be sold for 10/6 money units. It is obvious that in this case labour remains the unique factor of production. But the general rule is that capital should be positively remunerated; this is so because capital is a form of savings and savers demand interest. In order to satisfy this demand, the company must gain a positive amount of profit from which interest will be taken. Let us suppose therefore that the unit of product, one shirt, is sold at a price such that a profit-interest of 1,000 units of money will be formed through the sale of the national product. The price of one shirt is therefore of 10/3 units of money; the price of the total number of produced shirts mounts up to 2,000 units

68   Bernard Schmitt

of money; this results in a profit of 1,000 units of money, the labour cost of the product being 1,000 units of money.

Is it not correct in this case to conclude that labour is no longer the only factor of production? It seems that in our example labour produces 1,000 units of value (wages) and that capital produces an additional 1,000 units of value (profit-interest). It would be strange, under these conditions, to claim that labour produces 2,000 units of value. It would be strange as well to say that labour does produce only 1,000 units of value but, in spite of that, labour produces all the value (amounting to 2,000 units) of the macroeconomic product.

Let us simplify the problem while keeping the key points.

Once the amount of profit is positive, we know from scientific certainty that the increase in physical productivity is, at least partially, transformed into the production of units of value. In the numerical example that we are considering, the purchasing power, in physical terms, of the interest-earning households is equal to half of the global product of the national economy: it comprises 300 shirts out of the 600 produced. One can therefore induce in all certainty that the increase in physical productivity, production being multiplied by six, will lead to a positive increase, albeit by three times less, of the production in value, multiplied by two. If the use of capital had not enabled a multiplication by six of the *physical* production, the *value* produced by the national economy would still be of 1,000 units. As the use of capital constituted during previous periods enables the formation, during the current period, of positive interest, by 1,000 units of money in our example, this means that the capital produces the units of value in that period and even as many units of value as labour (in our example).

The only really logical analysis concerning profits is the following: it is not true that capital produces units of value; this is absolutely impossible for the reasons stated above, the main one being that only the issuing of wages gives the money form to the product. It is the production by labour – and no other production – that is transformed into a creation of money. The simplest of arguments in this respect is based on the distinction between the two markets, those of the producing-services and of the products: wages are formed on the first one whereas profits are formed on the second one; but then the producing-services market has exclusivity of the formation of the macroeconomic income. The market of products only comes in reference to two functions, neither of which being a creation of incomes. The products are withdrawn from money on the second market that also redistributes part of the spent wages into non-wage incomes, that is, all kinds of profits.

Instead of saying that capital produces units of value, it is better to say that capital multiplies by a coefficient greater than one the value produced by labour. If one maintains nevertheless that capital produces units of value, logically one can only be meaning by this that labour produces units of value through capital.

Transformation of productivity gains into productions of value units

It is the transformation of an increase in physical productivity into an increase of value production that explains the whole formation of non-wage incomes.

A macroeconomic analysis of unemployment 69

Using capital implies saving on labour. But one should be careful to note that *this does not mean that capital is driving labour out and that it reduces the level of national employment.* That would be absurd thinking. In reality capital does not increase employment (nor diminish it) but multiplies its efficiency. In our example, 1,000 workers keep their job, full employment is maintained; but these 1,000 workers are now worth 2,000. We can now enunciate a general rule: the level of employment, of production and of the product are only measured by wage units issued on the producing-services market in any national economy that would not use real capital (such an economy does not exist); but the measure of the level of employment, of production and of the product must in addition take into account the multiplying coefficient of the efficiency of labour in producing units of value, this coefficient being entirely determined by the transformation of physical productivity gains resulting from the use of real capital into a gain in the production of value.

Banks and capitalism

We have now reached the core study of capitalism. The twenty-first century will undoubtedly bring a (soft) reform of capitalism: in the post-capitalist regime, all the kinds of profits (all profits) will be formed *inside wages*, without any additional non-wage income. In the meantime, it is indisputable that all the profits are added on to the wages. However, wages are the only incomes issued on the producing-services market. Profits are not issued on this market. It is quite clear that profits could not be issued on the products market. It is important to distinguish the formation of profits from their emission. Profits are *formed* on the products market; we have insisted on that. But profits are not *issued* on this market. There is only one market where profits can be issued, namely, the financial market.

When the bank lends 1,000 units of money to the households, taken as a whole, it issues profits: it issues them through a loan; it is therefore on the financial market that it issues them. We should note at once that the emission of 1,000 units of money in a bank loan granted to the households is an emission of *wages*. In fact, households obtain in that way a part of their future incomes. How do we know that? The households will have to dip into their future incomes, those being wages, in order to repay the loans. Instead of saying – which is nevertheless true – that the bank lends 1,000 units of money to the households, it is more correct (more precise) to say that it lends 1,000 units of wages to the households.

We are now facing two different kinds of emissions and even emissions from two different sources. In our numerical example:

- 1,000 units of wages are issued on the producing-services market; it is the formation of wages in the proper sense;
- in addition, 1,000 units of wages are issued on the financial market; this is the formation or the 'pre-formation' of profits.

The households have now at their disposal a total of 2,000 units of wages, of which 1,000 units are the product of the current period, the other 1,000 units of

70   *Bernard Schmitt*

wages being advanced by the bank on their future incomes. The comparison between the income (2,000 wage units) available to the households and the value of the macroeconomic product (1,000 wage units) does not lead to the certain conclusion that the firms, taken as a whole, must make a profit equal to the difference (1,000 wage units). It could very well be that the households refuse to spend 2,000 wage units to buy a product of 1,000 units of measure; they may stop when they have reached an expenditure of 1,500 wage units to acquire a product whose value is 1,000 wage units. In this case, the firms face a clearing deficit; this deficit therefore cancels an equal amount of profit. But let us assume here that the households actually do spend 2,000 units of wages to purchase the product measured by 1,000 wage units. Then a profit of 1,000 wage units will form in the firms taken as a whole. This profit, as we know, is used in two possible ways: either distributed as interest to the households or retained in the possession of these firms.

Households are protected by the rule that profits cannot exceed wages

The following demonstration is a bit difficult but quite clear. We must prove that the amount of profit cannot exceed wages. We could be mistaken in this matter. To avoid any such mistake at the initial stage, we must from the onset indicate that profits may be higher than wages if we take into account *all* profits, including interest profits and profits *stricto sensu*, that is, the income retained by the firms as a whole. It could be then that total profit, the sum of the two kinds of profits, reaches a level twice as high as wages; at the limit, interest profit reaches 1,000 units of measure, while profit (retained by firms) reaches also 1,000 units of measure, whereas the emission of wages during this period amounts to 1,000 units. In these cases, it is obvious that total profit is twice as high as wages.

The demonstrations are therefore different: we have to prove that interest profit cannot exceed wages; the second proof is that invested or undistributed profit cannot exceed wages. Let us consider these two profits separately.

Let us assume initially that the invested profit is not positive, profit being entirely distributed as interest.

We have already remarked that the incomes advanced by the bank to households as a whole are future wages. If in every period we have a new loan and the repayment of a previous loan, we find that, once the equilibrium is reached, in each period households give back to the bank what they receive from it. We observe therefore that the loan cannot exceed the repayment capacity of households, that capacity being used up once they have spent the entire amount of their wages. The upper limit of the loan is therefore 1,000 wage units for 1,000 units of wages issued on the market of producing-services. It results that the profit, fed by the spending of money lent to households, cannot exceed the 1,000 units of wages issued period after period in the national economy. The conclusion is that interest profit cannot exceed wages. This result is true in the capitalist system but not in the post-capitalist system, which we will not deal with here.

A macroeconomic analysis of unemployment   71

Let us now set aside the interest profit to concentrate on invested profit. The argument in this case is exactly the same as for the interest profit: in order to repay the capital owed to the bank, households cannot have at their disposal on average in each period more than their current wages. This is absolutely certain, because the money granted by the bank is entirely absorbed, unit of money for unit of money, by the repayment of the capital previously lent. The new conclusive evidence that we were searching for has now been found: profit cannot exceed wages. Once again this induction (deductions are made from axioms, inductions are drawn from facts) is confirmed in the capitalist system, restrictively. The difficulty that immediately follows is without doubt greater than the problem we have just solved.

Possible coexistence, within the limit of wages, of an interest profit and
an invested profit, each one being equal to the amount of wages

One necessarily feels that households cannot take from their wages of 1,000 units both the amount to repay a loan that induced the formation of an interest profit of 1,000 units and the amount to repay a loan that led to the formation of an invested profit of 1,000 units: indeed, it is impossible to take 2,000 units of measure from 1,000 units of measure. If the question were confined within these observations, one would have to conclude that the economy of the nation produces a *total* amount of profit at most equal to wages. The distribution of this profit may therefore be of 600 units of interest and 400 units of profit (undistributed) for an amount of wages of 1,000 units. In reality however, the wages being of 1,000 units, the total profit may mount up to 2,000 units provided of course that 1,000 units of profits are actually distributed as interest to the households and that 1,000 units of profits are finally retained by firms.

The explanation of this strange result is quite obvious: if firms, as a whole, give back to households the profit of 1,000 units of money (units of wages), households have again at their disposal the wages issued in the period. The two groups have therefore gone back to the 'starting line' so that households may yet again pay a profit of 1,000 units of wages to firms, thus forming this time an undistributed profit.

Division of the economic activity of the nation in two sectors

The analysis only needs to move one step forward in order that the crucial division of the national economy in industrial sectors should be clearly perceived.

- The first sector produces the wage-goods proper.
- The second sector produces the interest-goods.
- The second sector also produces the profit-goods in the strict sense.

Let us proceed through didactical steps. Let us first build the distinction between the two sectors in the case where the amount of invested profit (undistributed) is

72   *Bernard Schmitt*

not positive. After that, we will study the case of a positive amount of profit-goods produced in the second sector. We shall prove, finally, that the second sector carries both the interest profit and the invested profit, without confusing them at all but on the contrary adding them up.

Production of interest-goods in the second sector in the case where the national economy does not produce new investment-goods (during the period under study); moving further on into the definition of capitalism

Let us study the limiting case, namely the interest-goods amounting to 1,000 units of value for an equivalent amount of wage-goods. If p_1 is the first period when capital is formed, let us start the analysis in a period, p_n, when capital has developed enough to cause an amount of interest equal to the amount of wages. In p_n the bank lends 1,000 wage units to the households as a whole, these repaying 1,000 wage units to the bank. It would be a mistake to cancel the current loan by the repayment of the previous loan (that from p_{n-1}): such a compensation would happen only if the *same households* were the new and the old borrowers. In this case that would mean abandoning the assumption of the repayment of the previous loan. The total income produced in the two sectors is 2,000 units of measure: the 1,000 units of measure that add up to the wages issued in the economy, 500 units in each sector, result, as we have understood above, from the transformation of a gain in physical productivity into an increase in the production of value.

Let us list one by one the relevant flows:

- the emission of wages amounts to 1,000 units in the national economy;
- the households have at their disposal in money 2,000 units of value;
- the multiplying coefficient of the value production by households is two;
- from these 2,000 units of value, households as a whole take 1,000 units of value and repay the previous loan.

A continuity is created between the issued wages of 1,000 units of value and the repayment of 1,000 units of value. These two flows are related to the households as a whole, one positively (formation of wages) and the other negatively (taken off the wages). These same flows are also related to the firm or the firms as a whole, one positively, the emission of 1,000 units of wages coming from the income that the households as a whole take off their assets, and the other negatively, the emission of wages considered in itself. The continuity that we have just described is the central point: through the bank and by the intermediation of the firms as a whole, households *pay to themselves*, as a whole, up to 1,000 units of income (units of value, units of wages).

Let us be precise on what we mean by the expression 'households pay to themselves'. It is always true that households pay themselves by their own labour. In this sense, it is certainly not abnormal but, on the contrary, the general rule that households pay themselves. But there are two utterly opposite cases: households may get, by the payment of their job, a purchasing power or a real income that is created in the emission of wages, and it may also be, in the opposite case, that households obtain in payment for part of their work a purchasing power or a real income that they have spent to buy a product. We observe then that households obtain a purchasing power or a real income *already spent by them*. It is in this precise case that we say households pay themselves.

In a national economy that would not produce any profit, the households would obtain for the whole of their income a purchasing power created in the emission of the wages, no part of real income received by households would be coming from a real income already spent by them. Capitalism is a production regime in which households, as a whole, obtain part of their real incomes in the form of a real income already spent by them. Let us now introduce an important piece of information: a purchasing power or a real income disappears when spent. If households, as a whole, are paid with an income already spent by them, they obtain, in money, a *zero product*. As it is certain that no unit of money is empty of product, the wages obtained in an 'empty emission' do contain a product that the workers, paid with fully 'filled' units of money, have to share with the producers of profit-goods in a broad sense.

The formation of any profit, distributed or invested, results from the fact that households as a whole obtain no product, up to the amount of profit, in exchange for their work. They then obtain a sum of money emptied of any product. The explanation continues in the distinction of the two profits: the product withdrawn from the households by the formation of distributed profit is given back to them through interest, whereas the product withdrawn by the formation of invested profit is definitively taken from the property of households without any compensation.

Let us offer another analysis of the definition of capitalism: it is the regime in which firms pay part of the labour by spending a purchasing power already positive and taken from households. The factors that produce the investment-goods receive in payment a real income already received by other households, that purchasing power having been transferred as a profit to firms. An equivalent amount of real money (products deposited in a sum of money) is therefore received by two distinct measures of labour. If the profit amounts to 1,000 units of wages, the households receive in payment of a labour measured by 2,000 units of value twice the same sum of 1,000 wage units.

Inertia over time of the formation of profits; increase (over space) of the amount in profits

It only requires that the bank grant an initial loan of 10 units of money to households as a whole in order that this loan, renewed from period to period, brings to the economy the financing for the formation of a 10 wage-units profit from period to period. It is a perfect inertia over time. On the basis of this inertia, an 'expansion' of the loan from the bank to households allows an increase in the profit's share of national income. When the limit is reached, we observe that in each period the emission of wages being of 1,000 units, the bank lends 1,000 units of money to households.

74 *Bernard Schmitt*

Production of profit-goods in the second sector

For this new enquiry, we can consider as one set all the households' incomes, namely wages and interest. As a matter of fact, these incomes are equal to the income of labour as a whole once the multiplying coefficient (which transforms the increase in physical productivity into a production of value) is applied. In our example, the labour production of value has been doubled because of the use of capital in the production process. As the emission of wages in the global economy is 1,000 units, the macroeconomic product has a value of 2,000 units of wages. Households own the whole of this value until the production of profit-goods in the strict sense, investment by the firms as a whole, becomes positive. Let us start with a zero profit even if later on the analysis shows that this profit is positive over that period. Initially we only see wages of 1,000 units and interest of 1,000 units: the production of the second sector is therefore already positive, equal to half of the national production. We meet again a problem already treated: how could we conceive of a production in the second sector that, in addition, would include the profit-goods? Is it not certain that Sector 2 cannot produce a greater amount than Sector 1? As the production of the second sector is already absorbed by the interest-goods, one does not understand clearly how positive profit-goods could be part of it. Now, by assumption, the production of profit-goods has also reached its upper limit, so that Sector 2 produces strict profit-goods of 1,000 units of value. Should we conclude that the production of the second sector is twice as high as the production of the first? That would be worrisome, because the analysis would be incoherent.

This is the point where we can offer an analysis that directly takes into account the multiplying coefficient of the production of measure units. On the one hand, the new increase of real capital absorbs a part of the new labour; on the other hand, the previous increase of real capital multiplies in each period the efficiency of labour in producing units of value. Let us recall that the two components of the problem to be solved are the following in the period under study:

- the firm has the factors of production working 50 per cent for itself;
- the capital already accumulated multiplies by two the production of value units carried out by labour.

We can observe that one only needs to multiply each of these two rates by the other to obtain the number 1, the meaning of which here is revealing: in the end, the factors of production work for themselves in spite of the fact that they provide the firm with a profit equal to their wages.

Production scheme of the two sectors when the upper limits of profits and interest are reached

Notice that the sectors have not yet been entirely explored at this stage of the analysis; additional considerations will have to be brought in. Figure 4.1 is correct within its own limits.

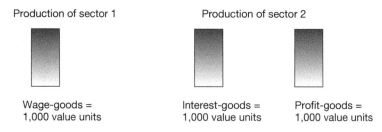

Figure 4.1 The production of the first two sectors.

The general explanation is the following. The multiplying coefficient of the production of value is three and not two. Indeed, the production of interest-goods is based, like the production of profit-goods, on the transformation of an increase in physical productivity into a production of value. Thanks to the capital previously accumulated, labour in the current period will bring 3,000 units of value, whereas it would only bring 1,000 units of value if the economy were operating without capital. The formation of an interest profit withdraws 1,000 value units from the 3,000 value units. Similarly, the formation of the invested profit withdraws 1,000 value units from the macroeconomic product of 3,000 value units. The factors of production keep in their possession 1,000 units of value.

Time has now come to apply to invested profit the analysis already carried out for interest profit. In the capitalist regime, invested profit is formed, like interest profit, through the use of a loan that the bank grants to the households as a whole. Let us suppose that the new loan (in relation with invested profit) has a time horizon of one period. During the first period when a profit is formed, no profit is yet spent. But as early as the second period, the new profit is faced with the spending of the profit from the immediately previous period.

Let us now consider the formation and the spending of a profit amounting to 1,000 units of measure in period p_n and let us suppose that the profit of period p_{n-1} was already of 1,000 units. We can see that in each period, from p_n to p_{n+x} (where x is as great as we wish), any income formed during the period is spent during the same period. This means that unemployment is left unexplained, global demand being also necessarily equal to global supply. The analysis must therefore be pursued and must take into account the role of amortization. Produced in the second sector and used in the first and second sectors, fixed capital undergoes wear and tear and obsolescence and must therefore be amortized. The amortization of fixed capital implies a new production of investment-goods that replace the old ones. The third sector is where this production takes place.

The amortization of fixed capital

The first, 'positive', conception of amortization identifies it to a net production of investment-goods. It would be too hasty to conclude that amortization conceived of as a net production would necessarily generate a positive measure of

76   *Bernard Schmitt*

unemployment. On the contrary, for many years during which capital increases, the production of amortization-goods in the third sector of the national economy does not prevent full employment. The relevant events unfold in the way described below. Let us analyse the situation where the limits have been reached in the second and third sectors, and the production, which measured in units of wages paid to the employees is equal to 1,000 units of value, is distributed uniformly between the three sectors:

- the 333 1/3 units of wages created in Sector 3 are spent in Sector 1 to clear the wage-goods, whose value is raised by 333 1/3;
- the firm finds in this way the financial resources needed to fund the production of the third sector.

It thus follows that employment in Sector 3 is assured. As employment is also assured in the other two sectors, the economy of the nation does not suffer from any unemployment.

The explanation that we have just given requires an important clarification: how is it possible to claim that the value of the wage-goods (produced in the first sector) is increased by the value of the amortization-goods (produced in the third sector)?

Here we observe again a case where the price of a collection of goods is greater than its value. Any formation of a positive profit requires the existence of such a difference. It is not surprising that this should also be the case with amortization because, precisely according to their positive definition, amortization-goods are final goods, exactly like investment-goods (profit). If we ignore here the formation of distributed profits, the firm sells the wage-goods that have a value of 333 1/3 units, at a price that is *twice* 333 1/3 units of money: it makes a gross profit of 333 1/3 units of wages, which allows the firm to pay the workers employed in the third sector.

We can express the same fact in the following way: by buying the wage-goods households buy simultaneously, in the same transactions, the amortization-goods on behalf of the firm. It is in the sales of the first sector that the firm finds the means of financing the production of the third sector. It is absolutely normal that it should be so, because the beneficiaries of amortization (the maintaining of capital) are households. If capital were decaying, the production of physical goods would decline over time, which would reduce the well-being of households. The conclusion is therefore that net production, including the production of amortization-goods, is obtained after deducing the reproduction cost of these goods.

The latter analysis leads to another perplexity.

We have just seen that the reproduction of capital is not a net production. Should we not deduce from this that the production of the third sector is not a net production?

If the answer were positive, it is quite clear that Sector 3 would not even exist, because each sector of the economy carries a *net* production. The subject of amortization is all the more interesting, from an analytical point of view, because it is complex: it does not allow for the application of the logical law of excluded middle but requires on the contrary the intervention of a more advanced, more modern logic. The two propositions indicated below are absolutely true, each one of them, even though they seem to contradict one another:

- the net contribution of capital can only be assessed, as we have argued, after the payment of its own reproduction cost;
- in spite of this fact, the 'reproduction goods' are entirely final goods, to the same extent as the consumption-goods and the investment-goods.

According to the first idea, the reproduction of capital does not bring any net value: it does not add any value to the national economy, because the capital itself absorbs for its maintenance and perenniality the value that it brings for its reproduction. However, according to the second idea, the reproduction of capital is the productive activity, *positive and net*, of the third sector. It is certain that Sector 3 carries only the reproduction of capital; it does not carry at all the production of capital that manifests itself in the other two sectors. It is in the production of consumption-goods and investment-goods that the production of capital is to be found. It is therefore indeed the reproduction of capital – and not its production – that is the net production of the third sector. One understands even intuitively the fact that the reproduction of capital is necessarily a net production of the national economy. Let us assume that a computer has to be replaced by a more sophisticated, more modern device: it is obvious that the new computer, which replaces the old one, must be produced exactly like the computers that constitute a new investment in the period under scrutiny. In this respect, there can be no difference between production goods and reproduction goods.

We are therefore compelled to conclude that both contrary definitions of the amortization-goods are true (factoring out the law of excluded middle): amortization-goods are both pure reproduction goods and true production goods. In their strict definition as pure reproduction goods, the amortization-goods bring no net value to the economy of the nation. But according to their other definition, also entirely correct, the amortization-goods bring to the economy of the nation their full value. It is in the totality of their value, 333 1/3 units of measure, that the amortization-goods are both a purely gross value (that cannot be added on to the value of national product) and a net value (that must be added on to national product).

The sectorial division of the national economy – which, far from being a purely theoretical construct, actually exists – enables the understanding of this duplication of value, gross and net, of amortization. In the first sector, amortization is purely a gross value, of 333 1/3 units in our example. In the third sector, where it is present simultaneously, amortization has an equal net value of 333 1/3 units.

Actual explanation of unemployment: evolution of capitalism through time within a logical pre-defined framework

It would be naïve indeed to think that "because the production of amortization-goods takes place in the third sector of the national economy, the macroeconomic

78 Bernard Schmitt

activity is actually divided in three sectors". It is again solely by applying logic that the question of the sectors can be solved. Are there one, two or three sectors in the economy of the nation? If we decide, without any analytical basis, that Sector 1 produces wage-goods, Sector 2 produces profit-goods (interest and investment) whereas Sector 3 produces amortization-goods, nothing is yet demonstrated: it could be that this division is artificial and that in reality all production does take place in the first sector or in the first two sectors. The relevant criterion is based on the very nature of money.

Let us assume, *horresco referens*, that money is an asset chasing, on the various markets, the real assets, each exchange involving money being composed of two movements in opposite directions, units of money moving the other way from or meeting the real goods. In this case, there would be no basis on which to distinguish production according to sectors. However, if we kept distinguishing sectors, we would be using a useless classification, because in the end the last two sectors are logically part of the first. It is always possible to split a unique reality into 'sections' in order to treat these separately even though it is only a unique magnitude.

The reason why it is *essential* to analyse the activity of the economy in distinct sectors is that money, in itself, independently from its content or tenor, is an asset–liability, strictly a zero asset, a pure number. The most important consequence that follows is the fact that goods are exchanged against goods, no unit of money is ever the final end of an exchange. The immediate consequence of this first consequence is that real money, meaning money's content, is always, without any exception, *at first a wage-good in the strict sense*. If we were to ask a firm to inject directly an investment-good or, even, an amortization-good into a sum of money, it would be completely unable to do it. No one can escape the law of money that forces itself on everybody; even politicians are helpless and powerless in this matter.

At the moment one unit of money fills itself with a real good, it is certain that this object is a wage-good in the strictest sense, a good that can only be destined to end up in the property of a household. There is no way, neither in a formally correct analysis nor in the concrete world, that a unit of money could be endowed directly with an investment-good or an amortization-good. If we could, in a laboratory, capture under a microscope a unit of money at the very moment when it is created by a bank, we could only detect a real core made up of wage-goods, these being at once the exclusive property of the factors of production, which is not the case for either investment-goods or amortization-goods.

The production of wage-goods is a flow that comprises only one stage. The production of profit-goods (investment-goods) is a two-stage flow: the first stage of this flow is a production of wage-goods; its second stage is the transformation of wage-goods into profit-goods. Similarly, the production of amortization-goods is an operation comprising two stages: no amortization-good can be injected directly into a sum of money. The first injection that undergoes a sum of money, which will eventually contain amortization-good, gives it a tenor in wage-goods; only a transformation of these goods will allow it *in fine* to contain amortization-goods.

A macroeconomic analysis of unemployment   79

We have just formulated the law of the division of economic activity into three *logically* distinct sectors; these differ not just in name. The first sector is where each unit of money is issued only once, no money previously issued can be issued a second time in this sector. The second and third sectors are where any unit of money is issued for the second time. It is quite clear that these definitions are mutually exclusive. They are incompatible. We see therefore that the division into sectors is a logical necessity: it is imposed, not by words, but by the concrete reality of how national economies operate.

Even though they are employed in producing amortization-goods, the workers of the third sector *receive their wages in consumption-goods*, therefore in goods on which they have full ownership within their assets, not in goods that repair capital in the firms. We observe therefore the existence of a complete *dissociation* between the object produced by the workers in Sector 3 and the object they receive in payment: the first of these objects is by definition a good that is gained and kept by firms as a whole, whereas the second relevant object is obtained by households as a whole. It is obvious, however, that the production is no more doubled up in the third sector than in the first. It is inconceivable that the product of Sector 3 should exist to the extent of 333 1/3 units of value as amortization-goods and in addition to the extent of 333 1/3 units of value as consumption-goods. Measured on the producing-services market, the product of one sector, whether the third or the first, is exactly equivalent to the units of wages that are issued therein. In this instance, the product of Sector 3 is therefore 333 1/3 units of value and nothing more.

Again a deeply thought-out solution is required, because the problem is itself very deep. In this respect, only one analysis is correct from the logical point of view and in reality: *consumption-goods already incorporated in the wages issued in the first sector are 'served' to the producers employed in the third sector*. It is certain that the amortization costs contribute to the transformation of a gain in physical productivity into a gain in units of value. That is because it would be absurd to claim that capital has the ability to produce interest-goods but that it is unable to finance its own reproduction. It is the opposite chronology that prevails: capital has first to reproduce itself; only afterwards will it be able to produce interest. By the way, there is no need to fight in order to impose this idea that every economist will accept without discussion. If capital brings a net value, it means that it still has some 'power' left after it has reproduced itself. In the relation between the productions of the two sectors, the first and the third, we observe that the production of units of value in the first sector is augmented, *within this same sector*, by all the value produced in the third sector.

The inescapable rule is the following: in order to produce amortization-goods, the workers must first produce consumption-goods, in the strict sense, and then transform them in reproductions of capital. The real world does not allow, in the capitalist regime, the *direct* production of amortization-goods: the production of amortization-goods must be carried out through the intermediary of the production of wages-goods in the strict sense.

It is the loans of deposited profits that impose the division in sectors of the economic activity of the nation. The third sector exists positively therefore and, as

80 Bernard Schmitt

we have shown, it can employ at its highest extension a third of the workers, 333 1/3 units of employment on a full employment of 1,000 workers (measured in wage units). But it is the employment in the activity of the second sector that is our first concern. Once the upper limits of the last two sectors are reached, we know that 333 1/3 workers are employed in Sector 2. A consequence immediately follows: the interest and the profits produced in units of value in the second sector cannot exceed, in total, twice the sum of 1,000 units of money. A first sum of 1,000 units of money is the monetary value (again expressed in wage units) of the interest-goods (which include the dividend-goods). The second sum of 1,000 units of money issued in the second sector is the monetary value of profit-goods (new investments in the current period). It is the first sum of 1,000 units of money, issued in the second sector, that must first draw our attention: *it is distributed among the successive layers of capital accumulated in the previous periods.*

The capital added on during the current period does not yet bring any interest. But any previous addition to capital does produce positive interest.

A 'law' mainly discovered by Karl Marx, the so-called "tendency of the rate of profit to fall", calculates the ratio of the sum of the interest produced during a period divided by *the sum of real capital accumulated during all the previous periods.* Let us consider a numerical example. The accumulated capital reaches the sum of 100,000 units of value in the current period: we see clearly, then, that the interest allocated to the total accumulated capital, amounting to a maximum of 1,000 units of value in each period, determine a ratio of 1 per cent. In other words, the interest rate is only of 1 per cent per unit of capital. It is legitimate, in this respect, to speak, as suggested by Knut Wicksell, of a *natural rate* of interest. Let us never forget that the great authors of the past are useful. They have not worked in vain. They have efficiently prepared the reform of capitalism of which they are, in advance, the co-authors. Why then is the rate just described, a *natural* rate? The reason is that it is worked out by the nature of things, precisely by the accumulation of capital over time. Once the new investments in each period bring about in the current period a total accumulation of 100,000 units of wages, it is *objectively certain*, 'natural', that the interest produced in the current period should be related to a capital of 100,000 units of wages. It is also as much natural and objective that the interest produced in a given period cannot exceed the value brought or added, with the help of capital, by a third of the factors of production employed in the economy of the nation. Consequently, and once again naturally, objectively, the average rate of interest per unit of capital cannot exceed 1 per cent.

It is obvious that this example is arbitrary. But what is not arbitrary is the fact that *capital increases continuously, from period to period, thanks to every new investment, whereas the production of interest in each period reaches a limit that will never be surpassed.* It is the conjunction of this limit imposed on the production of interest related to a continuous increase in the capital to be remunerated (with the interest) that constitutes the expression of the objective or natural law of the capital's dynamics, the tendency of the rate of profit (interest) to fall.

There is nothing worrying yet, because one might imagine that the interest may fall down to zero or may tend indefinitely towards zero. But on a second point, of

A macroeconomic analysis of unemployment 81

equal importance to the first, Wicksell increases our concern. The *natural interest* is not the only category of interest that exists in the real national economies that experience, in fact, a second category of interest, namely the *monetary interest*.

How, given scientific progress since Wicksell, can we interpret the *monetary* interest? It is simply the '*Leihzins*' (a term that comes from Böhm-Bawerk (1851–1914) to whom Wicksell (1851–1926) was close). The current rate of interest on the financial market is determined by two independent actions: the rate is decided, for example each week, by the central bank of the country and it is discussed between lenders and borrowers. It is obvious that although these two determinations are, as we have just mentioned, independent from each other, one is nevertheless subordinated to the other: once the effective rate in relation to the national currency has been decided by the central bank, the rates discussed within the country by the participants on the financial market must fall in line. *The central piece of information here is the fact that the monetary or financial interest is determined in each period and regulates the confrontation of the* new incomes *likely to be lent and the financial needs of economic agents willing to run a deficit in order to spend in the current period a sum of income greater than the incomes they received from production.*

We fully understand then that there comes a time when, capital having already developed considerably and been accumulated in great measure, the *monetary rate* will exceed the *natural rate* of interest. It then becomes more interesting, in the true sense, for capital holders to use it on the financial market, where it 'earns' the monetary interest, rather than using it on the producing-services markets, where its yield would be equal to the natural rate. It is a simple rule of good management of available funds. On our way to understanding unemployment, its aetiology, there is only one obstacle left. We have to grasp the exact meaning of using capital on the financial market when maintaining full employment would require that it should be used on the producing-services market.

Once again Wicksell – whose perspicacity regarding unemployment is without doubt greater than Keynes's, although the latter wrote a few decades later – gives us the correct idea. The monetary funds in possession of the firms may be definitively withheld from the new production in order to be spent in a purely financial way that has no outcome whatsoever on the products market. Rightly, once the natural rate of interest becomes lower than the monetary rates newly determined in the successive periods, the firms' interest (again, no pun intended) is to throw funds period after period into the circle of production. Instead of buying a positive amount of new product in each period, which would constitute a positive demand on their market, the firms then finance the production process in its two aspects simultaneously, *formation and expenditure of incomes*. It is clear that a capital assigned to both the formation of a macroeconomic income and to its expenditure will not actually finance any purchase, any net demand. In actual fact, it means that firms give up producing new investment-goods in the second sector – that would aggravate the negative difference between the natural rate and the monetary rate of interest – and instead produce amortization-goods: *the production of the third sector is thereby substituted to the production of the second sector.* Full employment would only be maintained if amortization-goods were produced in the third sector, kept separate from the second sector. But that would require a natural rate of interest at least equal to the monetary rate of interest. The production of amortization-goods causes a positive level of unemployment in the exact measure that these goods are being produced in the second sector instead of the third, which defines a reduction of the production circle, the only cause of which is the discrepancy between the two interest rates to the disadvantage of the natural rate of interest.

If full employment were maintained, the value of the new product of each period would amount to 5,000 units of measure. Indeed, all the wages issued in the economy of the nation define a product of 1,000 units of value located in the first sector; the interest-goods and the investment-goods, located in the second sector, have a value of 2,000 units; the amortization-goods, in their capacity of final goods, are produced to the level of 1,000 units of value in the third sector; finally the value of the amortization-goods is added on to the value of the wage-goods or, identically, to the consumption-goods produced in the first sector. In case unemployment reaches its maximum level in manufacturing, the amortization-goods are produced in place of investment-goods in the second sector. It is quite natural that, in their capacity as final goods, the amortization-goods should be investment-goods. But the value produced by the economy of the nation is thereby reduced by 1,000 units of value, which corresponds to the wages of a third of the workforce that would be employed in a full employment situation: unemployment affects, therefore, a third of the workforce in the manufacturing sector.

The reform to defeat unemployment: recalling a few essential ideas

Man transforms himself into a demiurge and he will truly master only a world that he will have contributed to create. One cannot deny that human beings are subject to the ills of capitalism, namely inflation and unemployment. It is on these precise points that progress in the economic, and therefore social, organization is possible. When this is accomplished, we shall live in a reformed capitalism, free from its disorders. Humanity will have more than enough problems to solve, particularly of a political, moral and religious, and even sociological, nature, such as the education of children and adults. The nobility of our discipline resides entirely in its objective: like any product, political economy must be useful to society and so must the economists themselves.

It is only in the capitalist system – and not in the logical order of things – that the division of the economic activity in three different sectors is enforced. In post-capitalism, the production of the nation will be entirely carried out in only one sector. We can already guess that the existence of the other two sectors, which could be joined to the first, is clinging only to a thread, namely the channel of the loans granted by the banking system to the households as a whole. Once this thread is severed, Sectors 2 and 3 will no longer be supplied and all the macroeconomic activity will take place in only one sector.

A macroeconomic analysis of unemployment 83

One idea that we have mentioned several times, but only allusively, is crucial here: any profit, whether interest profit or invested profit, is formed as a deposit in a bank. It is the deposits that come about at the moment when profits are formed that feed the loans of the bank (the banks as a whole) to households (as a whole). We know very well that it is not true to say that any deposit of a newly formed profit will lead to a new loan, net of redeemed loans. This would ignore the inertia of loans over time. Indeed, in the concatenation of the successive loans of this type, only the first one will have, in the period when it is formed, no corresponding repayment of previous loans (that do not yet exist). For the other loans, there are in parallel repayments of an equal amount. But one can well conceive that it is possible, by way of a reform, to nip in the bud the loan of any bank deposit formed by a profit. Once this is achieved, the two other sectors of the national economy will no longer be able to materialize.

Again, why is it that the formation of profits is associated with the formation of 'loanable funds'? This is so because the bank does not distinguish, in its resources, deposits according to the category of depositors: the deposits are deemed important, not the depositors. Any deposit, whatever its origin, is a sum of incomes that the bank may, and even must, lend, by its very function of linking together agents with a surplus (depositors) and agents with a deficit (borrowers). In its function as a financial intermediary the bank lends, automatically, we might say, any deposit that it has received. Let us analyse the deposit of a profit in the strict sense (that is, one to be invested) amounting to 1,000 units of measure at the moment it is formed initially. In the world as it is now (capitalism), profit is based on a loan that the banking system grants to households as a whole: to the profit of 1,000 units of measure corresponds then such a loan of 1,000 units of measure. We see, therefore, the deep meaning of profit: households obtain these incomes of 1,000 units of (advanced) wages through the formation of a debt. As soon as households have at their disposal 2,000 units of wages, of which 1,000 are borrowed from the banking system, the purchasing power that they own is only of 1,000 units of wages, because no one owns the value that he has borrowed, which is, by definition, the property of someone else. We know, however, that the value of the product from the factors of production (the workers) is, in the situation we are describing, of 2,000 units of measure. It would be legitimate therefore that the households should obtain in full ownership a product (in monetary form) of 2,000 units of measure, instead of only 1,000. One is compelled to observe then that profit is an income that is taken from the households whereas it should logically be theirs and stay so.

It might at once be objected that profit is the necessary sustenance of capital and that capital is the multiplying factor in the production of units of value by labour. To suppress profit would imply suppressing the growth of capital. This is not correct: the growth of capital is not stopped, not even slowed down, once profits are in the possession of the households. Profits that would no longer mean, as in the capitalist regime, a loss of income to the households, would be as positive and as efficient as the profits defined by the definitive loss of value units suffered by households. The only difference, but its effects will be important, is that the profits kept in the possession of households reduce on the one hand the amount of income at their disposal (this is the very definition of invested profits) but on the other hand increase households' wealth in capital by the same amount: any new profit will be exactly represented by new financial securities *in possession of households*, namely shares and bonds.

5 National banking reform

Alvaro Cencini

Introduction

Although its initial meaning, derived from the Latin *reformare*, was 'to bring back to the original condition', the verb *to reform* is actually used in the sense of 'making changes in an institution or practice in order to improve it'. This is what the reform advocated by Schmitt, mainly in his 1984 volume and in his unpublished manuscript of 1998, is all about (Schmitt 1984a and 1998a, respectively).

The aim of this chapter is to show the changes that would improve the working of the present system of domestic payments so as to avoid once and for all the possibility of monetary disorders. In particular, our explicit goal in this chapter is to advocate a change in the way monetary transactions are entered in banks' ledgers, which will result in the eradication of inflation and involuntary unemployment. It is immediately clear that, normative analysis being necessarily founded on positive analysis, the principles of such a reform are derived from the study of the mechanism giving rise to these two pathological states. If inflation and unemployment were due to economic agents' behaviour, their eradication would simply be impossible, the task for economists being reduced to finding a set of measures capable of limiting their growth. Yet, if their cause is a lack of consistency between the logical laws applying to economics and the system of domestic payments implemented by banks, it becomes realistic to look for a solution that allows them to be wiped out. This is indeed one of Schmitt's strong messages: inflation and unemployment have a common 'structural' cause that can be permanently removed through a banking reform.

In order to determine what are the changes the present system of domestic payments must undergo it is necessary to know the logical laws the system should comply with and why it is actually at odds with them. This is why the presentation of Schmitt's reform is preceded by a short summary of the key components of his analysis, which explain the pathological origin of both inflation and involuntary unemployment.

86   *Alvaro Cencini*

The fundamental analytic principles

The crucial distinction between money and income

The traditional concept of money as a stock has led economists to reason in physical terms and posit the existence of a fictive world where a quantity of money is made to circulate more or less rapidly between economic agents that exchange it against an amount of goods of equivalent value. In this hypothetical framework, the goal of monetary policy is to find the best possible equilibrium between a quantity of money and the quantity of goods according with the stability of their prices. Since the stock of money is determined by monetary authorities whereas the stock of goods is determined by firms, their equilibrium is unavoidably unstable, and the whole exercise amounts to adjusting the former to the latter in a constant search for equilibrium that will never come to pass. Now, this search is not only frustrating but also altogether meaningless, because it is entirely at odds with the reality of our monetary systems, where banks must comply with the principles of double-entry bookkeeping and money can never be issued as a net asset.

The first building block of Schmitt's analysis is the distinction between money as such, which is a mere numerical form present as an a-dimensional means of payment in an instantaneous circulation or flow from and to the bank issuing it, and income, which is the result of the association between money and output and defines the real object of any payment. The relevance of this distinction lies in its implications for the definition of economic production and for the understanding of the meaning and genesis of inflation and deflation. In particular, the instantaneous nature of economic production derives from its identification with a creation of money that is made possible by a payment whose real object is a product. Indeed, it is through the payment of wages that the emission of money by banks acquires its significance and gives way to the formation of a positive income.

The strict relationship that exists between money, a numerical form, and product, its real content, as a result of production, makes it useless to reason in terms of equilibrium between two distinct stock magnitudes, and forces economists to abandon the use of physical concepts and mathematical tools to determine the origin of economic pathologies and their remedies. Macroeconomic analysis is an autonomous science founded on its own logical, macroeconomic laws derived from the double-entry nature of bank money – rigorously defined by Schmitt (1966a) as an "asset–liability" – and the way it is created through its association with produced output. Let us summarize the three most important laws on which Schmitt's quantum macroeconomics rests.

The macroeconomic identity of supply and demand

The first logical law of macroeconomics results from production and establishes the necessary equality between each new output and its demand. Since economic production is an instantaneous event through which produced output is given a monetary form, and since income, the result of this monetization, is best defined as 'the-product-in-the-money', it is immediately clear that each new production defines at the same time a macroeconomic output (supply) and a macroeconomic income (demand) as the two identical sides of the same object. In short, the first law of macroeconomics states that each production creates simultaneously a product and the income necessary for its final purchase. It is because production gives rise to 'the-product-in-the-money' that no difference can be found between macroeconomic supply and demand. This is particularly clear when we refer to national production. Indeed, global supply is nothing other than national output, which, as national accountants know well, is identical to national income. But national income is also the rigorous definition of global demand (it should indeed be obvious that economic demand can only be measured in terms of available income, a demand that cannot be financed being purely imaginary, and it should equally be clear that, being necessarily deposited with the banking system, the totality of national income is available and defines an equivalent demand). National output and national income are thus the two faces of one and the same reality: national production.

From an empirical viewpoint, the payment of wages is the transaction that, by giving produced output a numerical form, brings about the identification of economic output with the remuneration of wage earners. Wages have current output as their real object so that no difference can arise between the monetary and the real aspects of current production. The identity between macroeconomic supply and demand is the direct result of the payment of wages, the only original transaction defining economic production. Any explanation of inflation and deflation has to deal with this identity, which sets the theoretical framework of positive analysis. The challenge is therefore to show how it is possible for demand to be numerically greater or lesser than supply without introducing any difference between macroeconomic demand and supply.

As Schmitt's analysis shows, far from representing an obstacle to the definition of inflation and deflation, the identity between macroeconomic supply and demand is the key to understanding both the meaning of these two pathologies and what has to be done in order to guarantee the perfect correspondence between the substantial and the numerical equality of global supply and demand. As a matter of fact, the identity is always upheld, even if this implies the equality between two terms numerically different. Hence, in the case of inflation a given income measured in wage units, say 100 wage units, is distributed over an increased number of money units, say 110 money units: the identity between a demand, numerically increased from 100 to 110 money units, and a supply, defined by the amount of income formed in wage units, 100 wage units, being the mark of a pathological decrease in money's purchasing power.

The law of the necessary equality between each agent's sales and purchases

This law, first advocated by Schmitt in his 1975 book *Théorie unitaire de la monnaie* (1975a), is a direct consequence of the principle of double-entry bookkeeping applied to payments as they occur on the labour, financial and goods markets. Substantially, it states that no economic agent can purchase on one of

88   *Alvaro Cencini*

these markets without selling at the same time on another (or on the same) market, and vice versa. This means that the terms of every transaction are real, and that money intervenes merely as an intermediary, as a flow, and shall never be transformed into the object of a payment. It also establishes a strict relationship between the formation of income and its expenditure for the purchase of the output of the same period. Indeed, this law is central for the existence of a circuit of both money and income. If the actual system of domestic payments complied with this law, no disorder would occur: money would merely be used as a flow and the income formed in a given period would never be spent for the purchase of the output of another period.

The law of the identity of macroeconomic saving and investment

Considered by most economists as a kind of tautology derived directly from Keynes's equality between Y and $C + I$ and from the identification of saving, S, with $Y - C$ (to wit, with the part of current national income that is not spent for the purchase of consumption goods), the equality $S = I$ is, in reality, a true macroeconomic law establishing the identity between macroeconomic saving and investment. Quantum macroeconomic analysis shows, indeed, that it is only through investment, and particularly through the investment of profit, that income is transformed into an irreversible saving: fixed capital. The piece of information derived from this law is all important, both for positive and normative analysis, since it makes clear that an income transformed into fixed capital is an income that is forever withdrawn from consumption. The nature of macroeconomic saving is such that the sum saved is identical to that invested in the production of fixed-capital goods.

Whereas the identity between macroeconomic supply and demand establishes the strictest possible relationship between the creation of income (production) and its destruction (the final purchase of consumption and investment goods), the identity $I \equiv S$ establishes the perfect correspondence between the investment of income in the production of investment goods and its final transformation into fixed capital. It thus follows that, if the system of domestic payments complied with the logical macroeconomic law establishing the identity between S and I, not even a single fraction of the sum invested in the production of instrumental goods should still be available as a loanable fund on the financial market. Positive analysis, however, shows that this is not actually the case, and that it is precisely because of this lack of conformity between the present system and the identity $I \equiv S$ that the process of fixed-capital accumulation is subjected to a pathology that unavoidably leads to inflation and unemployment. At the same time, the law allowing for the positive analysis of the present, pathological state allows also for a normative analysis showing what amendments should be introduced in order to transform today's pathological system into a sound structure whose working will never generate inflation and involuntary unemployment.

Let us now refer to Schmitt's macroeconomic laws and demonstrate the principles of the reform that has to be implemented nationally, and how payments

National banking reform 89

will have to be entered by banks into their books to avoid creating a discrepancy between empirical transactions and logical laws.

The fundamental principles of normative analysis

The differentiation between the department of emissions (Department I) and the department of saving (Department II)

The first principle, to be implemented by every commercial bank operating in a given national banking system, is a direct consequence of the need to respect the identity of macroeconomic supply and demand, and the necessary equality between each single agent's sales and purchases. In particular, it derives from the necessity of avoiding the expenditure of an income formed by the production of any given period, say p_0, in the purchase of the production of any successive period. This logical necessity does clearly not concern the behaviour of economic agents, who are free to spend their income as they like, on the purchase of whatever production they prefer. Any income being a perfect substitute for any other, the freedom of economic agents can easily be guaranteed even if payments are entered in banks' balance sheets in such a way as to avoid any superposition of incomes formed in successive periods. Since the cause of the economic pathologies affecting our system is of a macroeconomic nature, the remedy has nothing to do with economic agents' behaviour and is not in the least affected by it.

As shown by Schmitt in his 1984 book on inflation and unemployment, the distinction between Departments I and II is necessary to avoid the formation of an excess demand due to the addition of incomes of different periods.

> Excess demands can only result from the imperfect separation between monetary emissions and financial intermediations. It has to be made sure that incomes lent on the financial market be spent for the purchase of the product of savers, otherwise they would increase the global demand of goods produced in another period.
>
> (Schmitt 1984a: 308–9, our translation)

Earlier on in this book, Schmitt had used another argument to show how a 'benign inflation' can arise from the lack of distinction between the two departments. Referring to the 'golden rule' followed by banks, he had shown that the equality between loans and deposits is not enough to avoid entirely the risk of over-lending. Based on the principle of double-entry bookkeeping, the golden rule seems to comply both with the equality of assets and liabilities and with the requirement that loans be financed by savings. This would indeed be the case if bank deposits were only made up of saved income, that is, if they could never be increased by a mere emission of money dissociated from any economic production. In other words, if banks acted as pure financial intermediaries, they would lend to borrowers what had been lent to them by depositors and nothing more. When no clear distinction is drawn between monetary emission and financial intermediation,

90   *Alvaro Cencini*

however, banks have no means of knowing at every instant of time the exact amount of income they can lend, and may finance their loans through a mere creation of money. This risk is nonetheless extremely reduced for the twofold reason that banks avoid as much as possible mutual indebtedness (which is almost unavoidable when a bank lends more than the income it has contributed to form through the payment of wages), and that their possible over-emission is not cumulative in time.

The distinction between Department I and Department II fulfils two tasks: it reduces to zero the risk of banks' over-emission, and avoids the formation of an excess demand due to the superposition of incomes formed in successive periods. Let us consider a numerical example of the way payments would be entered in the two departments within any given period and at its end (Table 5.1).

Entries (1) and (1') refer to the payment of wages corresponding to the production of p_0 and taking place at any instant of time, say t_1, which we suppose to be situated within that same period (any other assumption would do equally well). Entry (1) defines the amount of money issued by the department of emission to the benefit of firms, whose debt towards the banking system is initially monetary. On the other hand, entry (1') shows that the result of the payment of wages is the formation of a positive income, saved and deposited with banks by income earners. Firms are initially entered on the department of money emissions because banks pay out wages on their behalf, while wage earners are entered in the saving department because they are the owners of a new income. Starting from t_1, wage earners are the owners of the income saved in Department II. If we suppose that the successive payment of wages, referring to the production of period p_1, will take place at t_2 (a week from t_1 if wages are paid weekly, a fortnight if they are paid every two weeks, or a month if they are paid monthly), during the whole period of time separating t_1 from t_2, the credit–debit relationship between Departments I and II will define the exact amount of income referring to the production of p_0 that banks can lend without risk of fostering excessive demand.

Table 5.1 The payment of wages as entered in Departments I and II

	Banks B		
	Department of emissions (I)		
Assets		*Liabilities*	
(1) Firms F	100 m.u.	Saving department (II)	100 m.u.

	Banks B		
	Saving department (II)		
Assets		*Liabilities*	
(1') Department of emissions (I)	100 m.u.	Wage earners	100 m.u.

Key: m.u. = money units

National banking reform 91

Let us call the economic agents who own the income deposited in the saving department after wages have been redistributed among households 'income holders'. In the interval of time t_1–t_2, income holders can spend their savings and banks can lend to their clients the amount of income still available in the second department. If we take the final expenditure of income by savers and borrowers to be equal to 40 money units after two days in a system where wages are paid weekly, entries in the two departments will be as shown by Table 5.2.

Entries (1) and (1') represent the situation after the payment of wages and the redistribution of income among households. The successive two entries, (2) and (2'), concern the final expenditure of 30 wage units carried out by income holders. The income holders' final purchase reduces their deposits with Banks B by 30 wage units; the banks in turn credit firms, in the first department, with an equal amount of money units. The implication of Banks B's lending of 10 wage units is represented in entry (3'), where borrowers are credited with part of the income saved by income holders. At the same time, being charged to carry out the payment of F on behalf of their clients, Banks B debit borrowers, in the second department, and credit firms, in Department I. Entries (4) and (4') account for the final expenditure of 10 income units (wage units) by borrowers, while entries (5) and (5') describe the situation as it presents itself after the final expenditure of income holders and borrowers. Since "[a]t every instant 'loanable' savings are precisely defined by *the sum total of the credit rights of the first department on the second*" (Schmitt 1984a: 310, our translation, italics in the original), entries (5) and (5') tell banks that they can still lend 60 money units to their clients two days after the payment of wages occurring at t_1.

Table 5.2 The evolution of loanable funds within period p_0

	Banks B		
	Department of emissions (I)		
Assets		*Liabilities*	
(1) Firms F	100 m.u.	Saving department (II)	100 m.u.
(2) Saving department (II)	30 m.u.	Firms F	30 m.u.
(4) Saving department (II)	10 m.u.	Firms F	10 m.u.
(5) Firms F	60 m.u.	Saving department (II)	60 m.u.
	Banks B		
	Saving department (II)		
Assets		*Liabilities*	
(1') Department of emissions (I)	100 m.u.	Income holders	100 m.u.
(2') Income holders	30 m.u.	Department of emissions (I)	30 m.u.
(3') Income holders	10 m.u.	Borrowers	10 m.u.
(4') Borrowers	10 m.u.	Department of emissions (I)	10 m.u.
(5') Department of emissions (I)	60 m.u.	Income holders	60 m.u.

Key: m.u. = money units

92   Alvaro Cencini

In the following days, before the next payment of wages at t_2, bank deposits are further reduced by other final expenditures and so is the credit–debit relationship between Departments I and II. In order to describe what happens at the end of the day preceding the new payment of wages, let us assume that after a week 10 units of income are still available in the second department. To avoid these 10 units of income feeding an additional demand of the goods produced in period p_1 one applies this simple rule: at the end of period p_0 entries in Department I must be cancelled out, any credit balance being automatically transferred to Department II (Table 5.3).

The situation just before the end of period p_0 is represented in entries (1) and (1'), while entries (2) and (2') are those allowing the transfer of the monetary credit of Department I *vis-à-vis* Firms F to Department II. The meaning of this transfer is clear: F's monetary debt is transformed into a financial debt. This is so because at the end of period p_0 any product unsold on the goods market is forcefully purchased by F, which covers their costs of production through the expenditure of the income still saved by income holders. During the interval of time t_0–t_1 income holders own unsold output; at the end of the period it is owned by firms in the form of a stock of real goods. Yet, this does not mean that firms are the final owners of unsold output, because they finance their purchase by a loan. They own it, because they spend an income and cover its costs of production, but they also owe it because they do so thanks to the income saved by income holders and lent by B. Firms' stock is formed through the expenditure of a sum of saved-up income, which is why Firms F are now entered on Department II only. And the fact that firms are entered on the assets side of the saving department is a further proof that their purchase of unsold output is not final, because it is financed by an equal sale of financial claims.

Table 5.3 Bookkeeping entries at the end of period p_0

	Banks B		
	Department of emissions (I)		
Assets		Liabilities	
(1) Firms F	10 m.u.	Saving department (II)	10 m.u.
(2) Saving department (II)	10 m.u.	Firms F	10 m.u.
	0 m.u.		0 m.u.

	Banks B		
	Saving department (II)		
Assets		Liabilities	
(1') Department of emissions (I)	10 m.u.	Income holders	10 m.u.
(2') Firms F	10 m.u.	Department of emissions	10 m.u.
(3') Firms F	10 m.u.	Income holders	10 m.u.

Key: m.u. = money units

In our numerical example, the 10 units of income saved by households are lent by them to banks in exchange for a financial claim on B (they own a claim on a bank deposit of 10 money units), and Firms F owe B the amount lent to them and spent for the purchase of their stock of real goods (banks own a claim of 10 money units on firms). By guaranteeing that any income still available in the saving department at the end of period p_0 is lent to firms and spent by them in the purchase of unsold output of *this very period*, the rule advocated by Schmitt makes it impossible for any fraction of the income formed by the production of a given period to be spent for the purchase of the production of a successive period. From t_1 to t_2 the income formed by the payment of wages and not yet spent on the market for produced goods and services is saved and thereby immediately transformed into what Schmitt calls 'capital-time'. The final expenditure of income holders and the financial intermediation of banks, which enable their clients to spend what income holders have saved, reduces the amount of capital-time. If a positive amount of savings (capital-time) were still available in Department II at the end of any period, it would be lent to firms and would be spent by them in the purchase of that part of their output still unsold. In this case, part of the wage goods initially produced would be transformed into a stock of goods whose cost of production is covered by firms thanks to the loan obtained from banks. Simultaneously, the capital-time would be destroyed, and the economy would not benefit from the production of any investment goods. What is still missing in this analysis is the formation of a positive macroeconomic capital. The presence of fixed capital of a permanent nature is essential to economic growth. As we shall see in the next section, the existence of fixed capital is subordinated to the investment of profit and requires the introduction of a third department in banks' ledgers in order to avoid the pathologies generated by today's system of domestic payments.

The structure of a fixed-capital department

Although necessary, the distinction between the department of emissions and the saving department is not sufficient to avoid the pathological formation of fixed capital, which is the common source of inflation and involuntary unemployment. A third department has to be introduced, namely the fixed-capital department (Department III). In order to better understand the role played by this new department, it is worth recalling the reasons why fixed capital is currently formed in a way that is inconsistent with the logical laws of monetary macroeconomics.

The first reason for the creation of Department III is the same as the one imposing the distinction between Departments I and II: the need to avoid that an income formed in any given period be spent on the purchase of the output of any other period. Schmitt first established the existence of a vertical and a horizontal circuit for every single firm in 1977 (see Cencini and Schmitt 1977). Based on the identity between macroeconomic supply and demand, this principle states that the income formed in any given production is necessarily spent for the purchase of its output, either by wage earners (vertical circuit) or by firms (horizontal circuit). This logical requirement has to be translated into a set of rules whose

94   *Alvaro Cencini*

implementation guarantees its consistency with the way payments are entered into banks' ledgers. The distinction between the first two departments fulfils this task as far as savings are concerned, no income saved in period p_0 being available in p_1 to finance the purchase of p_1's production. What the introduction of Department III must avoid is the possibility for a profit formed in p_0 to be invested in p_1 in the production of new capital goods. If this result could not be attained, firms would spend their profit in the labour market and purchase part of the production of p_1 since its very formation (that is, since the payment of wages of p_1), a purchase that is the mark of the pathological formation of fixed capital.

Let us observe that what has to be avoided is neither a firm's decision to invest its profit, nor its actual production of new investment goods. Fixed-capital formation and accumulation are essential features of any efficient economic system and firms are and will be free to plan their production of consumption and investment goods as they like and can. Errors in forecasting notwithstanding, the production of fixed-capital goods can even be determined before the formation of profits through their advanced expenditure. As always in quantum macroeconomic analysis, economic agents' behaviour can never be the cause of the anomalies affecting our economies, which are due to 'structural' causes, that is, the lack of conformity between the structure of our system of payments and the logical laws deriving from the nature of money, income, and fixed capital. In short, this means that the reform must introduce the bookkeeping mechanism necessary to guarantee this conformity irrespective of the decisions taken by firms and households. In the specific case we are analysing here, the reform suggested by Schmitt does not restrain the activity of firms, but merely makes it technically impossible for profits formed in a given period to be spent to finance the production of another period. Profits would still be formed as they currently are, and firms would still invest in the production of new capital goods, yet it will no longer be possible for profits formed in p_0 (or in any other period) to be spent in the payment of wages of p_1 or any successive period.

To illustrate why the reform must impede the expenditure of profits in the payment of wages of a period different from the one whose production leads, through its sale at a mark-up, to the formation of these profits, let us refer to Table 5.4.

If we consider both entry (1), which originates from the formation of a profit equal to 20 money units in period p_0, and entry (2), which results from the investment by firms of 20 money units in the production of fixed-capital goods in

Table 5.4 The investment of profit in the absence of Department III

	Banks B		
	Saving department (II)		
Assets		*Liabilities*	
(1) Stock	20 m.u.	Firms F	20 m.u.
(2) Firms F	20 m.u.	Wage earners	20 m.u.

Key: m.u. = money units

period p_1, we immediately observe that the payment of wages in p_1 implies the expenditure of the profit formed in p_0. The consequence of this expenditure is the final purchase by Firms F of wage earners' output at the point of its very production. Indeed, by spending a positive income, namely their profit, firms acquire the final ownership over the goods that should have been obtained by wage earners as real content of their wages. In other words, firms empty wages of their real object and wage earners are literally dispossessed of part of their output. As an effect, fixed-capital goods are immediately lost to income holders, alienated from them and appropriated by what Schmitt calls 'disembodied' or 'depersonalized' firms. Instrumental goods are from the outset prevented from becoming the real object of income holders' credit with banks, which is why their appropriation by firms is pathological. This is to say that instrumental goods physically stocked by firms should keep defining the real content of income holders' macroeconomic saving. This would indeed happen if firms were only 'personalized' ones, because in that case profit would precisely define income holders' macroeconomic saving, and fixed-capital goods would still represent its real content.

The objective of preserving the income holders' economic ownership of fixed-capital goods stocked by firms is reached by avoiding the expenditure of the profit formed in p_0 within the payment of wages of p_1, namely, by transferring to the fixed-capital department the profit that firms invest in the production of instrumental goods. From the moment that investment defines a macroeconomic saving through which income (profit) is irreversibly transformed into fixed capital, it is logical to enter it into Department III, thereby preserving a financial relationship between the instrumental goods stocked with firms and the profit of which they are the real object. Entries in the second and third departments are as shown in Table 5.5.

Entry (1) describes the situation as it presents itself at the end of period p_0 given the formation of a positive profit of 20 money units derived from the sale of p_0's output at a mark-up. The profit matches the stock of wage goods still unsold: these same wage goods are the real content of profit. In our numerical example, it is

Table 5.5 The transfer of invested profit in Department III

Banks B			
Saving department (II)			
Assets		*Liabilities*	
(1) Stock	20 m.u.	Firms F	20 m.u.
(2) Firms F	20 m.u.	Fixed-capital department (III)	20 m.u.

Banks B			
Fixed-capital department (III)			
Assets		*Liabilities*	
(2') Saving department (II)	20 m.u.	Firms F	20 m.u.

Key: m.u. = money units

96   *Alvaro Cencini*

assumed that the totality of F's profit will be invested in the production of instrumental goods and thus transformed into fixed capital. Entries (2) and (2') show how invested profit (which defines an irreversible macroeconomic saving) is transferred to the fixed-capital department. Being subtracted from the saving department, profit can no longer feed any payment of wages of p_1, which prevents 'disembodied' firms from purchasing wage earners' output. Rather than being paid out of pre-existing profit, wages corresponding to the production of fixed-capital goods are paid, as any other production, through an emission of money that gives wage earners the ownership over produced output. It is true that instrumental goods are stocked with firms and that households will never purchase them on the goods market. Yet, this apparent ambiguity is easily overcome by reference to generalized exchange, which enables firms to exchange their stock of unsold consumption goods with the fixed-capital goods produced by wage earners. The 20 units of consumption goods produced in p_0 and purchased at the end of that same period by firms, are exchanged, at equal value, against the 20 units of fixed-capital goods produced in p_1 and owned by wage earners.

Table 5.6 reproduces the bookkeeping entries corresponding to these transactions.

The first entries, (1) and (1'), describe the transfer to Department III of the profit invested by Firms F. The successive entries, (2) and (3), define the production of fixed-capital goods in p_1 and the final purchase of the consumption goods produced in p_0 and still stocked with F respectively. Finally, entry (4) and entry (1') show the end result of the transactions leading to the formation of a positive fixed capital owned by firms on behalf of income holders.

The aim of Schmitt's reform is to modify the actual system of domestic payments in such a way that it would become impossible for the profit formed in p_0 to be spent in p_1 for the purchase of fixed-capital goods produced in that period.

Table 5.6 The production of fixed-capital goods

<table>
<tr><td colspan="5" align="center">*Banks B*</td></tr>
<tr><td colspan="5" align="center">*Saving department (II)*</td></tr>
<tr><td colspan="2">*Assets*</td><td colspan="3">*Liabilities*</td></tr>
<tr><td>(1) Stock</td><td>20 m.u.</td><td>Fixed-capital department (III)</td><td></td><td>20 m.u.</td></tr>
<tr><td>(2) Fixed-capital goods</td><td>20 m.u.</td><td>Wage earners</td><td></td><td>20 m.u.</td></tr>
<tr><td>(3) Wage earners</td><td>20 m.u.</td><td>Stock</td><td></td><td>20 m.u.</td></tr>
<tr><td>(4) Fixed-capital goods</td><td>20 m.u.</td><td>Fixed-capital department (III)</td><td></td><td>20 m.u.</td></tr>
</table>

<table>
<tr><td colspan="4" align="center">*Banks B*</td></tr>
<tr><td colspan="4" align="center">*Fixed-capital department (III)*</td></tr>
<tr><td colspan="2">*Assets*</td><td colspan="2">*Liabilities*</td></tr>
<tr><td>(1') Saving department (II)</td><td>20 m.u.</td><td>Firms F</td><td>20 m.u.</td></tr>
</table>

Key: m.u. = money units

This is necessary in order to avoid the loss of income holders' economic ownership over fixed capital. Let us explain it again in some detail.

In either of its two forms, capital derives from saving. Capital-time results from the reversible transformation of income, which, precisely because it is saved and deposited in continuous time as capital, can be spent in any instant (of a given period) different from the one in which it is formed. Fixed capital results instead from the irreversible transformation of income. In this case the income saved will no longer recover its initial form, because its investment will give rise to the production of fixed-capital goods. Macroeconomic saving is defined precisely by the amount of income that will never be spent for the purchase of consumption goods, a result that is obtained by giving savings the form of fixed capital.

The production of instrumental goods requires an initial sacrifice by income holders, who must save part of their income to form a stock of wage goods that will provide the real fund necessary to start a process of fixed-capital accumulation. In our economies, firms are charged with collecting that part of saving that is transformed into fixed capital. The expression 'personalized firms' conveys clearly the idea that firms are mere intermediaries, acting on behalf of households or income holders; or, rather, that they *should* be nothing more than the representative of income holders. If this were the case, the totality of profit, that is, of the income transferred from wage earners to firms, would define a saving held by firms on behalf of income holders. In particular, and from a macroeconomic viewpoint, income holders would own the fixed-capital goods produced through the investment of profit, and stocked with firms. It is through the formation of profit and its successive investment that part of current income can be saved by an economy and given the irreversible form of a fixed capital. Thanks to Schmitt's reform, this process would take place without erasing the financial relationship between fixed-capital goods and macroeconomic saving, that is, without allowing for the expenditure of profit formed in a given period within the payment of wages of a successive period.

Today's pathological formation of fixed capital is caused by the lack of distinction between saving and fixed-capital departments, which allows for the payment of wages to be financed out of a pre-existing income. From mere intermediaries, firms are thus transformed into disembodied economic agents that expropriate income holders of part of their income and consequently of the fixed-capital goods obtained through its investment. The nature of the pathology is such that depersonalized firms (which cannot be identified with any income holder, shareholders and entrepreneurs included) become the purchasers of labour itself, which is thus transformed into a commodity. This is an outright anomaly, of course, because labour is a macroeconomic factor of production, the source of economic output and, as such, it cannot be identified with the result of production. Yet, this is precisely what happens when a positive income (profit) is spent in the payment of wages: wage earners alienate their labour and depersonalized firms appropriate fixed-capital goods. The link between fixed-capital goods and financial capital is severed, and income holders lose their economic ownership over instrumental capital.

98   *Alvaro Cencini*

Tables 5.5 and 5.6 show what has to be done to avoid the formation of pathological capital (or, which amounts to the same thing, of depersonalized firms). Entries in these two tables refer to invested profit only, because it is the investment of profit that, when not correctly entered into banks' ledgers, leads to the pathological process of fixed-capital accumulation. However, from a practical point of view, the totality of profit will be transferred from the second to the third department. That part of profit that will then be redistributed as interests or dividends will simply be transferred back from the third to the second department, where it will recover its original form of income and be spent for the purchase of consumption goods. The only entries remaining in Department III will be those defining the amount of profit transformed into fixed capital and thus withdrawn forever from consumption.

A further proof of the necessity of introducing a distinction between saving and fixed-capital departments

The analysis presented in this section refers to the one developed by Schmitt in his 1998 manuscript on the eradication of unemployment (1998a). In this unpublished manuscript, rather than distinguishing between periods and reasoning in value terms, Schmitt distinguishes between productions and shows how values can be increased to the level of prices without contradicting the principle that labour is the unique macroeconomic factor of production. The principle he applies is that of the increased value produced by labour when it can benefit from the presence of fixed capital. Labour is still considered to be the unique source of economic value, yet it is claimed that the increase in physical productivity allowed by instrumental capital multiplies the value generated by labour by a coefficient greater than one. The problem arising from the increase in value is how to explain the purchase of current output given that wages are the only source of income. Schmitt endeavours to show that in the present system of domestic payments income is increased to the level of prices thanks to a macroeconomic loan granted by banks and financed by the deposits of profit. He is thereby able to prove that, because of this new loan, investment goods are *de facto* produced by firms in a sector distinct from the one devoted to the production of consumption goods, a situation that deprives income holders of the economic ownership over fixed-capital goods.

Let us consider our numerical example once again. This time we do not distinguish between successive periods, but assume that firms produce two sorts of goods, namely consumption and investment goods, and that the wages paid in each production are, respectively, of 80 and 20 wage units. If we accept the idea that the increase in physical productivity due to the presence of fixed-capital goods is transformed into an increase in the value produced by labour, we can assume the value to be equal to 120 wage units: 100 units of value are derived from labour, while the 20 additional units are the measure of the increased value of labour ascribable to fixed capital. Now, in order to purchase an output that is sold at a price of 120 wage units and whose value is also equal to 120 wage units, the banking system must provide a total income of 120 wage units. Schmitt's

National banking reform 99

analysis shows that things change radically according to the way this is done. If banks provide the 20 additional units of income through a macroeconomic loan financed by the deposits of profit, the production of investment goods is dissociated from that of consumption goods and defines the formation of its own sector, distinct from the one devoted to the production of wage goods. This is what happens today, the formation of profit giving rise to bank deposits that, as any other bank deposit, are lent on the financial market.

The subtraction of investment or fixed-capital goods from households (to wit, income holders), which was earlier explained by the formation of depersonalized firms, is linked here to the macroeconomic loan households have to take recourse to in order to finance their purchase of consumption goods. The fact that consumption and investment goods are produced in two distinct sectors shows that income holders never own the latter. The analysis runs as follows.

The payment of wages being the only transaction allowing for the physical product to find a monetary form, the totality of output takes necessarily the form of wage goods. This means that investment goods cannot be immediately issued as such: "in no case, neither in a formally correct analysis, nor in the concrete world, can a unit of money be directly enriched by an investment or an amortization good" (Schmitt 1998a: 119, our translation). Hence, the production of investment (and amortization) goods can only take place in two stages, where the first one corresponds to the production of wage goods and the second to their transformation in investment (and amortization) goods. Two emissions are necessary to introduce investment goods into a monetary form. In the first emission, money units are given wage goods as real content; in the second emission investment goods replace wage goods. The same sum of money units is issued twice and given two different real contents. This is what explains the division of production into three sectors. In the first sector money units are issued a first time, the totality of output consisting of wage goods, whereas in the other two sectors the money units are issued for a second time and find another real content, profit and amortization goods respectively.

As we know, through the payment of wages workers become the owner of produced output in the form of money-income. This is what happens in the first sector: wage goods are the real content of workers' monetary remuneration. Things change in the second and third sectors, where wage earners do not obtain their own output as the real content of their wages. In particular, producers of investment goods obtain, as the real object of their wages, a sum of wage goods already issued to the benefit of wage earners working in the first sector. As in the preceding analysis, the production of investment goods is financed by profits. The financing of the production of investment goods out of profits means that the payment of wages is 'nourished' by an income already formed in a previous payment of wages. It is because the payment of wages to workers producing investment goods is in reality a re-emission of wages that the division between the first and second sector is a logical necessity. Wages paid to workers in the second sector are deprived of their real content, investment goods being replaced by part of the wage goods already issued in the first sector. The appropriation of investment

100 *Alvaro Cencini*

goods by firms is the mark of the pathological formation of fixed capital as previously explained. In the present analysis, the anomaly is explained by showing that the emission of wages in the sector producing investment goods is in fact a re-emission, wage earners being paid by the re-emission of the wages paid out in the sector producing consumption or wage goods.

The determinant here is the additional macroeconomic loan granted by banks to income holders or households, which allows for the clearing of markets, where produced output is sold at a mark-up. It is because of this loan that households end up losing part of national output and that national production occurs in three different sectors. The transformation of the increase in labour's physical productivity into an increase in value requires the availability of a greater amount of income to avoid deflation. The way this requirement is met enables us to distinguish between an orderly and a disorderly system of domestic payments. In the present system, where no distinction between issue, saving and fixed-capital departments exists in banks' ledgers, profits give immediately rise to bank deposits, which are lent on the financial market. When this loan is financed out of invested profit, that is, out of an income irreversibly transformed into fixed capital, a serious problem arises. It is indeed highly illogical that an income transformed into fixed capital be still available on the financial market. The loan thereby financed amounts to an emission of profit that adds up to that of wages and increases the amount of income households can spend for the purchase of consumption goods.

The analysis based on the increased productivity of labour made possible by fixed-capital accumulation shows that, today, profits are formed on the market for produced goods and services, and issued, as an additional macroeconomic loan, on the financial market. As a result, households incur a debt equal to the amount of wages paid for the production of investment goods, which is a further proof that instrumental goods are lost by income holders and appropriated by firms. The loan of the deposits formed from the investment of profit by banks, which defines the emission of profit on the financial market, allows households to purchase the totality of the consumption goods produced in the first sector. Yet, households can do so only by incurring a debt that they will have to repay in a subsequent period by using part of their income, that is, of their wages. The macroeconomic nature of this loan lies precisely in the fact that it amounts to an emission of wages. Since profits are themselves derived from wages, this should not come as a surprise, but merely confirm that what leads to the distinction between sectors is a pathology that burdens households with a debt. This is tantamount to saying that households can purchase the entire output of the first sector (wage goods) only by giving up the ownership of the investment goods produced in the second sector.

When profit is invested, its transformation into fixed capital is irreversible and defines a sum of income forever subtracted from consumption, that is, a macroeconomic saving. If invested profit can nevertheless finance a loan, this can only result in a pathological increase in demand on the product market, which is clear evidence that inflation is the first consequence of capital accumulation. The pathological increase in demand resulting from the additional macroeconomic loan granted by banks is not due to the presence of an increased amount of income that households can spend, but is made possible by the availability of invested profits as bank deposits. What increases demand pathologically is the expenditure of profits taking place on the labour market when they are invested in the production of instrumental goods. It is because invested profits are still available as bank deposits on the financial market that they feed banks' macroeconomic loan to households, and it is because they are spent within the payment of wages that they are still available as bank deposits. The origin of the pathology lies here: in the fact that invested profits are not withdrawn from the financial market.

In order to avoid the loan of the deposits formed following the investment of profit, a mechanism must be introduced at the bookkeeping banking level allowing for the automatic transfer of invested profits from the saving to the fixed-capital department. If entries were as shown in Table 5.5, the totality of the profit invested in the production of instrumental goods would be preserved in the third department of banks and subtracted from the second. Having been deleted from the second department, invested profit would no longer be available to finance an additional loan on the financial market. At the same time, being entered in the third department, it would keep maintaining the all-important relationship between instrumental goods and fixed capital, the essential objective of which is to preserve the economic ownership of fixed-capital goods by households (or income holders) considered as a whole. "The 'grab' carried out in the second department is but the sanction of an irreversible fact: invested profits are the indelible saving of households [...] [who] are the only owners of instrumental capital, now fixed in the set of income holders" (Schmitt 1984a: 330, our translation).

Conclusion

As Schmitt's analysis shows, the origin of the pathology leading to inflation and unemployment is to be found in the process of fixed-capital formation. Whether we explain it by referring to the appropriation of fixed capital by depersonalized or disembodied firms, or by considering the sub-division of the economy into sectors and the loan of invested profit, the conclusion is unchanged. In both cases, households forever lose the ownership of fixed capital and its accumulation leads to an unavoidable increase in the work wage earners have to devote to its amortization. From the moment analysis incorporates fixed-capital amortization, a satisfying explanation of inflation and unemployment can be found. Yet, it is because fixed capital is formed in a pathological way that its amortization ends up being the cause of a ghastly economic crisis. Schmitt's reform provides a satisfactory and easy-to-implement solution that would free the countries adopting it from the disorders arising within their domestic payment systems. Let us hope that it will be implemented in the nearest future.

Part II
Analysing the international economy

6 From reparations to (net) interest payments on external debt

Same script, different cast

Edoardo Beretta

Introduction

Admittedly, it is a difficult task to write on Bernard Schmitt's economic research. He is perhaps one of the last economists to have explored in great depth a plurality of aspects of the (inter)national payments system. If we think of his contribution to economics, several key terms predictably spring to mind: from "money" to "inflation" and from "disorder" to "reform". At the same time, there is even less doubt that his legacy is, for its international monetary part, nourished by long years of study of (net) interest payments on external debt. As we will duly explain, this is an economic state of affairs (where interest due on external liabilities are greater than yields on foreign assets) which mostly affects Less and Least Developed Countries (LCD), seriously endangering their economic wellbeing as nations. In fact, as Bernard Schmitt has amply demonstrated, the current system of international settlements allows for interest to be paid by the residents, and additionally by the nation as a whole; the baleful consequence being a supplementary loss of foreign reserves. Preposterous as it may seem, these countries are deprived of the same amount – not only in terms of domestic output (transferred by the residents), but also of external resources (stored in their foreign reserves) – leading to a double economic loss. But where does this groundbreaking intuition come from? And to what do we owe such a detrimental malfunctioning of the current international economic order?

The link between reparation and (net) interest payments on external debt

Bernard Schmitt's innovative analysis is arguably connected to economic history, more particularly to an episode often discussed by scholars, namely the Keynes–Ohlin–Rueff debate (1929) on German reparation payments. Although Schmitt may not have probed into this specific event, it is quite clear that the origins trace back to it. Indeed, as pointed out by Beretta (2013) and being a particular typology of external indebtedness, the process involving the German government at that time suffered from the same pathology. As Keynes (1929: 1) duly showed,

106 *Edoardo Beretta*

The Dawes Committee divided the problem of the payment of German Reparations into two parts – into the Budgetary Problem of extracting the necessary sums of money out of the pockets of the German people and paying them to the account of the Agent-General, and the Transfer Problem of converting the German money so received into foreign currency.

Let us analyse these argumentations using a step-by-step approach. In fact, up to this point, reference had been made mainly to net interest payments without exploring war reparations. The external debt service is now a far more common phenomenon, because after World War I reparations have been infrequent. As demonstrated by daily experience, wars between nations no longer lead to extended reparative payments. At the same time, war reparations in cash have been largely replaced by supplies of goods or services, that is, by payments in kind. Although their assertions cannot be compared to those of quantum economics, other economists have worked out that cash transfers entail a secondary, twofold burden:

how economists and policymakers thought reparations affected reconstruction and the restoration of peace in Europe in the 1920s had serious practical significance some twenty-five years later. At the end of World War II, Allied decisions regarding reparations were coloured in large measure by what happened in Germany during the 1920s.

(Morrison 1992: 390)

Indeed, most of the considerations made for net interest easily match any made in the case of war reparations. As we have already anticipated, the former involve a twofold loss of resources – the first, in domestic currency, represents the actual amount of the payment; the second is given by the (cost-bearing) monetary vehicle represented by foreign currency in order to convey the domestic income through the international monetary space. In economic literature the first flow has always been seen as the source of a "budgetary problem" (dependent on finding sufficient internal resources representing the real content of the payment) and the second flow as a potential cause of the "transfer problem", which evidently refers to the need to convey the microeconomic payment outside the national currency area. To quote a statement by a Harvard economist, which highlights the controversy on the additivity of both economic resource flows, "[t]he budgetary view sees a single difficulty, and the transfer view a double one" (Williams 1930: 76).

Sadly, economists have paid too little attention to this phenomenon; although few researchers have been close to understanding that the reparation payments presuppose a second transfer of resources by the nation as a whole. In fact, after the earlier theoretical contributions of John Maynard Keynes in the wake of the Treaty of Versailles requiring Germany to transfer an exorbitant amount of reparations (132 billion gold marks equivalent to nearly 32 billion US dollars (Staley 1935)), many researchers have analysed their functioning using Keynes's famous terminology: "budgetary problem" *versus* "transfer problem". As a logical consequence, there is a clear distinction between the ability to pay and the ability to transfer the payment.

The latter is a question of foreign trade; the former is primarily a question of national resources and income, when viewed from the standpoint of the German people, and primarily a question of the budget, when viewed from the standpoint of their government. That these and the foreign trade are but different aspects of the same problem, and closely interrelated, is of course obvious.

(Williams 1922: 482)

Precisely these sorts of assertions confirm the theoretical analysis by quantum economics. Indeed, already in 1922 some economists were aware of the fact that Germany would need to not only find internal resources ("ability to pay"), but also retrieve a corresponding amount of foreign currencies in order to convey the residents' payment through the international monetary space ("ability to transfer"). It does seem surprising that, although some of these economists were aware of that anomalous double payment of war reparations, none of them (at least, before quantum economics) were aware in the current non-system of international payments of the primary cause of this double loss to national wealth. Therefore, we have to agree that this is an "idea that is either utter nonsense or truly 'revolutionary'" (Schmitt 2004: 1). It is no less true that many economists have found it unimaginable that the first (microeconomic) payment entails a second, macroeconomic one. Having established that this system inflicts a double loss on the debtor country (DC), let us investigate what, in economic terms, lies behind each of them. On the one hand, interest payable to the creditor nations (CC) constitutes the yields on an initial loan by countries (having earned a trade surplus) to developing countries. This means that in period t_0 the latter countries have benefited from an inflow of foreign capital, which has increased the internal resources at their disposal. On the other hand, reparations begin *ex nihilo*, that is, by the will of the victorious powers after a military conflict. From a financial point of view, the last consideration means that the defeated nation may not have received, during time period t_0, any foreign capital now to be paid back. The gratuitousness of the transfer of resources is even more evident (Figure 6.1).

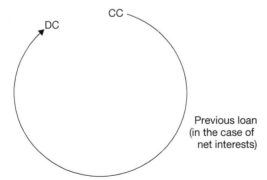

Figure 6.1 Net interest on external debt versus reparations: the previous-loan difference.

108 *Edoardo Beretta*

In fact, it is "important to note that a country's external debt is first incurred by its residents and not by the country itself" (Cencini 2005: 270). With specific regard to reparation payments, conversely, we must bear in mind that these originate out of nothing. As a consequence, the payment of war indemnities cannot be attributed to the economic decision to import more than export. War reparations have no real recipient in a specific resident of the creditor nation. Nonetheless, this payment typology exhibits significant similarities with net interest income on foreign debt – for instance, with specific regard to its registration in the current account of the balance of payments and its inherent one-sidedness. Thus, both types of transactions may be analysed in a similar way, although conceivably reparation payments (being imposed from scratch) are not only exposed to the same monetary disease affecting the external debt service, but are also economically more damaging.

Demonstrating the secondary burden weighing on (net) interest on external debt

If reparation payments are a unique class of international transactions, it is equally evident that Bernard Schmitt's analysis has focused on net interest on external debt, which remains one of the greatest concerns of developing and – as the euro crisis has duly shown – even post-industrial countries. Therefore, if a pathology is discovered, it is obviously worth scrutinising its causes. In the last decades, quantum economists guided by Bernard Schmitt's thoughts have had the opportunity to analyse from different angles the double charge weighing on net interest payments. Each publication explores a particular aspect of the problem. For instance, in Cencini and Schmitt's *External Debt Servicing: A Vicious Circle* (1991) the focus is mainly on the ensuing detrimental downward pressure on the exchange rates of the debtor country: "[r]atio of money S's devaluation $= \frac{\text{value of current external debt servicing}}{\text{value of commercial goods current imports}}$. [...] If nevertheless country S is able to service its foreign creditors in period p this can only mean that it gets into a new equivalent debt" (Cencini and Schmitt 1991: 175). In more recent publications attention has been drawn to the negative consequences of reimbursing external debts as expressed by an additional, fully preposterous obligation towards the rest of the world:

> in fact, being forced to incur a new debt to recover from the partial loss of its domestic income, country W_w allows creditor countries to import goods and services giving in exchange the very income transferred to them by its residents.
>
> (Cencini 1997a: 318)

Given the forbidding complexity of the question, hard to analyse exhaustively, we will confine ourselves to a specific approach and so demonstrate the anomaly affecting today's external indebtedness.

Consequently, in the following pages we will continue our analysis by concentrating on Bernard Schmitt's newest findings, published in *Modern Monetary Macroeconomics: A New Paradigm for Economic Policy* (Gnos and

From reparations to (net) interest payments   109

Rossi 2012). Where needed, we will complete the argumentation by adding evidence from past works. To this end, our starting point is the profound distinction between "sovereign debt", which is a combination between private and public obligations towards the rest of the world, and "public debt", which is nothing more than the State's indebtedness (either towards national or foreign residents). In other words, liabilities can be divided into the following categories:

- private internal debt (1);
- public internal debt (2);
- private external debt (3);
- public external debt (4).

Sovereign debt is thus represented by cases (3) and (4), while public indebtedness is represented by cases (2) and (4). Therefore, net interest payments on external obligations – the specific topic of this chapter – weigh on sovereign indebtedness, which, in Bernard Schmitt's analysis, is twice as high as it should be in a "normal", non-pathological state of the economy. Once again, the very reasons of this apparently absurd finding lie in the wrong perception of money, known in today's parlance as "book money", as opposed to a physical quantity of economic wealth (such as metallic coins). Despite its modern (and immaterial) essence, money remains (in people's and economists' minds, too) the direct counterpart in transactions for goods and services. According to this anachronistic interpretation, money is exchanged against real products tracing an apparently dogmatic separation of each (inter)national transaction into a monetary and a real counterpart. It is self-evident that post-modern money is quite the opposite of a material mass to be transferred from one agent to another:

> money, especially electronic money, would be completely neutral and could never create any 'distortion'. […] the currency is seen as an asset in that its presence in transactions sheds light on the fact that the only assets (being the terms of trade) are non-monetary assets.
>
> (Schmitt 2000c: 7, our translation)

This first observation, derived from daily evidence and confirmed by Bernard Schmitt's analysis, summed up in the previous chapters of this volume, is of crucial relevance. Indeed, it explains why external debts weigh on the shoulders of a nation's economy (represented by private or public individual agents) as well as on the foreign reserves, namely,

> those external assets that are readily available to and controlled by monetary authorities for meeting balance of payments financing needs, for intervention in exchange markets to affect the currency exchange rate, and for other related purposes (such as maintaining confidence in the currency and the economy, and serving as a basis for foreign borrowing).
>
> (International Monetary Fund 2009: 111)

110   *Edoardo Beretta*

This apparently inconceivable result can be demonstrated in several ways – the following being perhaps the most recent one. The starting point of the proof is obviously enough the equivalence (or identity) between the sum of commercial/financial imports of a country ($im_c + im_f = IM$) and the sum of commercial/financial exports of a country ($ex_c + ex_f = EX$): $IM = EX$.

As any accurate look at the balance of payments will show, commercial exports (imports) can be equal to or greater/lower than commercial imports (exports) – the same principle is also verified for financial imports/exports. This, however, does not contradict the fact that the total aggregate amount of exports of goods, services or financial securities is necessarily equivalent to their respective importations. To put it differently, the first are the counterpart of the second.

Let us therefore analyse the case of an indebted nation (for instance, DC), which has to disburse net interest on its external obligations. As we already pointed out with regard to the differences between reparation payments and external debt reimbursements, transferring interest on foreign liabilities means that DC has previously benefited from an inflow of external resources (that is, a loan), which has boosted its commercial imports over its exports of goods and services. As proved by evidence itself, DC and, more precisely, its residents have to repay a part of the yields of the capital previously borrowed: hence, S(DC) owe S(CC), namely the individuals in the creditor country, a sum x. On this basis, there seems to be no need at all to plead – as mainstream economists often do – for a generally balanced trade between nations. In fact, the debtor economy has benefited from an increased output (y) to be reduced by the interest due (in) leading nonetheless to a positive net inflow of resources ($y - in$), while the creditor country takes advantage from the subsequent interest transfer (in) to be added to its trade surplus. Net interest on external debt (in) therefore means that a corresponding domestic product ($pr_{in} = in$) is owed to the creditors in CC from its very formation. In other words, pr_{in} is owned by residents of the rest of the world (CC) despite having been produced by subjects in DC. The crucial question we need to answer now is whether the interest creditors receive a purchasing power over pr(DC) or pr(CC), namely foreign or their own resources. To solve the problem we need to identify the involved account of the balance of payments:

- if it is the financial account, the rest of the world lends to DC the resources necessary to make the real payment;
- if it is the current account, DC sacrifices its own resources to make the real payment.

Let us therefore have a closer look at each case separately. If (net) interest payments on external debt are registered as a debit in the financial account, DC does not subtract its own resources from its economy, because *in* is paid through a new net loan disbursement. As any accurate analysis of the balance of payments will show, the inflowing (borrowed) foreign currencies:

- are first of all a credit to the financial account;

From reparations to (net) interest payments 111

- mean a net gain of foreign resources coming from the rest of the world and increasing DC's international reserves ("the State, [understood as] the nation, is not a resident. It follows that foreign exchange gains do not belong to any resident, because they are owned by the State of surplus countries" (Schmitt 1996e: 47, our translation));
- are followed by an equivalent expenditure by DC's official reserves for the payment of its net interest (*in*).

The same procedure does not apply, if the payment of net interest on external debts – as actually happens – is debited to the current account. In addition, "[e] conomists maintain that *in* is debited in the current account simply because the expenditure carried out by the debtors of interest (DI) is entered in this account. This is a poor claim" (Schmitt 2012c: 254).

Before further refining this reasoning, it is necessary to understand that pr_{in} is a part of *EX*, namely the aggregation of commercial/financial exports. This is undeniably so, because the interest amount is transferred to the rest of the world as the yield of the financial capital previously lent to DC. The product transferred abroad is nothing other than pr_{in} ("in order to pay their debt [...] the [debtor] residents are 'forced' to realise a saving corresponding to [pr_{in}] against non-residents. To do so, they avoid buying a domestic product in order to spend the corresponding income for the redemption of their bonds" (Schmitt 1996f: 9, our translation)). More precisely, the rest of the world is the juridical owner of pr_{in} from the very production by the national debtor economy meaning that the owing of $pr_{in} = in$ occurs even before its exportation. Following this chain of reasoning, it is possible to assert that pr_{in} as a part of *EX* has no power to import, as it is already a legal and factual property of the economy of the rest of the world. It therefore appears manifest that a part of DC's imports (say im_{in}) is unfunded: $IM - im_{in} < EX$.

Since there can be no doubt about the equivalence between *IM* and *EX*, expenditures in foreign currencies have to exceed by the same sum (*in*) the total amount received through *EX*. But what does it mean? Odd as it may seem, every expenditure in terms of foreign money units is nothing else than an outflow from official reserves, which deprives the country as a whole of a corresponding amount. More precisely, if im_{in} represents the amount left unfunded by the rest of the world, ex_{in} is in turn the exports left unpaid by the creditor nation. These two aspects symbolise the pathological export (not backed by import) weighing on DC's shoulders.

To be even more explicit, it may be worth mentioning all the effects caused by today's way of reimbursing net interest on external debt. If there can be no doubt that only the real payment of *x* actually reduces DC's international reserves by a corresponding amount, DC's external indebtedness increases by *in* at the very moment interest is due. This conclusion is confirmed by a careful look at the International Investment Position (IIP), which is

a statistical statement that shows at a point in time the value and composition of (a) financial assets of residents of an economy that are claims on

112 *Edoardo Beretta*

non-residents and gold bullion held as reserve assets, and (b) liabilities of residents of an economy to non-residents.

(International Monetary Fund 2009: 119)

In fact, the IIP represents the country as a whole (and not its residents). In this specific regard, DC experiences a variation in its IIP marked by the difference between rising external obligations and shrinking official reserves:

Δ(IIP) = external debt increase + reduction of international reserves = *in*

Although the IIP deteriorates not only at the very moment interest is due, but also at the moment of the actual payment of *in*, these two negative forces (Δ(IIP) = 2z) become a single one (Δ(IIP) = z). As explained by the founder of the quantum school of economic thought himself,

> When official reserves are reduced by [*in*] in foreign currency, the variation of [DC]'s IIP changes form: it is initially an increase equal to [*in*] of [DC]'s external debt (+ [*im* as an increase of its external debt]); and it is transformed into an equivalent reduction of [DC]'s official reserves by the real payment of [*in*] (− [*in* as a reduction of its official reserves]).
>
> (Schmitt 2012c: 257)

In other words, as soon as the second manifestation (Δ(IIP)) appears, the first one (Δ(IIP)) disappears leading to the conclusion that the real cost of the net interest corresponds to *in* (and not to 2*in*).

As we have already anticipated, this conclusion does not mean that the payment process does not entail a pathological component redoubling the total economic efforts. In fact, in a normal state of affairs the transfer of *in* as the real content of the interest payment (real aspect) as well as the *in* total as expressed by a sum of foreign currencies (monetary aspect) would come to the same thing. Who can, for instance, claim that the real production of goods and services contributing to Gross Domestic Product (GDP) is anything other than the total income originated in the economy as a whole during a one-year period? Or who can safely assert that buying (importing) goods and services (real aspect) is nothing other than disbursing (exporting) securities or claims on the buyer's income (monetary aspect)? If, on the other hand, these aspects were to represent an additional characteristic, then we could claim that something anomalous and pathological is going on. As it happens, this is true for net interest on external debt, as we are about to demonstrate.

In order to do so, it is appropriate to distinguish between the total inflows (*EX*) and outflows (*IM*) of foreign currency into DC's economy and to explain each item with a step-by-step approach. Foreign currency outflows are not only represented by *IM*, namely the sum of commercial and financial imports, but also by *in*, namely the amount of net interest on external debt:

From reparations to (net) interest payments 113

IM (= aggregation of commercial/financial imports by DC)

$+ in$ (= interest on DC's external debt)

$IM + in$ (= foreign currency outflows)

We should bear in mind that DC's economy is deprived by in in terms of official reserves. To put it differently, if the aggregation of total foreign currency inflows were simply equal to $IM + LD_{in}$, this would mean that DC's international reserves would be definitely deprived of in. Not only that, but the debtor country also experiences an increase in its external indebtedness as a consequence of interest becoming due.

As it has been already mentioned, the payment of in from EX not only reduces DC's currency inflows, but it also leaves imports equal to im_{in} uncovered. The first step in financing the gap in the macroeconomic identity between IM and EX is therefore represented by the transformation from $IM - im_{in}$, namely the shrunken importing power, to IM. Evidently enough, $IM - im_{in}$ results from the reduced importing capacity $(EX - ex_{in})$ due to the transfer of the real product (pr_{in}). Only a reduction in foreign currencies available to DC's international reserves can restore the importing power to the "normal" level as represented by IM. Nevertheless, as shown above, foreign currency outflows are equal to $IM + in$, meaning that in remains unfinanced despite DC's previous reduction of official reserves. In light of this, the missing amount has to be provided by incurring a new debt, which is widely called a "loan disbursement" (LD_{in}), and has to re-establish the equilibrium between foreign currency outflows $(IM + in)$ and inflows. If we now take a look at foreign currency inflows, the situation appears to be the following (since any other item than EX numerically corresponds to in):

EX (= aggregation of commercial/financial exports by DC)

$- ex_{in}$ (= export of the real product pr_{in} by DC)

$+ LD_{in}$ (= loan disbursement in favour of DC)

$EX - ex_{in} + LD_{in}$ (= foreign currency inflows)

The fact that both items become equal $(IM + in = EX - ex_{in} + LD_{in} + RR_{in})$, as soon as the official reserves are reduced by a corresponding amount (RR_{in}), best describes the pathological duplication of the cost weighing on DC's shoulders. In fact, filling the gap between $IM - im_{in}$ and IM occurs by reducing the official reserves (first economic loss), while financing the difference between $IM + in$ and IM implies running into debt afresh (second economic loss).

Summa summarum, the debtor country is affected by a preposterous "secondary burden" – to put it in the words used by Rodrik (1988: 15), Borchert (2001: 241) or Machlup (2003: 216) – which transforms the reimbursement of external debts into a Sisyphean labour. Although the "secondary burden" weighing on debtor countries has to be proved by the instruments of logic, we may usefully resort to statistical evidence too. For instance, there can be no doubt that Brazil (as well as

114 *Edoardo Beretta*

many other Latin American nations) has been particularly exposed to the harmful effects of large-scale external indebtedness. The 1960s and 1970s showed Brazil's vulnerability particularly well (Galano 1994). Though characterised by the great uncertainty and volatility of economic measures, Brazil's statistical figures seem to reflect the monetary pathology described above. As shown in Table 6.1, the correspondence between net interest payments on external debt (in), increase in external indebtedness (LD_{in}), and reduction in official reserves (RR_{in}) is particularly evident – this being true for the periods 1970–2013, 1980–2013, as well as 1990–2013 (Table 6.1).

Of course, nothing would have changed if the correlation had been weaker (which is of course possible too, given the time span considered and the country typologies). Nevertheless, it seems once again verified that the payment of interest on external debt causes not only a corresponding increase in external debt stocks (augmented by a new loan disbursement from the rest of the world), but also a depletion of international reserves. This additive effect is truly anomalous, because it deprives the debtor country of a double amount of resources ("the interest imposes a double burden: (1) the interest payment is the cost of a debt; (2) the debt thus alienated creates an empty debt; (3) the payment of this empty[1] (e.g. net) debt has still to be made" (Schmitt 1999e: 8, our translation)).

The reader should by now have been given all the elements needed to understand the profound causes of the problem. It may nonetheless be useful to recap the analysis in order to sum up the core elements of the argumentation. More precisely, the pathology may be ascribed to a series of causes:

- misconception of modern money;
- misrecognition of the macroeconomic sphere (as compared to the individual level);
- misrecognition of the reasons for the payment by the current account of the balance of payments.

If we look specifically at aspect (1), there can be no doubt that money is still conceived as a quantum of (physical) goods to be transferred against real products.

Table 6.1 The reimbursement of interest on external debt: the Brazilian case (billion US dollars)

	1970–2013		1980–2013		1990–2013	
	Total	*Variation*	*Total*	*Variation*	*Total*	*Variation*
Interest payments on external debt	412.60	–	395.43	–	304.18	–
External debt stock	–	+476.49	–	+482.47	–	+362.17
Total reserves (including gold)	–	–357.63	–	–351.94	–	–349.62

Source: author's calculation based on World Bank (2015a, 2015c and 2015d).

From reparations to (net) interest payments 115

We can claim without fear of being contradicted that today's units of account are no longer linked to the intrinsic value of the artefact (like precious metals) representing them. The dematerialisation process of currencies is a *status quo* as well as a consequence of the very existence of modern payment systems. E-banking, credit or debit cards, or the simultaneity of economic transactions on a global scale are concrete examples of the lack of physicality of modern bank money. Similarly, if the latter does not present aspects of materiality and therefore holds no intrinsic value, it cannot be the object of any commercial or financial exchange, but it can be merely used as an (inter)national payment instrument. The fact that goods and services have to be exchanged against equivalent goods, services or financial claims is also implied by the double-entry bookkeeping itself. In other words, trade can only take place between real assets, that is positive values, and certainly not between goods or services and money (respectively between values and non-values). An intermediary for executing payments, bank money flows back instantly after completion of the transaction without being retentive like a stock of goods (which is, evidently, endowed with physicality).

Aspect (2) highlights in turn the drawbacks of the microfoundation (instead of macrofoundation) of macroeconomics, namely basing any macroeconomic analysis on purely microeconomic principles. For instance, international reserves reflect the external sector of each central bank. But what are we really saying? Even mainstream economics does not grant ownership of reserve assets to a specific economic agent; and yet it stops short of addressing the problem in any depth ("underlying the BPM5 concept of reserves are the notions of 'effective control' by the monetary authorities of the assets and the 'usability' of the assets by the monetary authorities" (Kester 2001: 14)). Accordingly, official reserves do not belong to any specific economic agent – not even to the State, which simply administers them through the central bank (if not strongly independent by statute). At the same time, there can be no doubt that the residents of the country are at the origin of the formation of foreign exchange reserves accumulated through international trade, although they are not their legal owners. In fact, it is desirable to systematically distinguish between the "source" (that is, the agents of the economy as a whole including the State), the "belonging" (the entire national economy) and the "administration" competence (the central bank) of foreign exchange reserves. More precisely,

> Even the State of a country is among its residents. It's always subject DI (e.g. a group of residents, which may have a single member like the State) bearing the interest debt. The fact that the (official and, in the same sense, international) reserves of the indebted country carry out the interest payment occurs by implication rather than because the debt would be directly caused by the country as a whole (which is not the case).
>
> (Schmitt 1999d: 5, our translation)

116   *Edoardo Beretta*

Again, in Schmitt's own words,

> Only residents of the world and not their sets (called countries or nations)
> conduct economic transactions. All imports and exports including purchases
> and sales of securities are decided by residents of the world, while sets
> defining nations do not add any transaction in terms of importations and
> exportations of their residents.
>
> (Schmitt 1999f: 14, our translation)

In order to better comprehend point (2), it is indispensable to analyse the
implications of concepts like "nation" or "country" (that is, the macroeconomic
sphere), "State" and "residents" (the microeconomic sphere). For instance, the
first one can be assimilated to the "set of economic residents", which is directly
involved in each international commercial or financial transaction by national
private or public sector's residents. This segmentation does not derive from any
hypothesis to simplify the proof. On the contrary, our conclusion derives from
simple observation of economic processes, characterised by directly acting
subjects (the microeconomic sphere), who are also at the origin of any commercial
or financial transaction, and the nation as a whole (the macroeconomic sphere),
whose intervention is necessary to carry out the payments of its national agents
and receive the counterpart from the rest of the world. "In fact", Schmitt writes,
"however, A carries the burden of interest only by implication; in the first place
the indebted person is not country A as such but merely a resident; even the State
of a country is one of its residents" (Schmitt 2000a: 7).

With specific regard to point (3), it is undeniable that there is a profound reason
why net interest payments on external debt are recorded in the current account
(rather than in the financial and capital account) of the balance of payments.
Merely claiming that this item pertains to this section (for instance, because the
corresponding expenditure by interest debtors is entered there) is unquestionably
a pointless tautology. Since we already know that foreign currency inflows (EX)
have to cover the outflows (IM), there can be no doubt that *in* (paying net interest
on external debt) is an excess expenditure, which also requires financing. If the
real product (pr_{in}) underlying the debt service had been borrowed from the rest of
the world, the transaction would have been entered into the capital and financial
account. Having proved that this is not the case, it being recorded (in the same
way as reparation payments) in the current account, we can now conclude that the
debt reimbursement occurs by transferring the country's own real product (pr_{in}),
which has obviously not been borrowed from abroad. The excess cost of servicing
net interest on external obligations becomes all the more evident.

Recapping the elements of pathology affecting (net) interest on external debt

In order to formulate a further visual proof of the pathology behind any service of
(net) interest on external debt, we adopt, following Bernard Schmitt, a zero-line

From reparations to (net) interest payments 117

approach. But what does it precisely mean? As already shown, the balance of payments itself implies that the sum of commercial and financial exports is equal to the aggregation of commercial and financial imports:

> The basic convention applied in constructing a balance of payments statement is that every recorded transaction is represented by two entries with equal values. One of these entries is designated as a credit with a positive arithmetic sign; the other is designated as a debit with a negative sign. In principle, the sum of all credit entries is identical to the sum of all debit entries, and the net balance of all entries in the statement is zero.
> (International Monetary Fund 2003: xxi)

Therefore, the graphic meaning of the identity relation $IM = EX$ can be represented as the perfect correspondence of foreign currency outflows (IM) and inflows (EX) (Figure 6.2).

This situation becomes a disequilibrium as soon as the payment of (net) interest on external liabilities (say, $in = 10$) is added to the foreign currency outflows. As a direct consequence, IM rises from 100 to 110 while EX remains stable at 100. A gap of 10 thus emerges, represented by the gap between the dotted line and the zero-line (Figure 6.3).

The anomalous functioning of the international payments system may not have been evident so far. As we already know, the crucial question is how this gap may be filled. Will it be financed by a loan from the rest of the world? Not precisely. What Figure 6.3 fails to show is a second implication caused by the discharge of (net) interest on external debt, namely the fact that a corresponding amount (10) in terms of real product originated in the debtor nation:

- not only has to be exported to the full advantage of the creditor country and corresponds to the yield of the capital initially lent;
- but it is owned *ab origine*, i.e. ever since it was produced, by the creditors themselves.

Put differently, a part of EX has no "power to import" at all and, therefore, EX has to be reduced by 10, the real product pr_{in} (10), to be transferred as a yield (Figure 6.4).

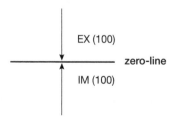

Figure 6.2 The identity relation between commercial/financial imports and exports.

118 *Edoardo Beretta*

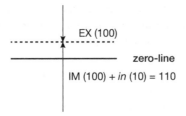

Figure 6.3 The disequilibrium after servicing (net) interest on external debt (1).

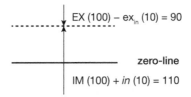

Figure 6.4 The disequilibrium after servicing (net) interest on external debt (2).

The gap between *IM* + *in* (110) and *EX* − *pr*$_{in}$ (90) has widened further and corresponds to 20 units to be financed. But how precisely would it work? The first balancing flow, which ideally has to cover *in* (10), comes from the official reserves of the debtor country. More precisely, the indebted nation depletes its own store of wealth in terms of foreign currencies (and, more limitedly, gold and Special Drawing Rights) by a sum corresponding to 10 units. Obviously enough, this is not the end of the story, because the identity relation (*IM* = *EX*) of the debtor country would still remain unbalanced, as shown in Figure 6.5.

Although the previous gap (20) has been reduced to 10, there is no doubt that this last one (10) has to be filled, too. This is not a convention, but is logically implied by the use of double-entry bookkeeping. That said, we have to clarify the origin of the flow filling the gap (10) still left. As already pointed out, a further loan disbursement coming from the rest of the world is required to re-establish the identity between commercial/financial imports and commercial/financial exports (Figure 6.6).

Although the relation may have rebalanced, this is no reason for complacency. In fact, receiving further loans from creditor countries is synonymous with soaring external indebtedness, very much the opposite of what the debtor nation wants, namely to reduce its liabilities towards the rest of the world. Not only that, but the economic damage caused by the malfunctioning of the current international payments system is also double: the increase in foreign indebtedness (10) and the loss affecting official reserves (10). Therefore, we can claim that a 10-unit payment of (net) interest on external debt lies behind a 20-unit economic effort, namely a secondary burden. If the subject of who should ideally receive the amount of official reserves (10) necessary to fill the first gap were to attract scepticism, we would simply answer that this sum is nothing other than a saving of resources by

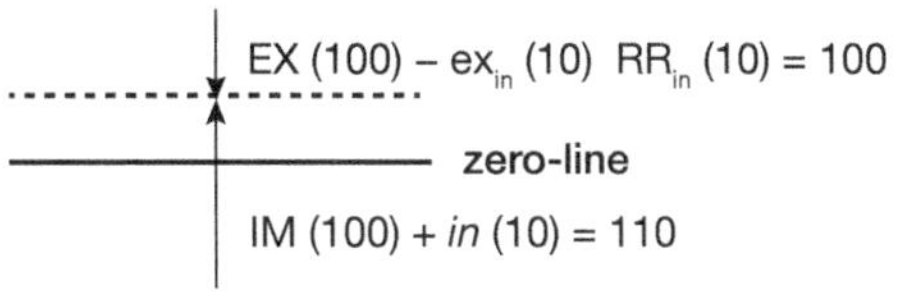

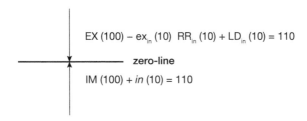

Figure 6.5 Re-establishing the identity relation after the service of (net) interest on external debt (1).

Figure 6.6 Re-establishing the identity relation after the service of (net) interest on external debt (2).

the rest of the world ("It is therefore never the case that deposits (unfairly) taken out of LDCs' international reserves enrich any residents of R: the relevant reserves are lost in favour of the macroeconomy of the rest of the world" (Schmitt 2000b: 17)).

A second doubt may arise and, more specifically, the claim that (net) interest on external debt (in) should be financed by the rest of the world through a loan disbursement (LD_{in}). If this were the precise mechanism behind what, for all intents and purposes, might be a (pathological) loan redemption, in would be directly financed by the creditor nations and (why not?) be entered into the financial and capital account of the balance of payments. However, this conclusion does not correspond to the reality of facts. By doing so, one might forget that:

- (net) interest payments are entered in the current account;
- the real products (representing the yields of the capital previously invested by the rest of the world) are owned, from the very moment of production, by the creditor countries. Hence, a part of EX, namely pr_{in}, has no "power to import" at all and, oddly enough, this crucial fact should not be forgotten ("Interest transfers to the rest of the world a right to withdraw a part of the national production of LDCs. The purchases to be financed by the rest of world on its own are therefore equal to $EX - ex_{in}$. If we add the foreign currencies lent to the LDCs, namely LD_{in}, the total inflowing amount to the benefit of the debtor nations corresponds to $EX - ex_{in} + LD_{in}$ and the gap between inflows/outflows precisely to in" (Cencini 2008: 377, our translation)).

Let us dispel a third doubt even before it sets in: why are mainstream economists worldwide still not alert to this detrimental process, which steadily deprives a high number of countries of billions of economic resources? This can be addressed

120   *Edoardo Beretta*

Table 6.2 Public debt *versus* external debt: the German case

	2004	2006	2008	2010	2012	2014	Variation (%)
General government gross debt (billion euros)	1,469.12	1,588.55	1,666.17	2,090.04	2,195.82	2,184.30	+48,68
Gross external debt position (billion US dollars)	2,932.99	3,402.51	5,397.00	5,542.03	6,010.34	5,409.02	+84,42

Sources: Eurostat (2015) and World Bank (2015b).

without necessarily referring to (equally correct) assertions like "the nature of bank money is still unrecognised". In order to refute such potential criticisms, we have to analyse why the two different terms of the problem, namely higher indebtedness and depletion of international reserves, go unnoticed by the general public. With specific regard to external liabilities there is no doubt at all that foreign indebtedness (as compared to public debt) is the "Cinderella" of economics, as Table 6.2 evidently shows.

Although the German Parliament reminds its members (and citizens) of the Government's indebtedness by making use of a "debt clock" (*Schuldenuhr*) (Bund der Steuerzahler Deutschland e.V. 2015), these numbers are somewhat unremarkable, not to say risible, compared to its steadily rising foreign obligations (Beretta 2014: 55), which increased by 84.42 percent in the 2004–14 period (Table 6.2). It is, therefore, no wonder policymakers feel that this type of indebtedness is not worth mentioning. However, there is another reason for this negligence by mainstream economists: if we take a look at official reserves, the situation is no better, because they do not belong to a specific agent, but to the nation as a whole ("As stated by Schmitt, the second payment of interest depletes LDC's official reserves, and, while it does not provide R with an additional capital, it allows R to avoid spending its domestic saving in order to finance part of its imports" (Cencini 2005: 273)).

Conclusion

The anomaly behind (net) interest payments on external debt remains generally undetected and continues to be responsible for further damaging the precarious recovery of debtor nations. As we mentioned, the starting point of Bernard Schmitt's vision was the Keynes–Ohlin–Rueff's debate on the distinction between a budgetary problem and a transfer problem in the German reparation case. Although this is not the right place to explore this particular historical episode further, there is sufficient empirical evidence to prove that war indemnity payments have been affected by the same pathology (Beretta 2013). This apparently astonishing conclusion seems less unlikely nowadays. Indeed, war reparations present a series of similarities to (net) interest on external debt:

From reparations to (net) interest payments 121

- they are entered into the current account of the balance of payments;
- they are also considered by mainstream economics as a "unilateral transfer" (Elliott 1936: 481; Fieleke 1996: 27), which cannot be assimilated to the "modern" item to be found in today's balance of payments statistics. In fact, the latter transfer typology is not really "unilateral" or "unrequited" (as war indemnities undoubtedly are) (Beretta 2013: 170), but respects double-entry bookkeeping principles;
- as we already pointed out, reparations originate *ex nihilo*, specifically by the decision of the victorious nations and without there having been a previous beneficial capital inflow;
- the same argument in terms of "power to import" can also be applied to war indemnities, which belong to the winners from the very moment the corresponding real product comes into being;
- war debts are a very particular category of external obligations, which are willy-nilly (at least in the current economic state of affairs) subject to an additional loss in terms of general wealth.

What is particularly sad is that the world is still – today, as it was yesterday – unaware of these major sources of instability, which should have no place in any post-modern society characterised by high technological standards and real-time gross payment and settlement systems like Fedwire in the United States or TARGET2 in the euro area. As the following chapters will show, reasonable solutions have already been put forward, but policymakers need to change their minds and, for instance, stop thinking that public debt is the sole threat to economic prosperity. If this were the only factor triggering already wobbly growth rates of GDP, then we would be already over the worst. Now we know that this is no foregone conclusion.

Acknowledgements

The author would like to thank Simona Cain for her precious editing work. His deep gratitude also goes to Alvaro Cencini and Sergio Rossi for their attentive reading of a previous version of this chapter.

Note

1 "Empty", which corresponds to the French word "vide" in Bernard Schmitt's original text, well indicates the pathological essence of the debt to be carried out by the debtor country.

7 Keynes's and Schumacher's plans and the failed attempt to understand international monetary relations

Nadia F. Piffaretti

Introduction

Modern macroeconomics was founded and tested around the two world wars. The heavy legacies of World War I had prompted a new generation of economists to formalize the conceptualization of national economies as 'whole economic systems' so as to better understand new challenges, and better devise policy solutions. By the time World War II was edging toward the end with a victory for the allied powers, Keynes had already used his new theory to shed light on key economic policy matters of the time. His macro-monetary analysis had highlighted the existence of insurmountable challenges leading to the impossibility of Germany fully paying for the requested reparations after World War I. Later, he was able to use the new theory to draw the macroeconomic contours of a 'war economy' in his 'How to Pay for the War' memorandum published in 1939 (Keynes 1978b). Quite a number of Keynes's recommendations remained unheeded. Still macroeconomic theory was proving to be a powerful tool able to provide insights into dynamics that economics had until then mostly ignored.

While World War II was still raging, great thinkers like Keynes, Kaldor, Lerner, Beveridge, and Stone, among others, mobilized their intellectual power to devise features of a new global economic system that would be rid of three features of the pre-war economic situation: unemployment, poverty, and inefficiency. This was part of a major effort planning for post-war reconstruction and a new international cooperation. Kaldor and Beveridge, working on economic recovery, were part of the Joint Committee of the Nuffield College Reconstruction Survey, which also included E.F. Schumacher. Work encompassed laying the basis for a new world monetary order, managing the tensions arising "in an era of quick transportation and intensive economic exchange" where "all economic phenomena are interconnected" (Schumacher 1943: 163), and facilitating recovery of long-term investment (Kalecki and Schumacher 1943).

Schumacher, born in the German Empire, had caught Keynes's attention with a draft piece on multilateral clearing. Keynes blamed the "impoverishment, social discontent and even wars and revolutions" on the "secular international problem" of balance of payment imbalances (Keynes 1980: 21). He traced its origins to a "single characteristic": existing systems "throw the main burden of adjustment on

Keynes's and Schumacher's plans 123

the country which is in the debtor position on the international balance of payments" (ibid.: 27). Keynes pointed out the deflationary effects of the resulting mechanisms, as rebalancing would lead to corrections through compression of imports, creating a "contractionist pressure against the world economy and, by repercussion, against the economy of the creditor country itself" (ibid.: 47). Rebalancing would have been more conducive of overall prosperity, Keynes argued, when occurring through expansion of opportunities of exports instead. This would have led, in the end, to more employment, less poverty, and better economic efficiency. The objective of Keynes's work was to support renewed social and political stability through prosperity, and foster international cooperation by supporting international investments, while at the same time grounding international trade on sounder monetary mechanisms (Piffaretti 2009). His proposal for an International Clearing Union was "a measure of financial disarmament" (Keynes 1980: 57).

The proposal for a new system of international payments

After an interwar period characterized by loss of domination of the pound sterling and expansion of the role of the US dollar, Keynes would work first at countering the German Funk–Schacht Plan (1940–42), and subsequently, over the 1943–44 period, at the design of the systems underpinning a post-war 'order'. Keynes argued that the use of money in international trade had only "worked" for "two periods of about fifty years each" in the past five hundred years (Keynes 1980: 21), and that the time had come for a far reaching reform that would have grounded international trade on an international system of multilateral clearing.

The core innovation of Keynes was the generalization of the principle of national banking to international transactions, creating an international clearing system operating within the "necessary equality of credits and debits" (ibid.: 44), very much similar to central bank clearing. The new system would have encouraged creditor countries to effectively use the purchasing power obtained on debtor countries (ibid.: 211). Keynes worked at various versions of his plan over the 1941–44 period, incessantly clarifying aspects of the proposed mechanisms, to address questions raised by colleagues as well as critics. It is, however, the version of the plan published (without consultation with Keynes) by E.F. Schumacher in *Economica* in May 1943 that brings the clearest formulation of the central feature of their two plans, notably that they do not entail the creation of a new 'international monetary asset'.

> It will be clear that the International Clearing Office requires no finance of its own, nor does it have to create a new international currency. If a new international currency were created, this would be of no economic significance. The holding of "a share in the Pool" would then be called a holding of "world currency", but the backing of the world currency would none the less be nothing else but the cash balances in the deficit countries. Since it is impossible to disentangle the mass of individual transactions, which give rise, during the

124   *Nadia F. Piffaretti*

course of business, to the various uncleared balances in the deficit countries and to ascribe any one particular balance, or part of it, to any particular surplus country, the Gordian knot is cut by making all the surplus countries the joint owners of the balances in all the deficit countries. [...] As a result of [the International Clearing Office's] (purely formal) operations, we get the following position: The Clearing Funds of surplus countries become indebted to their internal money markets and acquire an equivalent share in the Pool. [...] All individual sales and purchases have the same technical effect, irrespective of the country to which goods are sold or from which goods are purchased.

(Schumacher 1943: 154)

Increasing imports by creditor countries would lead, in the end, to increased overall global exports, avoiding the "restrictive forces" (ibid.: 158) of the debtor-led rebalancing mechanism, where the debtor country's lack of capacity to finance the current level of imports would lead to overall reduced exports by creditor countries.

The central aim of the Keynes Plan was fostering economic recovery and restoring international trade flows after World War II. This concern appears very central in the April 1943 final version of the Plan, presented as a 'white paper', which also suggested that the United States and the United Kingdom become the first two founding members of the Clearing Union:

This facility will be of particular importance as soon as the initial shortages of supply have been overcome. Many countries, including ourselves will find a difficulty in paying for their imports, and will need time and resources before they can establish a readjustment. The efforts of each of these debtor countries to preserve its own equilibrium, by forcing its exports and by cutting off all imports, which are not strictly necessary, will aggravate the problem of all the others. [...] The creditor countries will benefit, hardly less than the debtors, by being given an interval of time in which to adjust their economies, during which they can safely move at their own pace without the result of exercising deflationary pressure on the rest of the world, and by repercussion, on themselves.

(Keynes 1980: 46–7)

Foreign payments of trade flows would be paid through overdrafts. Surplus would be left unconvertible into assets, leaving it "tied up in the Pool" (Schumacher 1943: 157). This would leave the creditor country with the option of either increasing imports in the following period, or lending to the debtor country in support of investment that would have led in the medium term to increasing its export capacity and productivity. If the debtor country failed to use investment to increase exports capacity, then adjustment through other measures, such as devaluation, would have to be considered.

This expansionary objective of the Keynes Plan did not receive the necessary political consensus, as monetary stability considerations ended up occupying a

Keynes's and Schumacher's plans 125

prominent role in the negotiations leading up to the Bretton Woods agreements. In the "Joint Statement by Experts on the Establishment of the International Monetary Fund, April 1944" (Horsefield 1969), the provisions for placing on creditor countries some pressure to share adjustment were replaced by a new proposal requiring that the Fund monitor and issue a report on causes of sustained unbalanced creditor positions, and containing recommendations to address the situation. This new provision relied less on the inner technical mechanisms of an international monetary system, and more on the willingness to embrace international monetary cooperation among the domestic policy objectives of the members' countries (ibid.). Among the objectives stated in the final "questions and answers" document by the United States was to "minimize the deflationary monetary pressure that adverse balances of payments have had in the past" (ibid.: 139). This provision was considered more "far reaching", and in a way it was, as it allowed for some form of international intervention on domestic macroeconomic policy matters. But it abandoned the design of Keynes's system, which was meant to be intrinsically expansionist. Schumacher's (1943: 165) concluding words leave no doubt about the ultimate objective of the design of this system: "such a scheme, it is felt, should above all possess an inherent tendency toward expansion". Bernard Schmitt would decades later dismiss the system as intrinsically "inflationary" (Schmitt 1985c: 197), and propose a reform of the international system of payments that would go well beyond the mechanisms of Keynes's and Schumacher's Plans. What explains such divergent conclusions between Schmitt and these earlier economists? Let us address this question in the next section.

Schmitt's advances

Keynes used the emerging conceptualization of the nature of 'whole' economic systems to identify mechanisms to foster macroeconomic outcomes that would be more desirable from the political and social standpoints. Schmitt's understanding of macroeconomics further pushes these boundaries, highlighting that 'economies as a whole' have an intrinsic logic, which cannot be fully accounted for by economic dynamics of the aggregate, and that need to be analysed and understood separately. Accordingly, proper understanding of the internal working logic of 'whole economic systems' such as nations would lead to devising reforms that allow ridding systems of inconsistencies. For Schmitt, understanding the dynamics of whole economic systems comes down to comprehending the nature of monetary emissions, and the role of the banking sector and firms in defining the monetary expression of national production, that is, income. The theoretical underpinnings of international payments then follow logically the consequences of this original understanding of how monetary emissions define national economies 'as a whole'.

Keynes (1930/1971) had mastered the accounting nature of monetary emissions, the lack of intrinsic value of flows derived from double-entry bookkeeping as debits and credits, and used this understanding to suggest an international clearing union exclusively grounded on bancors' bookkeeping, with no need of assets-backing. He also had grasped the notion of economic system as a whole: his

126   *Nadia F. Piffaretti*

diagnosis of unemployment induced by lack of effective demand is an illustration of the relevance of his approach to economics. But this double achievement of Keynes, instead of strengthening Schmitt's admiration, fuelled a reaction of genuine frustration, which Schmitt made little effort to hide during his lectures: Keynes had gone far, but missed the logical conclusions of the foundations of macroeconomics he had himself laid out. Schmitt's puzzlement is also apparent in some of his writings. In his 1972 volume he managed to include in the same short paragraph that "A critical analyser of Keynesian thought always diagnoses serious contradictions" and "the basic lack of logic" with "Keynes' genius" (Schmitt 1972a: 113). He found Keynes's ideas "not fully mature" (Schmitt 1985c: 197, our translation), and hinted that "much larger post-war inflation" (ibid., our translation) would have occurred had the Keynes Plan been applied. Sardonically he commented that "it is often good that prudence and conservatism triumph first over genius" (ibid., our translation).

The problem with Keynes was that having left production out of his foundational framework, produced output had been left staring back at the monetary flows purchasing it: money still very much acquires the function of a net asset in most of Keynes's work, with the notable exception of passages in the first volume of his *Treatise on Money* (Keynes 1930/1971). Keynes's bancor balances define a positive amount of international purchasing power, and their recording in the balance sheet of the net exporting country gives raise to an equivalent amount of national money (Cencini and Schmitt 1991). While Keynes had been thinking and writing about it, the role of production is not consistently applied throughout most of his writings.

Schmitt set up to go further. In order to pursue the goals of its founding fathers, the foundational framework of macroeconomics needed to be logically consistent. He found it therefore necessary to bring production into the foundational monetary framework: national income is expressed by a circuit of monetary emissions, and double-entry bookkeeping of monetary emission constraints macroeconomic demand and supply of national income (of the economy taken as a whole) into a logical identity, defining a circuit in real terms (see Schmitt 1984a for a full exposition of the theory of monetary emissions).

This had far reaching consequences on how international payments are to be conceptualized, and on this basis managed within a coherent system. If distinct monetary spaces, which define distinct national economies of production, are what constitute 'national economies', then, international trade – a space where no production but only exchanges take place – appears quite exotic. It requires a supplementary theoretical effort. Schmitt (1975a: 83, our translation) marvels at the beauty of the intellectual challenge of framing an international monetary circuit: "[this is] probably one of the most beautiful problems of our science: its resolution requires effort, and it provides a true intellectual joy, which is rare in economic analysis."

While both Keynes and Schmitt call for a 'special framework' for multilateral monetary relations, their calls stem from very different reasoning. Keynes had observed the special problems caused by a lack of an international monetary system, and suggested that the logic of domestic central banking informs the structure of an international system: "[t]he idea underlying my proposal for a Currency Union is simple, namely to generalise the essential principle of banking" (Keynes 1980: 44). The approach of Schmitt is different. He found a much deeper reason for excluding national 'hard' currencies as a viable systemic solution: as there is no such thing as international production and international income, the set up of an international monetary system would serve the purpose of allowing payments between intrinsically heterogeneous national monetary systems. Let us turn to this question next.

A special set of financial relations

According to quantum macroeconomics, within the national economy, if the purchasing power of the newly produced income is not immediately consumed, it is immediately lent, resulting, at the end of the process of monetary creation that defines the new income, in new financial relations between two sets of economic agents, firms and wage earners. Saving part of their income, wage earners are sellers on the labour market and purchasers on the financial market, while, as borrowers, firms are sellers on the financial market and purchasers on the production factor's market. The payment of wages defines at the same time (Cencini 2005: 286) the domestic supply and the domestic demand of the period.

Every country that sells more goods, services and financial assets than it buys, during a given period, sees a demand exceeding the domestic demand (Schmitt 1975a: 65). Now, in the circuit of quantum macroeconomics, only net purchases can finance net sales. Framed this way, the essential question of international trade resides in balancing a country's own total net sales and net purchases (ibid.: 86). The juxtaposition between net purchases of one country and net sales by the trading partner, which lays at the core of Keynes's and Schumacher's expression of the problem, is therefore misunderstanding the theoretical terms of the problem of international payments. Schmitt sees no juxtaposition.

In the multilateral clearing proposed by Schumacher, the "pool clearing" gives "every country the right to discharge all its cash obligations to the rest of the world by paying its own national currency into its National Clearing Fund" (Schumacher 1943: 156). The National Clearing Fund in the payee's country subsequently makes a corresponding payment to the payee. An "overdraft quota" would allow this happen, and the corresponding surplus would be owned by the payee country but "tied up in the Pool" (ibid.: 157). In Schumacher's words, the overdraft allows "free access" to international trade (ibid.: 155). Subsequent authors have seen in this feature the need to address the world's 'liquidity problem'.

Schmitt's analysis is different. The international monetary flow is issued in an overdraft operation, analogous to the issuance of domestic currencies by the banking system. It does not define, however, an income, and presents no additional purchasing power (neither it is meant to address a liquidity problem). As such, it does not finance net purchases, but only pays for "reciprocal purchases" (Schmitt 1975b: 27, our translation). Let us clarify this point.

128 *Nadia F. Piffaretti*

Customarily in the literature, international systems are exemplified adopting the vantage point of the net importing country. This is the vantage point also adopted by Schmitt. For the sake of our explanation, we find it more advantageous to adopt instead the vantage point of the net exporting country. The net exporting country presents an excess export of its goods, the central question is to match this net sale with a net purchase. This requires the purchase of financial assets from the net importing country. It follows that financing of its net imports is provided by the net exporting country. The net sale of goods being matched by a net purchase of financial assets from the importing country, the 'closing of the monetary circuit' in the exporting country defines both the 'closing of the circuit' in the importing country and the "closing of the international monetary circuit" (Schmitt 1975a: 98, our translation). The only incomes consumed are the ones of the domestic economies of the trading partners, with no increase of overall purchasing power through the international payments system.

In his 1975 writings, Schmitt advocates promoting two fundamental economic 'freedoms': (1) allow countries wishing to sell an excess of commercial goods and buy an excess of financial assets, to do so; and (2) allow countries that wish to buy an excess of commercial goods and sell an excess of financial assets to do so (ibid.: 100). In the reality of international trade, these two freedoms are not respected. Countries wishing to buy excess commercial goods and sell financial assets (developing countries might wish to do so) are limited by the need to finance the acquisition of 'hard currency', which is additional to the limit established by the macro-framework and market forces, including the capacity to pay an appropriate level of return on the financial assets sold. As a result, countries have curbed their capacity to sustain a permanent deficit. Unless imports are compressed, countries may face the need to improve export performance through an increase of domestic productivity so dramatic as to be beyond what is feasible, or socially sustainable. Failure to curb the imbalance would push debt to unsustainable levels. Compression of the level of exports will result in corresponding negative pressure on exporting countries, as the potential global demand for their goods and services would be limited by the lack of availability of hard currency in the importers' markets. While the use of hard currency in international payments is overall inflationary, it promotes a parallel downward pressure on global economic activities.

Cencini and Schmitt (1991) observe that this is quite different from what takes place in inter-regional relations within the same country. There can be permanent trade imbalances between urban and rural regions of a country, without the rural areas of a country ever being compelled to correct the imbalances due to monetary factors. The only economic dynamics that count there are efficiency considerations, determined by the workings of local markets and prices. As a result, capital can be transferred from one region to another. International trade within the current international monetary cooperation arrangements does not allow for such freedom. Supplementary binding constraints due to the monetary arrangements apply. As the authors puts it:

Keynes's and Schumacher's plans 129

The international debt problem arises from the specific kind of relationships between national currencies that characterize the actual monetary system of international payments. It is the existence of a multi-currency world that creates the problem, and it is within this context that a solution has to be found.

(Cencini and Schmitt 1991: 19)

The dampening effect on international trade of the lack of a properly structured international payments system is among one of the least researched problems in macroeconomics. From a theoretical perspective, this issue essentially corresponds to the question of whether purchasing power can be transmitted between two countries through an international payment. Current currencies assuming the role of net assets, common wisdom suggests that this may obviously be the case. Hence there may seem to be no case for a research agenda. The insights offered by quantum macroeconomics, however, are quite clear: there is no such thing as a transfer of purchasing power within a non-production economy such as the international trade space.

It is interesting to note that a fundamental divergence of views on this matter fuelled a very public debate in the *Economic Journal* between Keynes and Ohlin around the question of the German reparations in 1929 (Ohlin 1929a, 1929b; Keynes 1971, 1978a). Keynes, who had been working at his *Treatise on Money*, argued that a reduction of Germany's purchasing power would not stem from a 'transfer', but from the reduction of wages of German workers in relation to wages in other countries. That is the 'compression of imports' stemming from the need to access hard currency to operate autonomous transfers. Keynes pointed out that such an effect would not have provided France with any 'additional' purchasing power, and would on the contrary have negatively affected France's own volume of exports in the end. Keynes argued that the domestic effects of the German reparations would have wrecked havoc on the German economy while at the same time lead to negative effects in the countries supposedly 'beneficiaries' of the net transfer.

The essential problem of international payments, so effectively identified by Schmitt's work, is that monetary payments cannot transmit purchasing power in the space of international trade, and neither can they transmit purchasing power over the temporal space. If such transfers of purchasing power were possible, we could, for example, as whole nations, save current income for future (maybe harder) times. Alas, this is only possible at agents' level, and this impossibility lies at the core of the challenges faced by our modern aging societies. Only future increased productivity, fostered through bottle-neck releasing investment, can provide enough future purchasing power for the pensions system to be sustainable as a whole, and to deliver on expectations. Purchase of financial assets at the individual level only creates a financial relation with the future banking system. In a way, it announces a transfer, but it does not guarantee that the macroeconomic conditions needed to honour this claim are realistic (Piffaretti 2010). This is similar to what Keynes pointed out as far as the question of German reparations was concerned: while the necessary budgetary arrangements for the payment of the German transfers had

130 *Nadia F. Piffaretti*

been put in place, the transfer could not be realized in macroeconomic terms. The mechanism requiring the purchase of hard currency was moreover at risk of creating a downward adjustment of the German domestic economy.

The special macroeconomic nature of financial relations derived from international trade is one of the most innovative contributions of Schmitt to economic thought. At the end of the relevant period, Keynes's bancor fulfils the role of a 'reserve asset', defining financial relations between net importing and net exporting countries. It is in this sense that his proposal of 'quotas' of bancor held by national central banks is interpreted. The bancor's holdings are lent by creditor to debtor countries, and what is left is a financial claim sold by net importing countries. As we did before, let us maintain the vantage point of the country that experienced excess sales (to wit, the net exporting country). Its purchase of the financial assets issued by the importing country guarantees the respect of the internal macro-monetary equilibrium, closing the domestic circuit. Does this financial relation define a claim on future incomes from the importing country (as a whole)? The agents holding this claim will certainly confirm they expect to access a corresponding future income, very much like holders of a pension insurance policy expect access to future income. In both cases, however, no additional purchasing power has been created at macroeconomic level by the simple act of formally registering the corresponding financial relation. Only production increases purchasing power, and operations not abiding to this fundamental principle result in inflationary pressures. Unfortunately, this is still the case in today's 'non-system' of international payments through hard currencies. The French economist Jacques Rueff had already pointed this out fifty years ago: "Entering the credit system of a creditor country, but remaining in the debtor country, the claims representing the deficit are thus doubled" (Rueff 1963: 324).

Macroeconomics' unfinished agenda: an international system of payments for the global village

The theoretical underpinnings for an international architecture have been laid out

After having established that the essential question of monetizing international trade is to ensure that the macro-monetary level coherence is safeguarded in both the net exporting country (A) and the net importing country (B), in 1973 Schmitt put forward a plan for a world monetary reform based on the principle of carrying out international payments through an algorithm that conforms to the needs of macro-monetary coherence within both countries A and B. Over the years, the insights offered by quantum macroeconomics' distinction of national monetary economies and international payments have proven to be an insightful framework for suggesting monetary institutional settings that address key international monetary challenges of the post-Bretton-Woods era. Quantum macroeconomic theory offered the elements for the design of a world monetary reform (Schmitt 1973), a European common system of international payments (Schmitt 1975b), an alternative framework for the introduction of the euro within a three-tier banking system without suppressing domestic European currencies (Rossi 1997), a plan for reforming external debt servicing (Cencini and Schmitt 1991), the design of a bilateral US–China settlement facility (Piffaretti and Rossi 2012), and the suggestion of a supra-national real-time gross-settlement protocol for reshaping the international monetary architecture after the global financial crisis (Rossi 2009a, 2015b). Despite the theoretical advances, thus far, policies have either remained within the domain of the 'international monetary cooperation' codified in the 1944 Joint Statement (Horsefield 1969), or have tried to address the challenge of increasingly dense cross-border transactions by unifying national economies into a single macroeconomic entity (as the European Union did with the introduction of a single European currency, that is, the euro). While policy pragmatism makes its way into understanding the necessary changes to the international architecture for economic prosperity in a hyper-globalized world, the theoretical progress in understanding the nature of monetary systems and cross-border transactions will prove to be invaluable.

Beyond a territory-based definition of macroeconomic systems

Schmitt's proposal for an international system of payments is in line with the notion of positive analysis setting the principles that normative analysis has to abide by (Schmitt 1975b: 70). These principles are logical derivatives of the positive analysis of the nature of a national macroeconomic system. On this basis, over the years, Schmitt highlighted the drawbacks of systems that do not comply with the positive laws of macroeconomics, namely, (1) the inconsistencies of the current non-system based on marketable hard currencies, (2) the inflationary nature of Keynes's Plan, (3) the limits of the European Currency Unit (ECU) and Special Drawing Rights (SDR) schemes, (4) the drawbacks of the euro, and (5) the highly problematic features of any single 'global currency' scheme.

While frustrated at times by what he perceived as an overall lack of attention within economics to the need of a rigorous understanding of cross-monetary systems' transfers, Schmitt remained constantly optimistic that in the future a better system would be put in place in the end. In the meantime, however, the global economy has been changing, and a constant feature of the problem of how it was formulated in the literature, namely that it is about national economies trading among themselves, may be itself not such a constant after all. As the world is rapidly evolving into an ever closely interconnected global 'economic village', it appears that the identification of a macroeconomic system with a nation-state may itself be a normative assumption. The rather recent era of nationalism, which led to the creation of a large number of nation-states with a vast array of institutions, including economic institutions, obscures the fact that the coincidence between national economies and macroeconomic systems is of normative nature, and an historical legacy. There can be macroeconomic systems that have little relation to a specific physical territory. Hyper-globalization, as well as growing internet-based production, open the possibility of future macroeconomic systems delinked

132 *Nadia F. Piffaretti*

from a very specific geographical region of the world, defined by 'resident professionals' scattered around the planet, perhaps even spending much of their time in and out of airports. Nevertheless, even macroeconomic systems that lack a very clear geographical demarcation would still be defined by their monetary structure, that is, the monetary space in which their income is defined. To maintain monetary coherence, exchanges between such macroeconomic systems would have to conform to the logic of payments outside of an economy of production, within the confines of an 'exchange economy'.

More immediately, current challenges facing the world economy can be informed by a deeper understanding of the principles of monetary-macroeconomic circuits. Modern monetary theory can contribute to the appropriate design of policy solutions and payment mechanisms. Increased interconnectivity, the blurring of the geographical demarcation of added value in highly complex global value chains, increased mobility of a globally growing population, and the stronger push to migrate toward higher performing economies, all raise the question of how a 'resident' should be understood. Virtual macroeconomic systems can be created. Piffaretti (2000) offers an extensive elaboration of these ideas. As an example, common wisdom suggests that economic migration implies physical travel to a new country. Standard economic theory seems to suggest that encouraging more freedom of circulation for people would increase overall global prosperity, but in view of the challenges of social integration in a new nation, the world is likely nowhere closer to allowing unrestrained freedom in choosing the country of physical residence. However, physical residence may not be what matters most in the end. Certainly, current advances in communications technology, the integration of global value chains, and the rise of very immaterial high-tech sectors open the opportunity for any resident of any country to be professionally active in an economic system that is not the one where the agent physically resides. But the laws of macroeconomic systems allow thinking a step further: poorer residents of unstable countries could be integrated into more stable macroeconomic systems by integrating the emission of their income into a different monetary system. The macro-system could move to them, instead of them moving physically to a new country to escape instability. 'Embedding' of foreign residents into a different macroeconomic system may be the essence of what some elites in oil-dependent countries manage to achieve, appropriating the hard currency-denominated rents and spending them on imported goods produced by the same country that both manages oil production and absorbs the exports. Analytically, they may already live in a different macroeconomic system than the one within which they officially and physically reside. If there is a lesson from Keynes's Plan, Schumacher's work, and the theoretical legacy of Schmitt, it is that logical thinking is only bounded by the limits of logic, not by physical or historical reality. Pure theory can, over time, shape reality in a way that might have surprised even its original authors.

Conclusion

Quantum macroeconomics and its theoretical framework of monetary systems started to be developed in the 1960s, but its origins date way back, to Ricardo's writings, and to Keynes's work among others. While World War II was still raging, a generation of economists recognized early on the need to ground international relations on a sounder monetary architecture. Political imperatives of that time finally led to the abandonment of the idea of a multilateral clearing union, leaving an unfinished agenda of international institutions that still reverberates today, as a multipolar world is taking shape and taking its very first uncertain steps. The world still lacks an international system of monetary relations that can facilitate the increasingly dense web of cross-border economic transactions.

While very much needed, Keynes's and Schumacher's Plans lacked internal coherence, as they rested on a theoretical framework still embryonic and imperfect. Early on in his career, while developing the theory of monetary emissions, Bernard Schmitt turned his attention to international payments and to Keynes's writings, notably his attempt to set up a clearing of traded goods and services based on a unit of account and the common agreement on how to deal with the balance. Schmitt's critique was scathing. Still Keynes's Plan provided the ground on which to test the international implications of Schmitt's maturing views of the meaning of domestic payments, and their logical implications. Indeed, Schmitt saw implications that Keynes had not suspected.

If both authors diverged in considering solutions, it is because of their essentially diverging research agendas. While Keynes was striving to find a solution to very practical problems in international payments and foster post-war recovery, Schmitt was looking to understand the nature of domestic payments and how they are to be carried out internationally. Keynes's lack of focus for the theoretical nature of the problem hampered the search for a logical solution. He was looking indeed for a mechanism to facilitate the development of international trade. Schmitt was looking instead to understand how international financial relations could be created and settled, and from that he built his original critique. At times, he appeared irritated by the realization that, finally, Keynes had not abandoned the notion of monetary phenomena as separated from real flows. Keynes had understood the importance of money and finance, but his framework remained unable to marry real and monetary phenomena in an integrated theory. In the end, Schmitt's approach shows a degree of superiority: it points to financial relations of different order than the ones within domestic monetary systems. Finally, this led him down the path of exploring the double nature of net international payments: how is the debt of the '*maison France*' created and settled? That would ultimately be the question Schmitt started to pursue while studying the Keynes Plan.

Successful management of an interconnected and interdependent planet can only be based on monetary relations that have overcome the twentieth-century structures and political confines, and can create macro-monetary systems that fully serve the economic needs and capability of people in the twenty-first century.

134 *Nadia F. Piffaretti*

But if the question of the setting up of an orderly-working international monetary system remains unresolved, so are its analytical underpinnings. The true nature of international monetary relations is still veiled in mystery, as Schmitt's writings in his last two decades of work on the double payment of interest clearly show. The dichotomic view of real goods and monetary flows still deeply hampers the fundamental understanding of the nature of international monetary and financial relations.

8 European monetary union

Sergio Rossi

Introduction

This chapter explains that Bernard Schmitt clearly predicted the euro-area crisis long before it occurred, as a result of his critical investigation of the conventional definition of money and the ensuing flawed conception of monetary union. The next section presents Schmitt's critiques in this regard. It thereby points out that money is not a financial asset, that its purchasing power does not depend on agents' confidence, that a payment is not a bilateral exchange, and that the balance of payments concerns a country as a whole and not merely its residents. This section also explains that monetary union does not imply necessarily the irrevocable fixing of its currencies' exchange rates, that there is an essential distinction between a single currency and a common currency, and that the member countries of the European Union (EU) do not need a single currency, which is actually a factor of crisis for them. In light of this, the third section briefly recalls that money is an 'asset–liability' whose purchasing power depends on production, and that each payment implies three parties (namely, the payer, the payee, and the banking system as a monetary intermediary). It then explains that a national central bank represents its country in the international monetary space, where a common (instead of a single) currency ought to be issued by an international settlement institution. If so, then the common European currency (let us call it the 'international euro', €_i) will not be used by residents for either their domestic or cross-border transactions, which they will settle using their own national currency – thereby recovering national monetary sovereignty. Between any two member countries of the European monetary union, by contrast, all payments will be settled using the international euro as a truly international currency that enables payments to be final also at the international level. This contrasts with the current situation in the so-called TARGET2 system, which does not imply payment finality at the international level, because, to date, the national central banks involved therein do not pay (and are not paid) finally when there is a transaction across that system. The fourth section is thus in a position to explain that the European single currency area is neither a truly monetary union (because actually the euro is not really a single currency for its member countries) nor a factor of economic as well as financial stability and macroeconomic convergence

136 Sergio Rossi

across these countries. In fact, the monetary policy of the European Central Bank (ECB) has been a factor of instability and crisis, because of its 'one-size-fits-all' stance as well as because of a lack of a true monetary integration as epitomised by huge TARGET2 imbalances. This section shows therefore that countries like Germany as a matter of fact exploited these problems to benefit from the situation unduly, since the free movement of financial capital across the euro area has increased (rather than reduced) actual macroeconomic divergence across that area. The conclusion recalls Bernard Schmitt's radical critiques of European monetary union and points out how his proposal for monetary integration is both urgent and appropriate to solve the euro-area crisis at the time of writing.

A radical critique of the conventional conception of money and monetary union

To understand (and to set up) a monetary union, one needs first of all to understand the nature of money deeply. This was also the starting point of Bernard Schmitt's research work in that domain. Contrary to conventional wisdom, and a widely-accepted belief in the economics profession, money is not a financial asset. If it were a financial asset, one would have to explain how it is indeed possible to issue a number of money units with a positive purchasing power starting from scratch (that is, from *tabula rasa*). Accordingly, 'global banker' Lloyd C. Blankfein claimed that he is doing "God's work", because he creates money out of nothing (Irvine 2009). In fact, however, banks can and do issue money as a purely book-entry item, whose purchasing power must be produced by some economic agent (usually a firm with its own wage earners). Clearly, without production, money would be deprived of any purchasing power, as logically speaking numbers have no purchasing power *per se*. As Schumpeter famously noted, no one would dispose of an umbrella in exchange for a number (particularly when it rains). Schmitt's starting point is precisely to explain how those numbers that banks enter into their ledgers, when they issue money, become endowed with a positive purchasing power. This led him to study the production process from a monetary macroeconomics standpoint (see Chapter 1, this volume). In respect of this, Schmitt (1971b) clearly noted two wrong conceptions of money: on the one hand, the idea that money is produced (by banks or by some other institutions) is wrong, because in that case one would need to find a standard of measurement of money itself – a problem that Ricardo (1823/1951) was unable to solve logically, as he was looking for an invariable standard of measurement within the set of commodities. On the other hand, the idea that money enters any transaction as a separate item with regard to those goods or services against which it is exchanged is also wrong, because in that case it is logically impossible to determine money's value before this exchange occurs. From the standpoint of neoclassical economics, Verdon (1996: 22) provides an internal critique to the 'commodity money' theory, when he notes that, logically, "money cannot be both a commodity and a measure of utility because it could not concurrently be something produced and exchanged (a commodity) and a simple medium of exchange and gauge of utility". Schmitt was indeed able to point out the logical inconsistency of

European monetary union 137

this theory, as in the latter the value of money depends on its purchasing power, which according to this theory can only be determined once all exchanges have already occurred. As noted by Cencini (1988: 122–3), neoclassical theory is unable to explain the value of money, as in this framework it "is said to depend on a value that can only be determined once exchange has finally related real goods to one another" (see Rossi 2001: Ch. 4).

In this regard, Schmitt (1966a) explained that a payment is not a bilateral transaction through which two separate objects (money on one hand, and some 'non-monetary' items on the other hand) are exchanged against each other. As also noted by Hicks (1967: 11), "[e]very transaction involves three parties, buyer, seller, and banker". A payment is indeed a trilateral transaction, as it implies the payer, the payee, and the banking system that monetises this transaction by issuing the (numerical) means of payment. To be sure, this emission of the relevant number of money units occurs always and everywhere, including when the physical support of this number is a piece of paper, namely, a bank note, whose emission is indeed recorded in the central bank ledger. This holds also when a resident in country A pays a resident in a different country, say B (for instance, as a result of foreign trade): both need to refer to a third 'pole' that issues the means of payment between them. To be sure, the balance of payments of each country involved thereby records the results of those cross-border transactions that its residents pay or are paid finally through the relevant banking system. Therefore, the balance of payments should concern at the same time the sum of a country's residents as well as the country itself (as a whole). Yet, as actually conceived, it is a rather primitive accounting device, since it is based on a single-entry bookkeeping system, rather than on a double-entry bookkeeping system (as is standard practice within countries to date): when a resident in country A disposes of a bank deposit to pay for the relevant imports, country A's balance of payments records just an entry (imports, with the minus sign) rather than two (imports and the expenditure of the corresponding amount of income); in a similar way, when a resident in country B is paid for some exports, country B's balance of payments records an entry (exports, with a positive sign) rather than two (exports and the earnings of the corresponding amount of income). This is enough to understand that balances of payments, to date, do not concern countries but merely their residents. As a matter of fact, cross-border payments are final for those residents that are concerned by them, but not for their countries yet, as the international payment boils down to a promise of payment (IOU) that the payer's country delivers to the payee's country, because no bank deposits can logically leave the monetary system in which they are formed. This is also the case, in fact, for the actual institutional design of the euro-area-wide payment system, named TARGET2: the participating national central banks are not in a position, to date, to pay (and to be paid) finally, because the ECB does not act as a settlement institution between them. Hence, the mushroom growth of TARGET2 imbalances since the crisis burst at the end of 2009 in the euro area (Rossi 2012).

A further contribution by Schmitt in this regard concerns the process of monetary union. Schmitt (1988a) explained that to form a monetary union, its

138 *Sergio Rossi*

would-be member countries do not need to fix their currencies' exchange rates irrevocably. They also do not need to dispose of their own national currencies in this regard. Indeed, conventional wisdom, as epitomised by Werner (1971: 21, our translation), considers that "exchange rate fixity is plain in a monetary union. Eventually, exchange rates are not only fixed but irrevocable. This situation amounts, essentially, to a single currency regime." With regard to this, Schmitt argued that a single currency is not the essence of monetary union, once we understand that the latter is a homogenous monetary space, that is, a uniform payment system, even when the homogenised currencies are subject to exchange rate flexibility (within some limits or fluctuation bands) over the long run. Now, in order for monetary homogeneity to exist, Schmitt (1988a) explained that foreign-exchange transactions should occur in a series of absolute exchanges, rather than in relative exchanges, as it has been occurring to date on the foreign-exchange market. An absolute exchange on the foreign-exchange market implies two different albeit homogeneous currencies, that is, a national currency and the international means of final payment. The latter vehiculates the former in a full instantaneous circle from and to its issuing country, thereby providing payment finality at international level, since it delivers to the payee's country a (real or financial) object rather than a mere promise of payment (IOU) in the form of a national currency whose corresponding bank deposit remains in the payer's country banking system (hence, the existence of trade "deficits without tears" as pointed out by Rueff (1963: 322)). On this subject, Schmitt (1988a) explains that euro-area residents do not need a single currency, which is actually a factor of crisis since it implies a single European monetary policy for a variety of heterogeneous national economies, whose structures have not converged but rather diverged with respect to real economic magnitudes, such as GDP growth and the rate of unemployment. In fact, the institution of the euro area has given rise to financial flows from the 'centre' to its 'peripheral' countries that have inflated the imbalances as well as a credit bubble within and across these countries – until the bubble burst in 2009 (see Rossi 2007a; Rossi and Dafflon 2012).

Contributions to a new theory of money and monetary union

Bernard Schmitt has greatly contributed to elaborating a modern monetary theory, based on logical thinking and rigorous conceptions of money and banking, within as well as across different monetary spaces. He notably provided constructive criticisms to both traditional monetary theory and the conventional understanding of monetary union, as pointed out in the previous section.

In providing his own theoretical contribution to monetary theory, Schmitt (1975a) starts from *tabula rasa* to explain how it is possible that a bank splits the number zero into a positive and a negative number (of money units): this occurs owing to the principle of double-entry bookkeeping. When it carries out a payment on behalf of a customer, the bank issues the relevant number of money units both positively and negatively: indeed, the addition of $+x$ and $-x$ (where x is the number of money units issued by the bank) is zero (so as to respect the logical principle of no net creation), but this separation of the number zero into $+x$ and $-x$ is crucial in order for every payment to occur finally; hence for a national economy to actually exist. Without this separation, in fact, no transaction, on any market, would be paid finally, as the issuance of an IOU by the purchaser of any items amounts to a promise of payment – and the circulation of a promise of payment in chronological time cannot transform it into a final payment logically unless this promise comes full circle (in which case we would have an intertemporal barter trade system, or a pure credit economy based on mutual confidence). Money is thus an "asset–liability", as Schmitt (1975a: 13) called it, because, logically speaking, banks cannot create without simultaneously destroying the same number of money units. In other words, money is a double-entry item: it features simultaneously both on the assets and the liabilities side of a bank's ledger when the latter issues it in payment of any (real or financial) item (like a good, service, or asset).

Now, as Chapters 1 and 2 in this volume have explained, the emission of money must be grounded on production, otherwise its purchasing power would be a figment of the imagination. This means that money and income are essentially different from each other: money conveys payments, while income finances them. Money must indeed be integrated with the economic activity of production, in order for the former to measure the latter (Schmitt 1971b). This is the essential reason why a payment implies three 'poles' (the payer, the payee, and the banking system) rather than being a bipolar transaction between a buyer and a seller on any kind of market.

As regards international transactions, the Schmitt analysis is consistent with the nature of money: there should be an international means of final payment, issued by a central bank for national central banks, which, as a matter of fact, act as settlement institutions for those banking institutions that exist within the domestic monetary system. The logic of this analysis is clear: as any payment implies three poles in order to be final, there is a need to have an international settlement institution for those payments that concern a country as a whole – namely, for the settlement of foreign trade on goods, services, and financial assets (Schmitt 1984c). In this respect, the national central bank must act as the monetary representative of the whole country in the rest of the world, recording through two separate but interrelated bookkeeping departments in its ledger all incoming as well as outgoing payments, as a result of those cross-border transactions that this country's residents carry out with their foreign counterparties (Schmitt 1984c). Elaborating on this international monetary architecture, Schmitt (1987a, 1988a) argued that a monetary union (or, better, monetary integration) necessitates a common (instead of a single) currency.

This analytical stance corroborates Keynes's (1980: 168) argument that

> We need an instrument of international currency having general acceptability between nations [...]; that is to say, an instrument of currency used by each nation in its transactions with other nations, operating through whatever national organ, such as a Treasury or a central bank, is most appropriate, private individuals, businesses and banks other than central banks, each continuing to use their own national currency as heretofore.

140   *Sergio Rossi*

As a matter of fact, both Keynes and Schmitt argued that countries need a common (and not a single) currency, so that each of them may keep its own national currency, thereby preserving its monetary sovereignty, which amounts to steering interest rate policy with a view to contributing to domestic financial stability and macroeconomic stabilization (see Rossi 2009a). Indeed, Keynes (1980: 33) pointed out that "[w]ithin any member-country or currency unit the provision of foreign exchange [has] to be concentrated in the hands of its central bank which would deal with the public through the usual banks". Schmitt, for his part, provided an operational plan of monetary–structural reform as he suggested splitting the national central bank's ledger into a domestic and a foreign department. The first department would record, in domestic currency units, the results of those international payments that are carried out by the international settlement institution, whose results in international monetary units would be recorded in the central bank's second department. A fundamental issue separates, however, Schmitt from Keynes in this regard: "the Keynes analysis was not able to separate strictly the monetary bancor from the financial bancor" (Schmitt 1988a: 143, our translation). Indeed, the 'Keynes Plan', presented at the Bretton Woods conference in July 1944, blurred the distinction between money and credit at the international level, because, at this level, it did not really distinguish between the means of payment and the purchasing power necessary for this payment to occur finally (Rossi 2007b).

To avoid this problem, Schmitt (1988a: 109, our translation) clearly pointed out what he dubs "the first principle of any international currency", notably, "that it is really defined in the space of international transactions". In this space, as a matter of fact, there is and can be no production, because all goods and services are produced within countries – as they are monetary economies of production in Keynes's (1933/1973) sense. The international economy, logically, can only be an exchange economy. Nevertheless, there are, in fact, two types of exchange economies: a barter economy (as in neoclassical economics) and a monetary economy of exchange (that is, an exchange economy where money plays the key role of providing for final payments to occur every time there is a transaction). This amounts to saying that the international economy might be either a barter economy or a monetary economy of exchange. In the former case, which is the actual "non-system" of international payments (Williamson 1977: 73), there are some so-called 'key currencies' (mainly the US dollar), which are considered as if they were international reserve assets – that is, financial products. International transactions are thus reduced to barter, since a 'non-monetary' item is exchanged against the "image" of a bank deposit that cannot but remain in the original banking system (Rueff 1963: 323–4). In the second case, which is the international monetary order proposed by Schmitt, international transactions provide for an absolute exchange whereby money is not an element of the terms of trade: it is an instrument (purely numerical) allowing this exchange to occur, as it vehiculates to those agents involved in it the object of the latter – that is, a good, service, or financial asset.

Schmitt (1988a: 160) explains therefore that the Keynes Plan must be amended, so that the international currency proposed by Keynes (the bancor) becomes a purely vehicular instrument, whose load will be provided by those national currencies that are disbursed by importers when they discharge their debts across their country borders. With regard to the European (single) currency, Schmitt (1988a: 160) considers that the euro must be, in fact, just the numerical vehicle of those goods, services, or assets that move across a country's borders: "being a vehicle in all its interventions, Europe's money will never be the object of a net supply or a net demand against any national currency whatsoever." The fact that the euro is actually not in a position to play this purely vehicular role is a clear evidence of its essential flaw, which explains that the monetary architecture of the euro area is the source of the euro-area crisis that burst in 2009.

The crisis-prone monetary architecture of the euro area

Schmitt foresaw the euro-area crisis, even though he never published his arguments in this respect – which he illustrated mainly in personal conversation. He was convinced that disposing of national currencies to adopt the euro as the single European currency would provide for free capital mobility across the euro area that would be profitable in fact for the 'core' countries of that area (see Cencini and Schmitt 1992), contrary to the mainstream view that considers free capital flows to be beneficial for less developed countries in need of closing the gap in regard to the most advanced economies (see, for instance, Fischer 2004 and the literature cited therein). Once peripheral countries in the euro area are "[p]ut at the same monetary level as that of the most capitalised as well as the most advanced technological production systems", as explained by Rossi (2007a: 326), "the less-advanced and slow-growing countries in the EMU experience a number of firms' closing down, while many [real] investments are being diverted towards more competitive regions." This gives rise to a widening gap with respect to productivity growth between the two groups of countries, that is, the core and 'peripheral' EMU (Economic and Monetary Union) countries, even more so when the single interest policy of the ECB induces a credit-led boom in the 'periphery' of the euro area. This means that the single European currency increases the rate of unemployment in the periphery of that area, which is not in a position to curb this phenomenon, because the domestic policy makers have lost the possibility to act on their currency exchange rates and they have tied their hands as regards national fiscal policy (owing to the Maastricht criteria and the ensuing straightjacket; see Rossi and Dafflon 2012). This problem has in fact been recognized, notably by Kenen (1969: 45–6), who pointed out that "[f]iscal and monetary policies must go hand in hand" to influence the economic system in the same direction and indeed from the same institutional level. It led Padoa-Schioppa (2004: 35) to understand the problematic institutional setting of the euro, which, in his own words, is "a currency without a state".

Elaborating on this along Schmitt's lines, one can easily understand that a country like Germany benefits from monetary union in a number of ways (Rossi 2013, 2015a). First, it is in a position to 'recycle' its net savings, corresponding to its trade surplus (on the assumption of a balanced government budget), by lending

142   *Sergio Rossi*

to peripheral countries in the EMU these savings in order for these countries to finance their 'twin deficits' and, as regards particularly Spain, to inflate a real-estate bubble so as to make the domestic economy appear to be closing the gap with the most 'competitive' ones within the same area. Secondly, by making it impossible for weak national economies to devalue their currencies' exchange rate, Germany forces them to compete on the grounds of the unit labour cost, making sure thereby that the German position remains prominent against other euro-area countries. Thirdly, the single interest rate policy of the ECB considers the situation of the euro area as a whole to determine its policy rates of interest, but, in fact, weighs the German economic situation more than it does with respect to that of any other national economy within the EMU (see Feldstein 2000, Lee and Crowley 2009, Krugman 2011).

The saddest outcome of this asymmetrical monetary union is that the euro-area crisis burst at the end of 2009, after the newly-elected Greek government announced that the debt and deficit figures of the country's public sector had been fudged by previous governments. This crisis represents the first 'crash test' to which the euro area has been confronted in a systemic way, and could lead to the euro dismissal as predicted by Schmitt. Although, in fact, Schmitt never elaborated on this prediction, he noted the lack of any 'viability' in the monetary architecture of the euro area. He did not imagine that some countries in that area would be pushed under financial as well as political stress to exit the EMU, but in some way he intuited that a major financial crisis was going to put the survival of the euro at stake in its present form. He was quite optimistic in this regard, as he considered that the euro crisis was a necessary – though not sufficient – event in order to transform the European currency into a common (instead of a single) currency. Another key factor of this essential transformation, which is still lacking, concerns the political attitude that European leaders will have to adopt against this view. Among them, the ECB is clearly, to date, the crucial stakeholder that must change its mind radically, if the transformation of the euro from a single into a common currency is ever to occur. Consistent with the nature of money, that Schmitt investigated deeply, he insisted on various occasions on an operationalization of his own plan for European monetary integration, explaining how it was going to (re)establish monetary order at the international level, where currencies are (to date) denatured into objects of trade and speculation. His arguments were centred on the structural reform of the domestic and international payments systems, elaborating on his *New Proposals for World Monetary Reform* (Schmitt 1973). He notably pointed out that the two-tier domestic banking system existing within any national economy must obtain a sort of 'supranational hat', which integrates at the international level the relevant national central banks under a 'common roof', namely an international settlement institution that issues the means of final payment needed to make sure that all central bank payments in the international economy are final for all countries involved.

As a 'second best' solution, Schmitt imagined that a national central bank (such as the German Bundesbank) could play also the purely technical role of settlement institution for all international transactions concerning any EU country, provided that it introduced a dedicated department in its own books. This department would thus be an '*Ersatz*' for the international settlement institution that Schmitt called for in several of his research works. Eventually, all national central banks across the EU would adopt such a solution, which boils down to the 'first best' solution, apart from the lack of a truly supranational institution carrying out the final payment at international level.

Conclusion

Bernard Schmitt had been very critical about the monetary architecture of the European single currency area since the first projects of monetary union in Europe. He rejected all of them on the grounds of logical thinking and conceptual rigour, providing also a series of constructive criticisms in a variety of scientific publications. His starting point was a deep understanding of the nature of money, its emission mechanism as well as its value or purchasing power. He used to say that he was a dwarf on a giant's shoulders, because he was extremely well read in the history of monetary thinking – and, more generally, in the history of economic thought. He was able to detect the most hidden logical flaw in a theoretical reasoning, as he never refrained from pointing out logical inconsistencies or lack of conceptual rigour in economic analysis. This overtly scientific attitude has been a source of major friction between Schmitt and all those economists whose research he criticised on logical-conceptual grounds. Uncompromising, he did not believe that for a new theory to emerge, its proponents should try to make some concessions, in order for them to obtain the necessary professional consensus. His life was marked by many harsh confrontations with the economics profession both within academia and in the most influential institutions around the world, like the International Monetary Fund and the World Bank. His personal and scientific integrity deserve to be recognized, and his untiring efforts for the common good must be paid a tribute – at least by inscribing his own theory in the history of economic thought. This is not enough to make sure that his proposals for European monetary integration will be put into practice. It will, however, provide a key reference in the economics literature – even though the large majority of academic economists are not interested anymore in reading ground-breaking work today. Nevertheless, as cogently emphasized by Machlup (1963: 259), "[t]he bank managers and others with practical experience ought to stop regarding anything that has never been tried as impractical, and the theorists ought not to give up attempts to advance their favourite schemes just because the bankers refuse to listen." This was the Schmitt intellectual stance, and time will vindicate it over the long run.

9 The sovereign debt crisis

Alvaro Cencini

Introduction

Correctly understood, the sovereign debt is a debt that affects a country taken as a whole, as the set of its residents. Hence, the term sovereign debt stands for a country's external debt, the two terms being essentially synonymous. The emphasis recently put on what has been dubbed the sovereign debt crisis, notably in the euro area, is therefore symptomatic of a renewed interest in a problem, known as the external debt crisis, that had already puzzled economists towards the end of the twentieth century. The main difference between these two expressions lies in the fact that the term 'external debt crisis' was mainly used to define the disorder affecting less developed countries, while the term 'sovereign debt crisis' has been widely used only recently to indicate a widespread disorder that affects also a relevant number of industrial countries, notably across the European Union. From a theoretical viewpoint, what matters is that these two expressions define the same concept, that is, the possible existence of a macroeconomic debt of the country itself. This specific topic was initially investigated by Schmitt as early as 1984 in his book *Les pays au régime du FMI*, where he addressed for the first time the problem of countries' external debt servicing (Schmitt 1984c). His great discovery, on which he was to work until 2011, concerned the duplication of the charge relative to the payment of countries' net interest on their external debts. Now, to show that indebted countries have to pay twice the net interest on external debts is tantamount to proving that they are twice as much indebted as they should be. It is therefore not surprising that Schmitt's analysis was ended up with an explanation of the origin of countries' external or sovereign debts. This chapter is devoted to his path-breaking discovery of the pathological character of sovereign debts.

The sovereign debt: a macroeconomic debt that should not exist

Once it is understood that the sovereign debt is nothing other than a country's external debt, it should immediately be clear that it cannot be identified with the country's public debt. The State is merely an element of the set of a country's residents. The debt incurred by the State when it sells public bonds either nationally or abroad is therefore that of a resident and not that of the country as a whole. The

The sovereign debt crisis   145

debt run by the State to foreign lenders may contribute to the formation of a country's external or sovereign debt, but is far from defining it. Debts incurred abroad by the private sector play also an important role in the formation of a country's external debt, which is best defined as the debt affecting a country as a consequence of the net foreign purchases of its residents, both of the public and private sectors.

Simply put, the question we have to answer is the following. Given a country, A, whose residents purchase more than they sell abroad, is it correct that, as a consequence of these net imports, the country itself, the set of its residents, runs an equivalent foreign debt? Schmitt's answer is uncompromisingly no: countries' sovereign debts are entirely illegitimate, the pathological result of a non-system of external payments that feeds the speculative financial bubble and is one of the main causes of the international financial crisis.

Let us investigate the problem by referring to a simplified numerical example. Consider country A with respect to the rest of the world, R, and suppose that A's total purchases or imports, both of commercial and financial assets, are equal to 14 units of money R, MR, while its total sales or exports, also of commercial and financial assets, are equal to 10 MR only. The difference, 4 MR, defines the amount of country A's net imports. Today this means that, theoretically and factually, country A incurs a debt of 4 MR to R in order to bring its inflow of foreign currency, 10 MR, to the level of its outflow, 14 MR. Apparently, this conclusion is entirely justified by the fact that A's sales fall short of its purchases, which have to be financed through a foreign loan.

Yet, this result would avoid criticism only if A's net imports were indeed paid by R and not by A's importers. The crucial point that has to be carefully examined is whether A's residents pay for their total imports or not. If it were to be verified that A's importers pay, in money A, MA, the equivalent of 14 MR, it would become difficult to conclude that the country still needs to borrow 4 MR abroad to finance its deficit. It is enough to observe what has been going on in Greece, Portugal, Spain, and Italy or in any other indebted European country to realise that their net purchases have indeed been fully paid by their residents. This simple state of affairs should be sufficient to show that the very existence of countries' sovereign debts is unjustified, and that a reform is urgently needed to free deficit countries from the burden of their external debts. Given the originality of Schmitt's discovery and the difficulty inherent in any analysis that seems to go against common sense, it is nevertheless necessary to provide further evidence of the illegitimate character of countries' external debts. Let us do it by first considering the specific problem posed to country A by the need to pay its net purchases in MR.

The case that we have to analyse is that of a country, A, whose net overall imports (commercial and financial) are financed through a foreign loan. The problem is of a macroeconomic nature: since, on the whole, A's expenditures are greater than its receipts, and since A has to pay its foreign creditors in MR, it seems perfectly logical to infer that the deficit country has to borrow the difference between its purchases and its sales from the rest of the world.

Internationally as well as nationally, payments are both real and monetary. When A's residents pay the residents of the rest of the world for their net imports,

146 *Alvaro Cencini*

they do so by transferring abroad part of the real resources of A's domestic economy. However, R's exporters must be paid in MR, which seems to justify the fact that country A runs necessarily into a debt with R since it has to borrow abroad the foreign currency required to convey the payment carried out by its residents in MA. Two requirements must be fulfilled:

- The payment of A's net imports of 4 MR must have part of A's domestic product as its real content.
- R's exporters must be paid in MR.

The intervention of country A is thus due to the necessity of transforming the payment of A's residents, carried out in MA, into a payment in MR. Does country A take over the payment of its residents and pay R in their stead and in MR? If this were the case, the foreign borrowing of 4 MR would be the only cost run by A, which would match its external debt with a positive inflow of the domestic income paid by its residents, net importers of commercial and financial assets produced by R's economy. However, this is not what happens in the present non-system of international payments, where the debt incurred by country A adds up to the payment in MA of its residents. The reason for this double charge deficit countries suffer from any time they pay their net imports through a foreign loan lies in the absence of a system providing countries, free of cost, with the currency required to convey internationally the real payments of their residents. Within any given country, the charge of domestic payments is single, for the simple reason that the banking system conveys them at zero cost from the payer to the payee. The unique charge payers must support is the national income attributing a real content to their payments. Among countries, the absence of a sound system of international payments doubles the charge of net imports, deficit countries being forced to get hold of, at a positive cost, the foreign currency needed to convey the real payment (in national income) of their residents.

No one denies the fact that country A's net importers pay their due in an income expressed in their own domestic currency, MA. Likewise, no one objects to the fact that R's exporters are paid in their own domestic currency, MR. Since A's imports are equal to 14 MR while its exports are of 10 MR, it is clear that A needs to find 4 MR more to convey the full payment of its net imports. What is less clear to mainstream economists is that, A's net imports having already been fully paid by its residents, the conversion of 4 MA into MR should be granted scot-free by the presence of a true system of international payments. What they seem to be unaware of is that it is illogical and profoundly unjust to force countries that have already lost part of their domestic resources to the benefit of the rest of the world to add a positive foreign debt to it. Logically, only two scenarios should be possible: either country A (its residents) does not pay at all its net commercial and financial imports, in which case its sovereign debt would be fully justified, or it pays them fully, in which case no external debt should add to the loss of domestic resources due to the real payment of its net purchases. By claiming that deficit countries have for long lived beyond their own resources, benefitting from 'free

The sovereign debt crisis 147

lunches' at the expense of surplus (and 'virtuous') countries, economists and experts of the main international institutions are backing the first scenario, regardless of the fact that deficit countries' residents have indeed paid for their total imports. As shown by Schmitt (2014), in reality it is the second scenario that applies, which means that, far from enjoying 'free lunches' at the expense of R, deficit countries have never stopped providing 'free lunches' to R, or, more precisely, to the financial bubble that has so far benefited from their pathological sovereign debts.

First formal proof of the double charge incurred by deficit countries

Let us consider again our numerical example, where country A represents a deficit country, that is, a country whose external purchases or imports are greater than its external sales or exports, and country R represents the rest of the world. All external transactions, commercial and financial, are taken into account and it is supposed that A's economy imports for 14 units of MR and exports for 10 units of MR, also called foreign currency. For the sake of simplicity, let us assume that the rate of exchange between A's currency, MA, and R's currency, MR, is of 1 MA for 1 MR.

The first thing to note is that the difference between A's imports and exports cannot be attributed to any particular importer or to any particular exporter of country A. In each period the sum of imports is confronted with the sum of exports, and if the former is greater than the latter, country A is said to run a deficit, without it being possible to pinpoint anyone responsible for that. The second observation concerns the fact that A's importers pay their foreign purchases in MA, and that A's exporters are paid in MA for their foreign sales. Up to 10 MA, the domestic income spent by A's importers is gained by A's exporters, that is, A's foreign purchases provide the amount of domestic income required to pay for A's foreign sales. But what happens to the 4 units of MA spent in excess by A's importers? It is certain that they are not obtained by country A's exporters, whose international transactions amount only to 10 MR (= 10 MA). It is also sure that, in the present non-system of international payments, they are also not obtained by country A itself or by any of its institutions. Only one logical possibility remains: 4 MA of A's national income are lost to A's economy because of the payment of country A's net imports.

The situation described above cannot be the final result of the foreign payment, carried out in MA, by A's residents. Country A has to re-establish the initial level of its national income, and this can only be done through a foreign loan. What mainstream economists have failed to notice is that importers pay, in MA, the totality of their foreign purchases, and that this first payment of its net imports costs A a foreign debt due to the necessity of obtaining an external loan in order to recover the domestic income spent in excess.

In reality, the 4 units of A's national income spent for the payment of A's net imports are never to be found abroad: R's net exporters are paid in MR and not in MA. It remains that these 4 units are lost to A's economy; A's national income is

148 *Alvaro Cencini*

reduced by 4 MA. The reduction in A's national income is explained by the fact that part of R's imports are paid by A, and can only be neutralised by a loan granted by R, whose object is a future income of A. If this loan were not granted, A's national income would drop from, say x units of MA to $x - 4$ units, and A would witness a parallel increase in its domestic unemployment. The first proof of the double charge of country A's net imports is thus almost completed. Indeed, it suffices to add the need to borrow abroad 4 MR – in order to bring A's inflow of MR to the level of its outflow (14 MR) – to the increase in unemployment caused by the loss of national income due to the domestic payment of A's net imports, to see that country A has to face a total cost twice as high as expected.

A's net imports are paid once by the importers and a second time by the country itself. The cost of the first payment is an increase in unemployment, while the cost of the second payment is an increase in A's external debt. One payment is carried out in MA and it reduces the amount of national income available in A, the other payment requires an expenditure of MR, which country A is forced to borrow abroad. The double payment results from the addition of these two payments. It is only if the national income spent in excess by importers were transferred to country A (its Sovereign Bureau in Schmitt's reform, where the Bureau would have to invest it in the financing of a new production, see Chapter 10), or if the sum of 4 MR borrowed abroad were to increase A's official reserves that A's payment would not be doubled. Unfortunately, neither of these conditions is actually satisfied. The transfer to A's Bureau of the sum of 4 MA spent by the importers is totally alien to the present non-system of transnational payments, so that an amount of national income is unavoidably lost to A in any period its importers of commercial and financial assets spend more than its exporters of commercial and financial assets earn. Likewise, it would be hopeless to look at A's official reserves to find that they increase by 4 MR when A borrows that sum from R.

At a first, superficial examination it might seem correct to claim that, since A's net imports have to be paid in MR, it suffices for A to borrow 4 MR in order to obtain the amount of foreign exchange it needs to finance its net foreign purchases. To pretend that the 4 MR borrowed abroad could increase A's official reserves is overtly at odds with the undisputable fact that R's exporters are paid in MR. This is certainly true, of course, but it must not be forgotten that it is also equally true that A's importers pay their foreign purchases in full. It is because A's net imports are fully paid by its residents that the sum borrowed abroad should not be lost by A. If this were the case, the debt incurred by A following the loan granted to it by R would be matched by an equivalent credit defined by the increase in A's official reserves (which would immediately be invested in the foreign-exchange market). This not being the case, it can only be inferred that the loss of foreign currency adds up to that of the national income spent by A's residents.

As previously suggested, the loss of A's domestic income can be avoided only through another foreign loan. This leads us to Schmitt's first proof of the double debt incurred by deficit countries that finance their net imports through a foreign loan. His argument concerns the need for the deficit country to finance both the

The sovereign debt crisis   149

real and the monetary payment of its net imports. Let us start with the real payment carried out by A's residents. Since A's imports of commercial and financial assets are greater than its exports, country A has to increase by 4 MR the amount of real assets it exports to R, a requirement it can actually fulfil only thanks to a loan of 4 MR obtained from R. Why is this so? Because in the present state of affairs A can only add to its actual exports of 10 MR the export of real goods, with a value of 4 MR, that it will produce in the future. A's total exports are thus increased to 14 MR by adding the export of future goods to that of the actual goods sold abroad by its residents. In the period when A imports for 14 MR and exports for 10 MR, A must find the way to make the value of its exports to equal that of its imports. A loan granted by R does the trick, because it allows country A to obtain in advance the sum it needs to finance the production of future goods, of value 4 MR, that it will give up to R at the moment the loan will be reimbursed. Even though it is true that A will produce and sell these goods only in the future, it is also true that R acquires them in advance: they are the very object of R's loan.

The reimbursement of the debt is the key element for the determination of its object. When its debt falls due, country A's economy will be able to meet its obligation by selling to R part of its domestic product and using the MR thus earned to pay back its creditors. By lending 4 MR to A in, say, period p_0, R is therefore increasing its imports in this very period, adding the purchase of 4 MR of A's future products to that of 10 MR of its current output. Even though R's residents will obtain A's future output only later, say in period p_1, A has lost its ownership over these products since period p_0. The loan granted by R allows A to obtain the 4 MR (changed into 4 MA) required to finance the production of the future goods that it will give up to R in p_1. The object of the debt incurred by A in p_0 is nothing other than a part, equal to 4 MR (= 4 MA), of A's future output (of p_1). It is through this loan that A is enabled to bring its exports to the level of its imports and thus pay, in real terms, its initial deficit, the difference between its foreign purchases, 14 MR, and its foreign sales, 10 MR.

What follows can be easily understood if Schmitt's law of the necessary equality or identity (in value terms) between each agent's sales and purchases is referred to. A corollary of the law defined by the identity between macroeconomic supply and macroeconomic demand, this law applies also in the international field, thus establishing the necessary equality between international sales and purchases for each country. In our example, country A imports (purchases) for 14 MR and exports (sells) for 10 MR. Schmitt's law establishes that A has necessarily to match its net purchases of 4 MR with equivalent sales. This should not surprise the reader: there is nothing extravagant in the claim that A can finance its real purchases only though equivalent real sales. In the case under investigation, A's sales of current output are equal to 10 MR, and country A can equalise its purchases with its sales only by adding 4 MR of its future output to what it sells to R. Yet, A will effectively give these goods to R only in the future period p_1. It has therefore to find the way to sell them before they are available, and this is precisely what is made possible by R's loan of 4 MR. The final result is that R advances to A , in period p_0, the income corresponding to the output that A will produce in p_1. Thanks to R's loan, A brings its sales of current and future output to the level of its purchases. By the same token, R's imports of A's current output, equal to 10 MR, are increased by the amount, equal to 4 MR, of its imports of A's future output.

Economists are well aware that countries' international transactions have to comply with the balance-of-payments identity $IM \equiv EX$, where IM stands for the totality of a country's imports, financial and commercial, and EX represents the totality of its exports, both commercial and financial, and that this is so even when their overall imports exceed their overall exports. Schmitt's law of the logical identity between each country's sales and purchases is nothing other than another version of the balance-of-payments identity. The respect of $IM \equiv EX$ is compulsory and explains why, in the present non-system of international payments, R's imports are brought to the level of its exports through a loan granted to A, which adds 4 MR to R's imports.

The loan we have investigated at length so far is what allows A to finance the real payment of its net imports. Let us say it once more: the goal of this loan is to allow R to increase its foreign purchases of A's output from 10 MR to 14 MR. By giving up to R part of its future output since period p_0, A's economy pays, in real terms, its net imports of 4 MR. However, this still leaves unpaid A's net purchases in monetary terms. In other words, R's exporters need to be paid in MR, a payment country A cannot carry out, because its inflows of MR are equal to 10 MR only. The first loan of 4 MR does not provide A with the amount of foreign currency it needs, since its object is an equivalent amount of A's income. Country A is therefore forced to borrow 4 more units of MR, bringing the total sum of its foreign borrowing to the level of 8 MR, that is, twice the amount of its net imports.

What Schmitt shows is that, in the present non-system, a sovereign debt, the result of the second loan needed to convey in monetary terms the real payment of A's net imports, adds up to the ordinary debt required to cover the difference between A's residents imports and exports. There are two debts: one real and one monetary (Figure 9.1).

The object of the real debt is the goods that A will produce in p_1, whereas the object of the monetary or sovereign debt is an amount of MR that country A is forced to borrow. Country A must finance a "*future* export of [4] MR value, and its present surplus import of [4] MR" (Schmitt 2014: 22, italics in the original). Since, as argued by Schmitt, "it is obviously unconceivable that the same loan of [4] MR pays for, at the same time and for the same period, an export of [4] MR

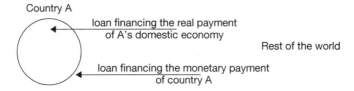

Figure 9.1 The two loans required to finance the real and monetary payments of A's net imports.

The sovereign debt crisis   151

and an import of [4] MR of the same economy" (ibid.: 22), country A has to incur a second debt. Now, this second debt, which is the very definition of the country's sovereign debt, is entirely pathological. Indeed, since A's economy has paid for its net imports, it is illogical to ask country A to incur a new debt to finance a payment that has already been fully carried out. As emphasised by Schmitt, economists take into account only the export of the deficit countries' current output, leaving inexplicably aside their export of future goods. They thus miss the fact that these countries' national economies pay their net imports in full.

Second formal proof of the pathological nature of deficit countries' sovereign debts

The second proof we have chosen to present in this chapter is, among the various proofs proposed by Schmitt in his astonishing 2014 paper, the one that might appeal the most to the reader with a penchant for physics. Indeed, Schmitt's argument is based on the principle, well known and unanimously accepted in physics, of the necessary coupling of any action with an equivalent and opposite reaction.

Let us consider once more our numerical example, where country A's total imports are equal to 14 MR and exceed its total exports, equal to 10 MR, by an amount of 4 MR. With respect to equilibrium, where A's imports and exports equalise at the level of 10 MR, the payment of A's net imports is an action. What is the reaction that necessarily accompanies it? The answer to this question comes through the understanding of the strict relationship existing between imports and exports. What has to be investigated is the impact of the payment of A's net imports on the payment, by country R, of A's exports. The first consideration is that A pays its net imports in MR, and that the payment is made possible by the loan granted to A by R. This is what is firmly believed by those economists who are also convinced that this payment is the only one imposed on country A and on its residents, and that A's external debt is the logical and fully justified consequence of A's net imports. Yet, what they fail to realise is that by paying R with an amount of MR obtained as a loan, A is eventually giving R the means to pay for its own imports, that is, they miss the fact that the payment of A's net imports reduces R's payment of A's exports.

The action (the payment of A's net imports) engenders a reaction that reduces by 4 MR the payment of A's exports; this is the crucial point of Schmitt's argument. This is so because A pays R with that part of R's national income that A borrows from it. In other words, it is with a domestic income of R that A pays R, which means that by paying for its net imports, country A allows R to recover the domestic income lent to A. By so doing, country A gives R the 4 units of MR it needs to pay for an equivalent part of its imports. But this clearly implies that, finally, it is country A itself that pays for part of its exports. The unity of action and reaction means that if R pays for part of A's imports, A must necessarily pay for a part of R's imports of equal value or, which is the same, for an equal part of its own exports.

152 *Alvaro Cencini*

Traditional theory ignores the essential relevance of the matter in hand and does not at all consider the fact, despite its key importance, that the rest of the world reduces the payment that it devotes to A's exports by the exact value of the payment it devotes to A's surplus imports.

(ibid.: 11)

Up to 10 MR, A's imports are paid for by its exports and no problem arises either for A or for R. Things change when A has to finance its net imports. What has to be asked in this particular case is whether the payment of A's net imports has, necessarily, an impact on the payment of its exports or not. To answer in the negative means to discard Newton's third law of classical mechanics, according to which every action is necessarily coupled with a reaction. The necessary, correct answer is that if A's imports increase from 10 to 14 MR (action), the payment of A's exports is necessarily affected, that is, subject to a reaction that reduces it from 10 to 6 MR. From R's viewpoint, this means that since it pays for A's net imports, that is, since it pays for A, it has to pay less for its own imports. Now, if the payment of A's deficit, equal to 4 MR, reduces the payment by R of A's exports from 10 to 6 MR, the total difference between the payments that A must finance, 14 MR, and the payments received from R, 6 MR, is equal to 8 MR and not to 4 MR only. As a consequence, A must borrow 8 MR from R in order to cover the full charge of its net imports, equal to 4 MR.

"Scholars' and experts' current thinking is simplistic", according to Schmitt, "in the sense that they 'forget' to add to A's imports paid by R, the unavoidable, blaring fact that an equal part of A's exports is paid by A instead of being paid by R" (ibid.: 11). What they ignore is that when A pays for its net imports by means of a loan of MR granted by R, its net purchases are financed by R, and that, when R pays for A's net imports, this action activates a reaction by which A pays for an equal part of R's imports.

Third formal proof of the duplication external debts are subject to in the present non-system of international payments

As shown by Schmitt towards the end of his 2014 paper, the double charge induced by the effect exerted by the payment of A's net purchases can be explained also by distinguishing between the period when A's deficit is paid through a loan granted by R and the subsequent period when the loan is reimbursed. Let us call the former period p_0 and the latter p_1, and suppose that in each period, from p_0 to p_n, country A runs a deficit of 4 MR. What is the total cost of A's deficit in each period from p_0 to p_n? If the answer were 4 MR, nothing would be wrong in the present system of international payments, and the duplication of the charge deficit countries are submitted to would be a figment of the imagination. On the contrary, if it were to be proven that the total cost is equal to 8 MR, it would be confirmed, once more, that deficit countries are forced to pay twice their net imports.

Let us consider what happens in period p_1, when the loan obtained from A is reimbursed by A's economy. According to our numerical example, in p_1 A's total

The sovereign debt crisis   153

purchases are of 14 MR, while its exports are equal to 10 MR. Since A has to reimburse the loan of 4 MR obtained in p_0, it must sacrifice 4 MR of the 10 MR obtained as payment of its exports in p_1. Following the reimbursement of its previous foreign debt, A's availability of MR is thereby reduced from 10 to 6 MR. Yet, its foreign purchases are still equal to 14 MR. Only 6 MR of these 14 MR are then financed by A's exports, the difference, equal to 8 MR, defining the amount of foreign currency country A has to obtain from R to cover its total costs.

Let us present Schmitt's argument once more. As any other loan, foreign loans have to be reimbursed, and it is by using part of its receipts in MR that country A can fulfil its engagements and pay back its foreign creditors. If country A's foreign sales or exports are equal to 10 MR, the amount of A's receipts in MR is indeed equal to 10 MR. It is out of this amount of foreign currency that A reimburses R's previous loan when it falls due. According to our assumption, country A's foreign borrowing is renewed for a number n of periods, and each new loan is reimbursed in the period following that of its formation. The loan of period 0 is reimbursed in period 1, the loan of period 1 in period 2, and so on, the last loan (of period $n - 1$) being reimbursed in p_n. As we assume also that in each period A's economy exports for 10 MR, it immediately follows that from p_1 to p_n the amount of MR still available for the financing of A's purchases after reimbursement of the debt incurred in the previous period is equal to 6 units of MR only. Given that in each period, between p_0 and p_n, A's foreign purchases are maintained equal to 14 MR, it is clear that A's foreign resources fall short of 8 MR $n - 1$ times. Things being what they are, in the following periods, $p_1, p_2, ..., p_n$ the situation will represent itself unchanged, two loans of 4 MR each being necessary to cover the cost of A's net imports.

> Each month, from p_0 to p_n, country A needs, at its disposition, a revenue of 14 dollars [MR], the value of its purchases (imports). This shows that, after repayment of the debt incurred in the previous month, country A's economy borrows each month 8 dollars abroad in order to settle the difference between the sum of its expenditures (14 dollars) and the sum of its receipts (10 dollars). We thus reach the conclusion that in each month, from p_1 to p_n, economy A borrows twice 4 dollars from the rest of the world.
>
> (ibid.: 87)

In order to cover its financial deficit, increased from 4 MR to 8 MR because of the reimbursement of previous debts, country A has to obtain a foreign loan of 8 MR in each successive period, thus increasing its external debt twice as much as the amount of its net imports, equal to 4 MR. The difference between A's total imports and exports being equal to 4 MR, logic would require that country A be submitted to an extra payment of 4 MR in order to fully cover the costs of its total purchases. This is unfortunately not so, and period after period country A is forced to borrow 8 MR to cover the difference between its imports, 14 MR, and the amount of MR still available after the repayment of its previous debt, 6 MR. This is the unacceptable effect of a non-system of international payments forcing deficit

154 Alvaro Cencini

countries to finance their net imports through a foreign loan: they must incur an extra debt of the same value as their net purchases (4 MR in our numerical example), which defines and explains the pathological sovereign debt they are subject to in the real world to date.

The reason why the double charge has gone unnoticed so far

Economists all over the world still believe that a single loan, equal to 4 MR in our numerical example, suffices to pay for the deficit due to a country's (A's) net foreign purchases. Their reasoning is simple: since country A's economy purchases are equal to 14 MR while its sales are only of 10 MR, the difference is settled through a foreign loan of 4 MR, which allows to equalise A's outflows of MR with its inflows. What they are well aware of is that A needs 14 units of MR in order to pay for its total imports of precisely 14 MR. This is correct, of course, but is it all? By answering yes, mainstream economists forget to take into account the real component of every payment. In fact, payments are both real and monetary: they include the transfer of goods and of money units. At the international level, every deficit country pays its net imports both in goods and in money units. What is necessary to investigate, therefore, is whether these two payments add to one another or not. Schmitt's all-important discovery consists in pointing out the fact that, actually, the two payments do not conflate into a single one, so that deficit countries pay twice their net imports. In this respect, it is worth pinpointing where and why most economists fail to detect the pathology that doubles the charge of deficit countries when their net imports are paid by a foreign loan. Let us do so following the argument introduced by Schmitt in the fifth section of his 2014 paper.

Schmitt's (2014) starting point is the traditional distinction between a sum of goods and a sum of money units. Accepting the assumption, unanimously shared, that a sum of foreign money units 'held' by a country defines a positive asset, a question may be asked concerning the units of MR obtained by A, the deficit country, to finance its net purchases. Do the 4 units of MR borrowed by A define a net asset or not? The answer would obviously be no if the credit of R, the lending country, were an amount of money units equal to 4 MR. This is indeed the case for every ordinary loan, the credit defined by the sum obtained from abroad being balanced by an equal debit defined by the debt incurred to the foreign lender. Yet, things change radically when the loan obtained from abroad is used to finance the borrowing country's net imports. In this case, indeed, the debt incurred by the borrowing country, A, has not a sum of MR as its object, but a sum of goods that A will produce in the future. "The units of foreign currencies borrowed to finance net imports are *monetary assets* and *real liabilities*" (ibid.: 37, italics in the original).

Economists know that the object of the loan obtained by A is a sum of goods that R, the lending country, will import in a later period, when the loan will be reimbursed by A. Unfortunately, they have failed to see the consequence of this fact, namely that "country R thus obtains the ownership of a future good, which country A's domestic economy will produce in a subsequent period" (ibid.: 37). This means that the 4 MR lent by R to A are, in reality, spent by R in the actual

The sovereign debt crisis   155

purchase of an equivalent part of A's future output. As we have already pointed out in the second section of this chapter, the loan granted by R re-establishes the balance-of-payments identity between *IM* and *EX* by bringing R's imports to the level of its exports, 14 MR. The equality between A's and R's total imports and total exports is thus guaranteed by adding to A's exports (R's imports) of currently produced goods the sum of goods that A will produce in p_1 and that R has acquired since period p_0.

What is crucial here is that

[a]s soon as the international loan of a currency has the function and effect to increase the revenues of a deficit country, to bring them to the level of its total imports, *it changes its nature: it becomes the payment of a future export of real goods.*

(ibid.: 38, italics in the original)

Now, the fact that the monetary asset obtained by A is matched by a real liability (A's future goods imported by R) has an unavoidable and unexpected consequence: the 4 units of MR obtained by A as a loan define a net asset. Although apparently surprising, this result is perfectly understandable: having equalised its total imports with its total exports through the sale of future goods of 4 MR value, A's economy acquires the ownership of the 4 units of MR borrowed from R. It is true that when its debt falls due, in p_1, A will have to reimburse it by paying 4 MR, but this will be done using the 4 MR obtained as payment of the goods previously financed by R. What must be clearly understood is that the problem spotted by Schmitt is of a macroeconomic nature, that is, it concerns the deficit country taken as a whole, as the set of its residents. If we consider only what applies to country A's residents, we cannot observe the pathological formation of A's external debt. As direct beneficiaries of R's loan, A's residents are credited with a sum of MR that they will have to reimburse in a later period. It is to country A as a whole that the previous reasoning applies: "[W]hat present-day scholars forget is to distinguish the assets and liabilities as they occur at the level of countries themselves, that is, as set of all their residents, from the assets and liabilities concerning simply a part of their residents" (ibid.: 39). This should not come as a surprise, since the balance-of-payments fundamental principle concerns countries themselves, and not any specific resident. The compliance with this principle explains the real (as opposed to monetary) nature of the object of R's loan to A and the consequent fact that the money lent by R defines a net asset of country A.

When a country benefits from a foreign loan that finances its net imports, it immediately gives up the ownership over part of its future output. If logic were complied with, this would allow country A to retain the ownership over the amount of foreign currency, 4 MR, borrowed from R. Indeed, by allowing R to increase its imports from 10 to 14 MR, country A pays, in real terms, for the totality of its current imports, equal to 14 MR. Yet, in the absence of a true system of international payments, deficit countries are forced to pay, in addition, for their net imports and end up losing part of their domestic output and incurring a foreign

156 *Alvaro Cencini*

debt. In the example, country A gives up 4 MR of its (future) national output and its sovereign or external debt increases by 4 MR. The 4 units of MR obtained by A as a loan, and which should be kept by A since they are defined as a net asset, are in reality lost by A in the (additional) monetary payment of its net imports. Finally, A pays twice its net imports of 4 MR, once by the transfer of goods worth 4 MR, and once by the payment of 4 MR. The great failure of economists and experts of the major national and international institutions has been to miss the macroeconomic aspect of international transactions and of their payments. Had they been aware of the macroeconomic implications of the payment of net imports via a foreign loan, they would have realised at once that a system forcing countries to add a monetary payment to their real payment is highly unjust and deeply in need of reform to avoid the very formation of countries' sovereign debts.

Neither deficit countries nor their residents should run an external debt because of their net imports

Let us be clear from the outset: the aim of this section is not to claim that a country's residents can incur no foreign debt. There is no need to insist on the fact that residents are free to import and export as much as they can, both on the commercial and on the financial market, and that anyone of them is free to borrow what s/he can. Any resident borrowing more than s/he lends on the foreign-exchange market incurs a net debt, and this applies equally well to the public and private sectors. Yet, these loans are part of the transactions that enter into the balance-of-payments identity and can therefore not define an external debt proper, which can only be linked with the difference between a country economy's total purchases or imports and its total sales or exports. What we want to present here is one of Schmitt's latest arguments concerning the payment by a deficit country and by its residents of its net imports. The external debt we are referring to is thus the one incurred by the country and its residents with respect to the payment of their net imports (commercial and financial).

The elements introduced in the previous sections suffice to prove the illegitimacy of both the external debt affecting country A and that incurred by its residents. In particular, it is enough to recall that (1) deficit countries' residents pay their imports in full, and (2) surplus countries bring their imports to the level of their exports to realise that no foreign debt should arise from the payment of countries' net imports. Indeed, it is true that (1) residents pay the totality of their foreign purchases in their own national currency, and (2) countries give up part of their future goods in exchange for part of the actual goods produced by their international partners.

If both country A as a whole and A's residents pay in full their net purchases, it would be highly unjust to pretend that they have nevertheless to borrow 4 MR each and increase correspondingly their external debt.

As a matter of fact, countries do not sell or purchase, only their residents do. It is therefore odd to speak of a country's debt, as if the country could import more than it exports. The idea that a country is a person is unacceptable, and so is the

The sovereign debt crisis   157

claim that it may run into debt as any of its residents may. It is thus immediately clear that it is greatly illogical to pretend that a country's debt can exist at all, let alone add up to the debt incurred by its residents. At this point, someone could venture to claim that, even though a county's debt does not exist on its own, it is possible to conceive it as the mere mirror image of the debt incurred by its residents. However, the fact is that a country's residents would incur a debt only if their net imports were to remain unpaid, which is not at all the case. Residents' imports are paid in full in the residents' national currency. Schmitt's final conclusion is therefore very clear:

> residents' purchases, even in excess, are fully paid at the level of 14 dollars [MR], the total value of all the economic goods supplied by the rest of the world, so that the external debt incurred by country A's residents is necessarily null and void. As the country's residents do not incur any external debt, it is necessarily the same for the country itself, the set of its residents.
>
> (ibid.: 94)

Whichever analysis is chosen among those developed by Schmitt in his last paper, the result does not vary: countries' sovereign debt is a pathological 'monster' that should not exist and its presence has dramatic consequences for deficit countries' populations, who are subject to a series of austerity measures that drastically reduce their well-being. The existence of sovereign debts is a fact, but it is also a fact that they are the result of a pathological system of international payments, which means that a reform of this system will suffice to get definitively rid of them. In his 2014 paper, Schmitt introduced the key elements of a reform that could be implemented by any single country willing to protect itself against the formation of a sovereign debt. The next chapter reproduces part of Schmitt's solution and completes the analytical presentation of the problem we have summarised here.

10 A one-country reform

The solution to the sovereign debt crisis

Bernard Schmitt

Introduction

Today the total external debt of a country is measured adding the debts as incurred by the country's residents. This is fundamentally wrong because the true criterion concerns the country as a whole and not merely its residents of the private or public sector. The question therefore belongs to macroeconomics, as does the law of international trade balance between each country's earnings (exports) and expenditures. In macroeconomics, where the measure of external debts is scientifically accurate, only the foreign currencies that are both received and spent by the country as a whole matter. The correct criterion is therefore consistent with the balance of payments: external debt increases by the exact value of the difference between international expenditures of foreign currencies and their gain.

Already today external purchases are first paid in units of the national currency of the importing country. It is even correct to say that importers pay for all of their purchases as if they were carried out within their own national economy. Payments carried out in money units transferred abroad, that is, in foreign currencies, 'come in' somehow later. It is foreign countries that demand to be paid in foreign currencies, most often in their own national currency.

To the extent of matched imports and exports ('imports-exports'), the payment of purchases abroad raises no problem, because the importing country obtains automatically, and therefore gratuitously, the total amount of foreign currency required by foreign exporters. The reform would not be necessary if imports were never in excess. But 'imports-without-exports' exist for many countries and for many periods. The sum of imports (always in its broadest sense) is first paid by an income formed in the country's domestic economy; it is the only payment that falls on residents. All external payments of imports are macroeconomic: it is the country as a whole that is subject to the obligation to pay R (the rest of the world) in foreign currencies.

The difficulty of understanding the crucial distinction between microeconomic and macroeconomic payments is one of the reasons for the error in which the present theory of imports' payment finds itself. Economists believe that imports are paid between residents of the world, in exporting countries as well as in importing countries. This is totally wrong, because only importers and exporters are residents, importing and exporting countries are entirely distinct from their residents.

The problem of the external debt crisis cannot be saddled on importing residents, even if they are members of the public sector. This 'crisis' is macroeconomic, because it is only the country considered as a whole that is sometimes unable to pay part of its external debts. One of the main functions of the reform is to avoid the very formation of sovereign debts, and prevent economies from 'running into a crisis'.

Basically, the only payment of imports that is justified is microeconomic. It is natural that importers pay for their purchases even though exporters are non-residents. The sums of money thus spent are part of the incomes formed domestically, in the countries where importers from the private or public sectors reside.

Let us repeat that the macroeconomic payment occurs at the expense of the importing country, even though its residents have paid for all of their purchases. Logical consistency dictates that the 'macro-payment' does not get added to the 'micro-payment', but becomes its simple translation.

This result of paramount importance, which is absent from today's system, will be achieved by the reform.

The main leading ideas of the reform

If their payment occurred between residents of a single country, imports would obviously not be paid using different currencies; they would be paid only by buyers' domestic income. Yet, it is a fact that the payment in the importers' domestic currency is not valid when addressed to exporting countries. A conversion is necessary. Yet, the conversion of the domestic deficit in foreign currencies is a cost-free transaction only to the extent that the country balances its imports and its exports. Indeed, exports bring the foreign currency needed to pay for imports. Within imports-exports the payment for external purchases is therefore simple.

Things are radically different in the case of imports-without-exports. This time the foreign currency gain is zero, because the export that would have provided it does not exist. The foreign currencies that are not earned must be purchased. As a consequence, the payment in foreign currency adds to the cost in domestic currency terms.

The reform will make this abnormal loss of foreign currency units impossible.

Let us call the new institution in charge of the reform the 'sovereign Bureau' or simply 'Bureau'. The sovereign Bureau will look after, on a nearly daily basis, the external debit (imports) and credit (exports) payments of its country's domestic economy. It would not be enough to obtain simple reports on the external debts incurred by its country, as released by the Bureau a mere few times a year. It is essential, on the contrary, that any new debt be seized in the very period it is formed. However, it is particularly important to note at once that the sovereign Bureau is not charged with the responsibility of controlling the transactions from a juridical or a customs point of view. The reform will, on the contrary, preserve the 'laissez-faire'; in particular the Inland Revenue will not benefit from it.

If the reform is implemented starting from January 2018, the function of the Bureau will be to oppose, already in this first period, the second charge that would

160 *Bernard Schmitt*

form because of the difference between the country's imports and exports. It is a matter of fighting against the double charge and not against imports as such.

The safest and simplest method of preventing the domestic economy from suffering the consequence of the second charge of debts is to guarantee that the external payments of the domestic economy are all carried out between residents. It is enough to this effect that the Bureau transforms every domestic payment addressed abroad (by considering it its own) into an external payment of which the Bureau is itself personally the only debtor.

The sum total of the reformed country's expenditures (imports) can be entrusted to the Bureau. It would therefore be unnecessarily complicated to retain only the payment of surplus imports. In pure theory, imports-exports do not require the intervention of the Bureau. These expenditures of the domestic economy are also and equally what it receives; in other words, their sum is zero. They thereby escape from any fault. But it would be a heavy and unnecessary charge to ask the Bureau to find and note the difference between the country's imports according to whether they are or not of a greater value than its exports. It is much easier and faster to enter all imports at the moment they take place.

Domestic payments to the credit of the rest of the world are carried out between residents, because the Bureau is itself part of its country's residents. The domestic payments of the Bureau do not prevent payments of foreign creditors being carried out at their full value. Put simply, it is the Bureau that carries out and obtains the payment for the transactions occurring between its country and the rest of the world.

That said, the explanation still has to be broadened, because the reform must indeed ensure that the domestic payments, in money A, be disconnected from external payments, defined in money R. The Bureau's intermediation is not enough. Nothing changes if it simply passes on the payments it receives. It is necessary and essential that the Bureau first cancels all foreign credits for its domestic economy's imports. It is not enough to replace the domestic payment; on the contrary it is necessary to suppress it entirely. Henceforth, from the reform onward, foreign purchases of country A's residents will be zero credits of R. Banks will just have to conform to this.

If the sovereign Bureau were merely interposed between R and A's domestic economy, nothing fundamentally would be changed, because R could always, as it does today, transform its credits in money A into credits in money R. The reform is more rigorous, because it no longer allows for a payment in domestic currency to be the object of a foreign loan. No purchaser and no lender abroad can include a sum of money A among their credits in country A.

The Bureau will address the banks as follows.

- *Addressed to exporters*: your only rights are defined in your national currency and the Bureau is your only debtor.
- *Addressed to importers*: your only debts are defined in your national currency and the Bureau is your only creditor.

A one-country reform   161

Concerning the equality between purchases and sales in international transactions carried out by residents of the private and public sectors, incomes in money A that are spent are also earned: their loss and their gain add up, therefore, to zero. But surplus imports are net expenditures; the income in money A that is so 'lost' is not recovered. Yet, is this income lost to everybody? It is certain that it is not, according to the reform, because surplus imports are zero purchases of domestic products.

If real goods produced by A's domestic economy remain 'covered' by their equality with the incomes formed, it is because the sum of money A spent for net imports is still available in the national economy. This simple ascertainment was valid also before the reform. However, the main dilemma is to know to whom these incomes belong.

Let us examine the case of country A. Its residents-importers spend 11 dollars, a sum that is thereby unavailable for the purchase of national output. It is replaced to the extent that there are exports; their value is assumed to be 10 dollars. Only one dollar is thus missing to equalise the monetary with the real income of A's national economy. This difference is covered by a foreign loan; it is precisely in this way that the actual disorder forms, with the effect that the debt is 'multiplied by 2' by the payment of net imports (see previous chapter).

The function of the reform is therefore not to bring the monetary income to the level of the real income, but 'only' to avoid the monetary income spent for net imports being 'captured' by R to the detriment of A's national economy. The sovereign Bureau, which obtains and spends all the sums of income in money A defining country A's exports and imports, spends the equivalent of 10 dollars for the exporters and includes in its net income the sum of 1 dollar (in money A, MA).

The domestic income entering the personal belongings of the Bureau is a final gain, which is not and will not be corrected by any future loss. From this it can immediately be deduced that the Bureau finally transfers this gain to its country's government. In our example, country A's budget obtains without any counterpart the equivalent of 1 dollar in the period considered. The government's net gain, that is its profit, is of n dollars (in MA) if, in the periods concerned, country A's net purchases (imports) are of n dollars.

A difficulty remains: how to be sure that foreign loans will not take possession, as is necessarily the case before the reform, of the gain in incomes A that the Bureau is supposed to transfer to the deficit country's government?

Certainty that the gains of the national budget in domestic money are net and final

The reform's principal aim is to assign to countries' governments the total of the sum of incomes in domestic currency spent for the payment of net imports. It is timely to observe here that this sum of income is indeed substantial, because it exceeds by far the value of national economies' net expenditures to the benefit of the rest of the world *before principal repayments of previously formed debts are taken into account.*

162 *Bernard Schmitt*

Following our example we can show very clearly the profit thus realised by country A's national budget. In the period considered, for example a month, A's net imports are to the value of 1 dollar (in billions). The national budget's gain without a counterpart of such a sum is already considerable. But it is possible and even likely that, in reality, the deficit country pays, in addition, part of its previous debt, still far from being reabsorbed. Hence, we can suppose, adding the payment of the principal of an external debt formed in previous periods, sometimes very far in the past, of say 2 dollars, that economy A's net imports reach 3 dollars in the period considered.

The great error of the so-called Troika (composed of representatives of the European Central Bank, the European Commission, and the International Monetary Fund) is to defend openly an already antiquated theory, which disastrously accuses deficit countries of living at the expense of more thrifty countries, which consume only the products of their own national economy. At the international level, Troika's experts say, countries whose imports are greater than their exports enable their residents to consume foreign goods through expenditures that remain unpaid in their respective homelands and that prevent other too generous countries from enjoying part of their own production. This would constitute an exemplary case of the proverbial 'free lunch'.

Not only is this completely wrong, but the error thus committed is literally multiplied by two: surplus countries rather than deficit countries get a free lunch at the time of writing. Deficit countries pay positively the totality of their foreign purchases, included their imports-without-exports. And surplus countries obtain twice the payment of their net exports, first to the credit of their lenders, then, a second time, to the benefit of a 'financial bubble'. Only making the first payment is logically, morally and economically justified. The second payment is but an unwitting extortion.

As we have just explained, the solution exists in preventing the deficit country's domestic income being 'gained', even in part, by the rest of the world. This is a loss that is naturally impossible to the extent of imports-exports, but the payment in domestic currency of net imports must be reformed; the income spent to this effect has to remain the domestic economy's property. The desirable result is reached as soon as the domestic income spent on the payment of net imports remains the property of the deficit country itself, as if purchases (imports) were carried out between residents. The Bureau must thereby be credited with a net gain and not as a result of a simple intermediation. But to concur that this sum of income A belongs definitively to the deficit country, initially placed with its sovereign Bureau and then with its government, shows nothing more than 'good will'. To want is not enough; it is necessary to be able to do. Now, the sum of income A that is spent by country A's national economy for the domestic payment of its surplus imports can still be appropriated by the rest of the world. This is precisely what has to be avoided. *For this, it is necessary and sufficient that the Bureau lends abroad, in foreign currency, the whole value of its country's net imports.*

It is obviously strange to contemplate that the deficit country must decide to lend funds abroad. Country A, whose imports' value is net to the extent of 1

A one-country reform   163

dollar, must borrow this sum abroad, yet it then has to lend 1 dollar to the rest of the world. If country A were satisfied to borrow foreign currencies abroad, it would certainly not become the owner of the equivalent in domestic money of the value of its net imports, to the benefit of its Bureau and then of its government. The loan of 1 dollar to the benefit of R has no other aim than to make sure of the gain in a domestic income of A of the equivalent of 1 dollar, the measure of economy A's net international expenditures, by the deficit country. It is therefore not a matter of preventing the foreign loan of 1 dollar that country A could not avoid but 'adding', negatively, the loan of 1 dollar to R.

In the end, the solution is simple: the sum of 1 dollar borrowed abroad is additionally (inversely) lent abroad. This loan makes it entirely impossible for A's government to lose the property of the income A obtained from the domestic payment that finances economy A's surplus imports.

Let us never forget that the general definition of imports and exports refers to all the expenditures and all the gains resulting from international transactions. The question that arises concerning the final profit derived by the deficit country's government refers to the difference between the sum of all expenditures (imports) and the sum of all receipts (exports) of the domestic economy of the nation concerned.

The subject becomes clearer when it is expressed in terms of two distinct incomes: the deficit economy (income in money A) and that of the rest of the world (income in money R). These incomes are both used in country A's imports. The residents-importers pay their purchases using a sum of income A. It is irrelevant whether the incomes thus spent are owned by importers or are borrowed by them within economy A. Yet, foreign exporters are paid, as they ask for it, in money R: it is income R, and not income A, that interests them.

The two payments involved are clearly defined: even though it is a question of the payment of non-residents, A's domestic economy carries it out using part of its national income, and therefore in money A, whereas, through its change in money R, the same imports are settled through the expenditure of a foreign income from the moment they are defined to the debit of country A, considered as a whole. In brief, imports are paid by the expenditure of a domestic income, and by the expenditure of a foreign income.

Do these two expenditures form one unique expenditure? The answer is both positive and negative.

- Imports balanced by exports are paid only in a foreign income.
- Net imports are paid both by a foreign income and by a domestic income.

Showing the crucial difference between these two cases is extremely simple. To the extent that imports are balanced by exports, exporters obtain from abroad the domestic income spent by importers: the sum of expenditures is hence zero. But to the extent that they are not, expenditures carried out by importers do not reach any exporter. Instead of being of a zero sum, they themselves are net.

164 *Bernard Schmitt*

Undeniably, therefore, there arises the problem of the acquisition of country A's domestic income that its economy spends on the payment in national currency of its imports-without-exports. Who exactly is the new owner of the sum of 1 dollar spent by importers in addition to their foreign purchases balanced by economy A's exports of the same period? We have just acknowledged that this income A is not obtained by anybody within economy A, which does not export anything with respect to its net imports. It is also certain that foreign exporters obtain only an income formed in money R. There only remain the lenders of funds, non-residents of A's economy. But does the loan of 1 dollar from abroad exist in favour of economy A? This loan must exist. Indeed, since to finance its net imports economy A 'gains' from abroad only a zero sum of money, it is forced to obtain it through a loan. What remains to be defined is the precise meaning of this loan at the very moment it is formed. It would be erroneous to claim that the rest of the world lends 1 dollar in order to feed the domestic purchases of A's residents; it is, on the contrary, a sum of foreign purchases to the value of 1 dollar that is thus covered. It is a loan; but what is its counterpart?

The conclusion we are seeking is as follows: income A spent for the domestic payment of surplus imports becomes the property of R's economy. The loan of 1 dollar by non-residents has two effects.

1 It means the appropriation of an income A, equivalent to 1 dollar, by R.
2 This sum of income A will be spent towards the future export of a product of economy A.

If we stopped here, the charge of external debt would inevitably be double, so that the reform would have no effect.

For what reason would the charge [of 1 dollar] be double, equal to 2 dollars? The sum borrowed, 1 dollar in an income R, would be spent, a debit that would add to the loss of the equivalent of 1 dollar in an income A.

For what reason would any reduction of this charge to 1 dollar be impossible? The payment of the net import in an income A would definitely be impossible. This is so because foreign sellers require to be paid in money R. The payment in money A occurs nonetheless, but the income A spent by importers is the monetary object of the loan granted by R, which will spend this sum of income A, equivalent to 1 dollar, to pay for the real goods produced in a future period and exported by A's economy.

There is a possible move, but only one, which avoids the loss of income A spent by the domestic economy of country A for the payment of surplus imports to the value of 1 dollar: that the country, mechanically, lends 1 dollar on the financial market to the rest of the world. The deficit country thus obtains, in financial assets, an external credit of 1 dollar that compensates exactly the debt of 1 dollar formed by the foreign borrowing of this sum. The result is the full success of the reform.

Instead of being paid both by a domestic income and by a foreign loan, surplus imports are paid abroad only by R itself, which lends the necessary sum of money

R to the deficit country. The fact remains that imports-without-exports are first settled by a domestic income. Country A's importers spend, for the equivalent of 1 dollar, an income formed by their national economy. What is entirely new is essential: the income A thus spent remains the property of country A, the rest of the world obtaining only the equivalent of this sum, in money R. The sovereign Bureau obtains free of cost 1 unit of income A, a profit that it transfers directly to its national government's budget.

Surplus imports, paid by the sovereign Bureau, no longer create an external debt for the deficit countries

This progress is so unexpected, bizarre we might say, that this crucial idea of the working of the reform is likely to be misunderstood and unenforceable. Moreover, would the nullity of deficit countries' external debts not amount to the pure and simple suppression of the justified credits of surplus countries? How would their net exports be paid if countries that import more than they export are not bound by any debt to the countries that export more than they import?

The first main ideas do not provide an advantage for deficit countries at the expense of countries whose exports are net. So far the reform creates a true 'system' of international payments favourable to all countries, to creditors as well as to debtors. Would the present main idea thus not be radically different and unacceptable? Would the country that granted itself the nullity of its foreign indebtedness despite its net imports, not be unjust to such a degree that it should be legitimately condemned and abandoned by the rest of the world?

In reality, however, the nullity of external debts is the only logical and scientifically accurate form of all international payments as far as deficit countries as well as surplus countries (thus deprived of any international claim) are concerned.

In brief, it is not at all true that the external payments of countries whose exports exceed their imports can only be completed if they obtain a credit on deficit countries. Instead of guaranteeing the credits of surplus countries, the formation of deficit countries' external debt is counterproductive and harmful to them. Countries whose exports are net are protected by the reform, one effect of which will be to cancel the formation of any external debt of deficit countries. Let us recall in a few words the reason why every country is positively paid without delay in the very period in which it has a surplus.

Let us consider again the analysis of countries A and R. Country A's 'deficit' is of 1 dollar. Before the reform, A contracts an external debt of 1 dollar to cover its deficit. The sovereign Bureau's action, on the contrary, will assure that country A's external debt will increase by 0 dollars. At this point what is of interest to us is not country A, but country R. Will it be injured by the cancellation of the deficit country's external debt? Quite to the contrary, country R is fully paid in the very period in which it is in surplus.

Let us compare the income obtained from abroad by country R with the external income obtained by country A. We find exactly the same gain when the reform is

166 *Bernard Schmitt*

implemented by country A. Indeed, country R obtains an external credit of 1 dollar. This is precisely the foreign credit of country A. Apart from the transfer generated by the Bureau, this initial credit of country A is the external payment of its net imports.

It is obvious that the credit obtained by R has exactly the same effect in the opposite direction: being of an external origin it brings to this country the payment of an import of equal value. This means that R's imports to the value of 1 dollar are paid by country A and not by country R. If we say, correctly, that country A obtains an income formed by the domestic production of economy R, it would be illogical and deeply unfair to judge that country R loses the benefit of its net sales, because it obtains the payment of part of its own imports by an external loan. The exact terms of the comparison are as follows.

1 Country A imports real assets equivalent to 11 dollars but pays 10 dollars for them, the additional value being provided by country R's economy.
2 Country R imports real assets equivalent to 10 dollars but pays for them only to the extent of 9 dollars, the difference being settled by economy A, from which a product equal to 1 dollar is lent by Bureau A to non-residents.

From this twofold fact we derive that R owes A exactly what A owes R. As a consequence, if country R does not get indebted to country A, it is logical, perfectly correct and just that country A does not get indebted to country R.

It would be pointless to directly discard the external loan of 1 dollar that country A obtains for its net imports of this value. We would simply go back to the starting position without a change. We thus maintain the loan as it stood before the reform. But the sovereign Bureau adds a reverse loan. We thus have the coexistence of two equal-size financial transactions, which 'contradict' one another: the loan of 1 dollar granted by R to A is offset by the loan of 1 dollar granted by A's Bureau to non-residents. It is understood that borrowers and lenders in the economy R are distinct residents.

The goal is thus achieved, because country R can no longer become the owner of real goods that country A will produce in the future (see Chapter 9); the loan made by R to A is of a zero sum. Thereby one precludes country A's net import to the value of 1 dollar costing 2 dollars.

According to what we already know about the task that will be carried out by the reform, the correct statement is that net imports cost nothing at all to the deficit country, which has 'borrowed-lent' instead of simply borrowing 1 dollar abroad. The essential goal is thus reached, because the sum to the value of 1 dollar formed in the domestic income of economy A is no longer earned by the rest of the world. As we know well, it is the property of its Bureau and, ultimately, of its government.

We can now complete the explanation of the reform.

Country A, which has so far carried out only a 'borrowing-lending', has still to borrow 1 dollar abroad in order to obtain the foreign currency it needs to settle its surplus import. The new external loan of 1 dollar brings at the precise level of 1 dollar the foreign currency obtained from abroad in addition to the payment of its imports-exports.

Borrowing-lending of 1 dollar + borrowing of 1 dollar =
1 dollar in net borrowing

The last act really worth mentioning concerns the external debt that country A carries because of its second indebtedness of 1 dollar contracted abroad. The challenge consists again in overcoming appearances to access factual reality. We first have the impression that the second loan simply confirms the first because it reproduces it. The first loan is cancelled by the loan that the Bureau grants to R. But the second loan has the immediate effect of replacing the first, giving country A the means to finance its net imports. Everything happens as if the third loan 'cancelled the cancellation' of the first. If this were indeed the case, the country's external debt would rise by 1 dollar as a result of its external debt contracted in each period by its deficit of 1 dollar. At the thirtieth period, for example of a month (therefore in a very short time), country A's external debt would already be thirty times higher than its current deficit, that is, 30 dollars instead than 1 dollar.

This is not at all the case. Reality is much simpler. The external debt does not increase at all: in the sum of periods elapsed, where imports are nevertheless 1 dollar in surplus in each period, country A's external debt is only equal to the current deficit of its imports, that is, 1 dollar only.

It is difficult to accept this conclusion, because it seems to contradict 'common sense'. The serious observation of facts nonetheless confirms it. It would be wrong to add to one another the two loans that country A contracts abroad in each period. The second loan is indeed only the reproduction of the first. It is certain therefore that the loan granted by country A compensates both the second and the first loan to country A. The total borrowing of the deficit country, which is equal to 1 dollar in each period, is thus finally and completely cancelled.

The economists of the sovereign Bureau will know well that their country borrows only once the value of its net imports. To cancel this loan only once and to renew it afterwards does not change anything, because the second loan identifies itself with the first. The identity of these two loans does not simply follow from the fact that their value is the same. There is much more to it, because the second loan produces a second time the first, nothing more. Deficit country A is therefore subject by its second borrowing to the only debt created by the first. Country A's external debt is initially of $(1 - 1=) 0$ dollars since the Bureau also lends 1 dollar. Eventually, the debt incurred is of 1 dollar because of the second loan. Since the credit that adds to it is of 1 dollar, the 'experts' of the Bureau have no choice but to add -1 dollar to $+1$ dollar, which gives the value of their country's indebtedness, at 0 dollars, an excellent conclusion, although a little unexpected.

However, the fact that deficit countries suffer no increase of their external debts is not really strange. Even scholars of the Troika recognise this sometimes; according to them the only external debts that increase in time are sovereign debts. That would be correct if, at least, sovereign debts really existed. But the reform

168   *Bernard Schmitt*

will prevent their existence. How are we to understand then that deficit countries will avoid any foreign debt? It is not as difficult as it seems. Let us think again about the fact that in each period country A runs a deficit of 1 dollar. If the value of its national production is of 150 dollars, this only means that 1 dollar out of these 150 dollars comes from abroad. This gap between the goods produced domestically, to the value of 149 dollars, and the goods produced abroad, to the value of 1 dollar, is repeated over time, in each period where the value of net imports is of 1 dollar. It is obvious that the country's external debt does not increase as much at all. By abolishing the sovereign debt, the Bureau will also enforce the cancellation of any external debt formed by net imports.

New presentation of the reform

Let us analyse, with reference to a given period, an outflow of foreign currency equal to 14 dollars and an inflow equal to 10 dollars. This gap in dollars between an outflow of 14 and an inflow of 10 is assumed to have existed for a long time in the same successive periods. There are two definitions of national income; in each period the new product is the real income produced, denoted $inc(A)\ P$; the corresponding monetary income is $inc(A)\ M$. We first show that the country's income would be 4 dollars higher if country A's exports were equal to its imports.

Domestic income = 154 dollars if $exp\ (A) = imp\ (A) = 14$ dollars

To the extent that there is equality between country A's exports and imports, the monetary income formed in money A remains fully available in economy A: the income A spent is replaced by the income A obtained. Yet, with respect to the net expenditures of foreign currency, 14 dollars are spent while only 10 dollars are earned.

There is a difference between monetary and real incomes caused by the net expenditures in dollars:

$inc(A)\ P - inc(A)\ M = 4$ dollars

If this difference were not taken into account, the value of the national product of each period would be $inc(A)\ P = 154$ dollars. Yet, the income produced in real goods cannot remain at this level; on the contrary it falls in line with the value of the monetary income available for the purchase of national output. As this value is reduced by 4 dollars, the level of real production is reduced accordingly, from the value of 154 to the value of 150 dollars. The value of the national product of each period is thus $inc(A)\ P = 150$ dollars.

It has just been shown that countries experience a decrease in their domestic employment to the extent that their expenditures exceed their receipts. It is not obvious at first that this is so, because the only money that matters in this respect is MA and not money R (MR). It is true that country A spends more MR (dollars) than it earns. But does country A spend more MA than it earns? If this is not the case, then net expenditures have no effect on the level of employment, since the expenditures of foreign currency (dollars) do not impact unemployment, which is in no way increased by it. Now, the net expenditure of money A is highly unlikely, since R is always paid in dollars; it is never paid in units of money A. We thus have the impression that employment cannot decrease despite the difference of 4 between expenditures and receipts in foreign currency.

Yet a doubt arises immediately, since we do not yet know the identity of those people who become the owners of the 4 units of money A spent for the net purchases. We consider the simplest of cases, where 1 unit of money A has the same value as 1 dollar.

The identity of people receiving money A spent on the imports balanced by exports is obvious: they are country A's exporters. But the surplus is a source of trouble, because the value of exports is, in this case, zero. Only a rather complicated reflection solves the problem. It is clear, first, that imports are fully paid; the expenditure corresponding to them is of 14 dollars and not of only 10 dollars. But what can be the use of the 4 units of money A that pay for no export of country A? To say that they remain available within economy A is a contradiction in terms, since these 4 units of MA are spent just like the 10 MA that pay compensated exports. But to claim, on the contrary, that this sum of 4 MA is finally to be found in the economy of the rest of the world is equally unsatisfactory, because all imports are paid abroad in foreign currency.

We have nevertheless promised a satisfactory explanation. Here it is. To the extent of its net expenditures of foreign currencies, precisely equal to 4 MR, net imports pay country R's exports; for their complement, of 4 MA, the domestic settlement of imports is but the payment of A's exports that this country is obliged to pay instead of R. The whole sum of income in money A that is spent in the purchase of dollars is thus obtained by A's exporters instead of being in part (4 value units) added to the income available for the purchase of national output. This explains why the domestic income of economy A, formed in money A, is reduced by 4 MA relative to real income, which is therefore also reduced accordingly. If, over time, country A's production was of 154 units of value per period, it would only be equal to 150 units owing to the effect caused by its net imports.

The aim of the reform can thus be defined in terms both simple and highly desirable: unemployment in the economy should in no way increase because of the highly undesirable but certain effect of its net expenditures of foreign currency (dollars). Thanks to the reform, the production of economy A will remain at the level of 154 units of value instead of being reduced to the value of 150 dollars by the (pernicious and not yet corrected) effect of the net expenditure, in each period, of a value of 4 dollars.

What we can show again, starting from the decrease of the domestic income of the deficit country, which has so far been ignored, is the fact that, without the reform, it pays twice its net purchases. The demonstration of this fact is especially easy now: the charge imposed by surplus purchases is at first the equal decrease of domestic employment. Even though country A suffers from the decrease in its employment, reduced from 154 to 150 units of value (dollars), it must still borrow

4 dollars abroad in order to cover the surplus of its expenditures in dollars; on the whole, country A is therefore debited for twice 4 dollars, while its net purchases of foreign currency are equal only to a value of 4 dollars.

But what is equally important to note here is the fact that the reduction of the employment of country A's domestic economy is harmful to the rest of the world. The reform is therefore necessary both for deficit countries and for their partners in the rest of the world.

The fundamental error of the Troika is not only to forcibly pursue deficit countries to ensure that they pay their sovereign debts; the authors of this 'trilogy' are wrong a second time, because they do not understand (yet) that creditor countries themselves suffer from the current regime of international payments. Reforming the foreign currency payment of 'poor' countries for their net purchases is also acting in favour of 'rich' countries. If the reform had no other purpose than to restore the justice with respect to deficit countries' external payments, it would still be fully justified, but its success would be doubtful, because 'rich' countries such as Germany would oppose it. It is fortunate that the reform concerns all countries, whether creditors or debtors. The essential action of the reform will be to prevent the pernicious effect of the surplus of foreign currency expenditures over receipts, that is, the decrease in the deficit country's employment. It is obviously favourable to countries whose sales exceed their purchases on the international scene that unemployment does not increase in their partners' economies. This is precisely the aim of the reform.

But how, by what factual method, can the reform be implemented? How is it possible to maintain economy A's employment at the level of 154 dollars when it spends 4 dollars more than its earnings?

Nothing is nevertheless modified if the government is satisfied with using this profit as an amount of income A corresponding simply to an income already waiting to be spent. The reform requires that the government's profit finances new, additional production in economy A (Figure 10.1).

Thanks to the reform, national production remains equal to 154 dollars. This gain provides a real advantage for both countries, R and A. Regarding country R, whose gain is unilaterally pursued by the Troika, it is good for it to become the owner of the value of 4 dollars that increases economy A's national production to the level of 154 dollars instead than 150 dollars. Concerning country A, this

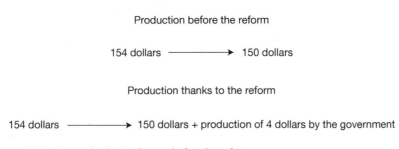

Figure 10.1 A's production before and after the reform.

A one-country reform   171

increase of its domestic production, being entirely due to the additional employment generated by the government's action, decreases in the proportion of 4/150 the level of unemployment of the country. This reduction of under-employment will add to the advantage already obtained through the cancellation of external debts.

Let us explain in some detail, albeit quickly, how the reform will work, the domestic income of the deficit country affecting production and not the national output already produced. Economists traditionally analyse the expenditures of income as 'purchases' of already existing products. The sale of national output, whose value is of 154 dollars, is the result of the expenditure of the corresponding monetary income. The entire expenditure of income A formed by national production belongs therefore to the transactions referring to the goods that have already been produced. In this sense production is prior to the expenditure of the income it creates. The case introduced by the reform is directly opposed to already existent expenditures. If expenditures of income formed in money A were all for purchases of pre-existent goods, the net expenditures of foreign currency (dollars) would compulsorily lead to the reduction of national income, whose value would only be of 150 instead than 154 dollars. It is the implementation of a completely different method of intervention that allows the reform to maintain national production at the value of 154 dollars. The solution presents no difficulty. It is necessary and sufficient that the domestic income spent for the payment of net expenditures be the gain of the government, a sum to be used only towards additional national production.

At the outset it is clear that R is not paid in units of money A. It is therefore 'normal' that country A pays in money R (dollars) for its net purchases of foreign assets. It is not at all surprising under these circumstances that the domestic income spent on these net purchases remains the property of country A even though it has been spent, as for balanced purchases, by its importers. Income in money A is of no interest to country R's exporters; it is therefore logical that this income remains the property of country A. On the other hand, it would be awkward if the income spent in domestic currency on the net imports of economy A were to be held as straightforward purchasing power by the government. In this truly inefficient case, country A's national production would remain reduced by the value of the net purchases of foreign assets.

In order to maintain the domestic production of its national economy unchanged at the level of a value equal to 154 dollars, it is imperative that its government or its budget obtains more than a mere purchasing power: it must obtain the power to produce and not just to buy. It is certain that the power to produce is legitimate and effective, and avoids inflation, only if the money available for this purpose defines, despite everything, a perfectly legitimate purchasing power. Properly defined, a 'power of production' is, at the same time, a positive purchasing power. The 4-dollar-value profit in national money (MA) obtained by the government of the deficit country is the power to purchase, to this extent, the domestic product unchanged. This, however, does not prevent the government from spending this amount of money A to employ people who would otherwise remain unemployed.

172   *Bernard Schmitt*

Let us say it once more: the rest of the world, R, is in no way disadvantaged since it is not interested in any payment in money A.

But what exactly is the gain that country R obtains from country A? It is necessary that this gain exists and is equal to 4 dollars since A's net expenditure is of this very amount. The correct answer is to say that the exporters of R receive the 4 dollars that country A borrows abroad. However the problem is a little more complicated. It is easy to understand that the foreign borrowing of 4 dollars brings to economy A the power to pay the surplus of its imports. But how is this loan repaid, paid back in turn? In this regard we note first the essential: country R becomes the owner not of the 'personal' product of A's government, but of the equivalent of this product in any of the goods of 150 dollars' value produced by economy A in addition to its government.

> Product of the government: value equal to 4 dollars
> Product of the domestic economy: value equal to 150 dollars
> Credit of economy R: 4 of these 150 dollars

Country R is thus paid twice a value of 4 dollars.

- It obtains the 4 dollars that A borrows abroad.
- It becomes the owner of real goods worth 4 dollars that are part of the product of the 150 dollars' value of country A's domestic economy created in addition to the goods of 4 dollars' value produced by its government.

Only one thing remains to be settled, namely that everyone gets what each expects out of the workings of the reform. Country A upholds the property of the total value, undiminished, of the income formed by its national economy; it is true that it 'loses' the 4 dollars that it spends in payment of its net imports, but in fact it obtains 4 dollars from this 'loss', the value of the foreign goods that it acquires through its zero export. Country R is not in the least harmed, because on one side it gives up real goods out of its own product, while on the other side it cancels this expenditure, because it obtains the equivalent of the additional goods produced by the government of country A. A's importers pay for the totality of their purchases, 10 for the imports balanced by exports of A, and 4 for the benefit of their government. R's exporters are paid in money R by R's importers, the missing payment being replaced by the loan of 4 dollars. This loan of R to A is cancelled by the loan in reverse that takes place at the moment country A sends 4 dollars to country R as payment for the equivalent of the domestic production of country A's government.

Afterword
Bernard Schmitt and heterodox economics

Sergio Rossi

Introduction

The research work of Bernard Schmitt is little known outside the French-speaking area, because the majority of his books are in French rather than English. To be true, there are an important and increasing number of (authored or coedited) volumes, as well as peer-reviewed papers, on quantum macroeconomics written in English. They concern either domestic or international issues in monetary macroeconomics, generally focusing on specific topics like inflation, unemployment, the international monetary architecture, European monetary union, the global financial crisis, and external debt servicing (see, for instance, Schmitt 1973, 1996a; Cencini and Schmitt 1991; Cencini 1996, 2010; Rossi 2001, 2004a, 2004b, 2006a, 2007a, 2007b, 2009a, 2010, 2011a; Bradley 2003; Cencini and Rossi 2015). Another set of published work concerns more theoretical and methodological issues, such as the nature, emission, and purchasing power of money, general equilibrium theory, Keynes's macroeconomic analysis, monetary circuit theory, and post-Keynesian economics (see, for example, Schmitt 1972a, 1982, 1986, 1988b, 1996b; Cencini 1982, 1984, 1988, 1995, 1997b, 2001, 2003, 2005; Schmitt and Cencini 1982; Bradley, Friboulet and Gnos 1996; Schmitt and Greppi 1996; Gnos 1998, 2003; Rossi 1998, 2003, 2006b; 2007c, 2008a, 2008b, 2009b, 2011b; Bailly 2003; Schmitt and De Gottardi 2003; Gnos and Rossi 2012).

In all these writings, Schmitt and his scholars widely discuss and provide criticisms of the relevant literature, be it in the orthodox or heterodox domain. In particular, Schmitt and Cencini are the authors, within quantum macroeconomics, who focus more on their critiques of orthodox economic thinking, whilst other scholars in the Schmitt school are more interested in heterodox economics.

Although a clear-cut classification of all these writings by the Schmitt school cannot be established, because a number of them refer to both orthodox and heterodox economics, either on conceptual and methodological grounds or as regards specific macroeconomic issues concerning the domestic or international economy, let us provide a structured and comprehensive survey of all these writings as regards, particularly, heterodox economics. The next section presents the similarities and differences with respect to other heterodox schools in economics at conceptual and methodological levels. The third section offers a

174   *Sergio Rossi*

synthesis of these similarities and differences in the investigation of specific real-world issues from a quantum macroeconomics perspective. The last section concludes briefly.

Similarities and differences on conceptual and methodological grounds

The starting point of Schmitt's investigation was triggered by his deep dissatisfaction with a theoretical approach to economic analysis that lacks conceptual rigour and is vitiated by logical contradictions, namely general equilibrium theory (Schmitt 1966a, 1972a; Cencini 1982). Considering the Walrasian model of a pure exchange economy, with n agents and n commodities, Schmitt was able to show that the existence of any (competitive) equilibrium is logically impossible. Further, he also proved that relative prices are a figment of the imagination, as they cannot be determined in such a model. Both these fundamental critiques have to do with the nature of money, which, as Schmitt argued, is not an essentially physical 'medium of exchange' but actually a purely numerical means of payment, issued by banks every time a payment has to be carried out. This argument has relevance in the debate between exogenous and endogenous money theorists (see Rochon and Rossi 2013). As such, it can be appreciated by heterodox economists who consider money to be of an endogenous magnitude. In fact, however, the majority of these economists are not really able to detach themselves from the (orthodox) view that sees money as the general equivalent of 'non-monetary' items (goods, services, and assets), as explained by Rossi (2001: Ch. 4). In other words, these economists are unaware that payments are not relative but absolute exchanges, whereby their objects are transformed from a real into a monetary form, or vice versa, depending on the kind of markets where these payments occur (see Schmitt 1984a).

Sticking to logical thinking, Schmitt explained that the logical starting point of analysis, in economics, must be production, because the objects of any payment must logically be produced before being sold on the marketplace. This principle may be easily accepted – and indeed is largely adopted – by heterodox economists, who argue against the view, adopted by neoclassical authors, that production and consumption are two faces of the same market event in chronological time. However, once again, Schmitt parts company with the other strands of heterodox economics, as he considers that production, as any other economic transaction, is an absolute rather than a relative exchange. When a wage earner is paid for his/her effort in any economic activity, s/he obtains the result of this effort in its monetary form, that is, a bank deposit, which is indeed the produced output. As Schmitt (1984a: 347, our translation) explained, in the payment of the wage bill,

> workers receive *their own product* in money. This transaction does not merely define an equivalence, but an identity: every worker gets a sum of money that, because of its being issued through the payment of the wage bill, identifies itself with the real output of this same worker.

Afterword 175

This absolute exchange, whereby a single object, produced output, is transformed (from a real into a monetary form), is essentially very different from a relative exchange, whereby money and non-monetary items are supposedly exchanged against each other. In an absolute exchange, produced output is transformed into a bank deposit and disappears as such when the payment of the relevant wage bill occurs, to reappear again once the deposit owner transforms this deposit into a real object and thereby consumes the latter in economic terms. This contrasts with all other heterodox explanations of market exchanges, which assume that 'money' (that is, bank deposits) and output co-exist as two essentially separate objects in chronological time.

The Schmitt analysis of production is also different from other heterodox views on this as regards the so-called factor market. Schmitt is the author who has most consistently, and rigorously, elaborated on Keynes's (1936: 213–14) argument that labour is the sole true factor of production. This is so because only the remuneration of labour gives rise to the relevant number of wage units, the total amount of which defining the current wage bill is the economic measure of all produced goods and services (inclusive of capital goods).

> So stated, this result seems to be very similar to the classical (pre-classical in Keynes' own terms) theory of value. In fact, it differs from it on a small but very essential point: the monetary measure of labour. According to the classics, labour is measured in physical units, whereas Keynes' basic unit is a monetary one. Wages are then the objective link between money and product, a link that is the direct result of the process of creation called production. Two main difficulties never overcome by the classics are thereby avoided, namely the physical heterogeneity of labour and the integration of money into the real world.
>
> (Cencini 1982: 134)

Hence, the Schmitt school agrees with other heterodox schools of economic thought that production factors are not really paid according to their 'marginal' product and that their compensation is rather a matter of power relations. It may also converge on arguing that capital is the result of labour, hence that profit is an income derived from wages. But the Schmitt school parts company with other heterodox approaches regarding the fact that a monetary production economy is actually based on the wage unit as the sole precise and objective measure of economic activity taken as a whole: "[u]ltimately, the *number* of wage units issued is the *measure* of the product of the economy" (Schmitt 1984a: 458; our translation). This contrasts with post-Keynesian economics, in so far as its authors consider the wage unit simply as a unit of money paid out to wage earners in a relative exchange (see, among several others, Bradford and Harcourt 1997). As Schmitt (1986: 118) explained, for the whole economic system "[t]he unit of measurement is the wage unit, because monetary wages define the equivalence of form and substance, that is, of the product and the number of units of money paid out in wages" across all production sectors (that is, those producing consumption goods and those producing capital goods).

176   *Sergio Rossi*

Analogously to production, consumption is also an absolute exchange, whereby income (in the form of bank deposits) is transformed into its physical object, that is, a good or a service that is thereby consumed in economic (though not necessarily in physical) terms when the relevant payment occurs.

The Schmitt approach to economics defines thereby a macroeconomic event as an event that concerns the economic system as a whole. Indeed both production and consumption affect the whole economic system as the former increases national income and the latter reduces it as a result of the underlying transactions. This approach provides therefore an original, and operational, understanding separating microeconomic and macroeconomic events, thereby rejecting any microfoundations of macroeconomics (see notably Cencini 2005). Clearly, it is logically impossible to aggregate individual behaviour or bundles of goods, to switch from micro- to macroeconomics. Hence, the representative agent is not in a position to deliver any input to macroeconomic analysis, as Martel (1996: 128) also pointed out when he argued that "the representative agent methodology described above is a gross fallacy of composition which disqualifies *any* kind of microfoundation from being a logically consistent and complete foundation for macroeconomics".

An analogous reasoning applies if we move from the domestic to the international level of economic analysis: the Schmitt school of thought points out that the international economy (not to be confused with the world economy) is the economic space where the agents are the countries themselves, each defined as the set of its own residents. This space, which of course does not exist on physical ground, is notably an exchange economy, because all output is the result of production – which cannot but occur within domestic economies, even though an increasing number of products are actually the result of a 'value chain' that involves several countries (each of them being a monetary economy of production). Now, as Schmitt and his scholars have explained, the international economy is affected by monetary disorder, in so far as international transactions are paid using a national – instead of a truly international – currency, considered 'as if' it were a net asset, which, moreover, can trespass the borders of the issuing banking system 'as if' it were similar to a commodity like gold.

Clearly, the so-called 'dollar standard', whereby the US dollar is considered as the 'key currency' of the world economy, is a non-system for international payments, because, in fact, no US dollar can leave the US banking system and is a purely numerical counter as the latter system enters it in its own books whenever it carries out a payment. This is not original of course, since both Rueff (1963) and Williamson (1977) pointed out that such a dollar-based international monetary regime is essentially vitiated. Nevertheless, there is an important contribution of the Schmitt analysis in this regard, namely its focus on a logical (rather than behavioural) critique of that regime as well as an operational way to solve the underlying monetary–structural problems with a fundamental reform proposal, as suggested by Schmitt (1973) originally.

Since the 1980s, Schmitt has been declining this reform proposal also at regional level, notably as regards the projects of European monetary union that

Afterword 177

were discussed at that time. A perusal of Schmitt (1988a) shows how his analysis was and still is relevant at the time of writing, to provide the European Union countries with a common currency that both is a means of final payment for their foreign trade and allows each of them to keep their monetary sovereignty (that is, their monetary policy decision-making process with regard, particularly, to the policy rates of interest). Both are indeed crucial, and the lack of them is a key factor of the euro-area crisis actually (see Rossi 2007b, 2012). This is a subject area where some post-Keynesian economists might find a strong argument that, on analytical grounds, strengthens their own critiques to the euro-area project and (lack of) governance. Elaborating on Keynes's proposals for an International Clearing Union, which he presented at the 1944 Bretton Woods conference unsuccessfully, these authors, working in the heterodox tradition, could find it useful to consider the Schmitt approach on endogenous money grounds with respect to the international monetary architecture – both in Europe and at the global level – provided that they are prepared to abandon the conventional view that considers money as an asset entering into a (relative) exchange, whereby money and 'non-monetary' items change their position in the relevant space, across time and country borders.

This leads us to discuss a variety of real-world issues analysed by the Schmitt school, to point out the similarities and differences with respect to other heterodox approaches that are worth considering in this regard.

Similarities and differences on real-world economic issues

As pointed out in the previous section, Schmitt provided an original analysis of money on conceptual grounds. This has given rise to a series of macroeconomic investigations, which we may consider dividing into domestic and international economic issues.

As regards the domestic economy, which Schmitt addressed first, we may single out the analysis of inflation and unemployment. This analysis is indeed original in Schmitt, as it distances itself from all other (orthodox or heterodox) studies in these domains, which, it is true to say, have been kept fundamentally separate by both traditions – whilst they are part of the same problem according to the Schmitt analysis (see Cencini 1996, 2005 and Cencini and Rossi 2015).

As regards inflation, one must first of all define this phenomenon conceptually, in order to assess (not to say measure) its outcome correctly, so that the appropriate policy could be adopted eventually. The Schmitt definition of inflation is rather unusual, because the emphasis is not put on its effect on the goods market (that is, an increase in prices), but rather on its essence – to wit, a loss in money's purchasing power. On this account, it is plain that the Schmitt analysis of inflation is ontologically different from all other ones, in both the orthodox and heterodox traditions (both of which define inflation simply as an increase in the relevant price level). As a matter of fact, there are different reasons in the real world behind an increase in a given price level, not all of which can be ascribed to a loss in the purchasing power of money (that is, inflation): State's intervention or the market

178   *Sergio Rossi*

structure may be such that the relevant price level increases, without there being any inflationary pressure, because the relationship between the amount of bank deposits and the volume of produced output is unaltered in the economic system as a whole (see Rossi 2001).

Schmitt (1984a) explains notably that inflation does not result from agents' behaviour, in contrast to so-called 'demand-pull' and 'cost-push' theories of inflation, but emerges as a result of a monetary–structural disorder affecting the domestic payments system. This, eventually, has to do with how banks enter these payments in their bookkeeping system, which is not in a position to distinguish money, credit and capital explicitly (see Cencini 2001). This disorder stems notably from the banks' recording of the investment of profit and accumulation of capital by the relevant firms. Notice that the problem is not, really, the functional distribution of income – as argued for instance by post-Keynesian authors in the Marxian tradition – but concerns the mechanics of banks' bookkeeping, which at the time of writing is quite rudimentary in this regard. As Schmitt (1984a) explains, there is an inflationary gap when the investment of profit gives rise to a new bank deposit that is 'empty', since its content (produced output) is appropriated, on the labour market, by what Schmitt (1984a) calls a "depersonified firm". Whilst this gap may be filled by output previously accumulated (when firms' profit has been formed), it remains void of content when firms amortize their accumulated capital, as the latter is owned by a depersonified firm, and thereby continues to increase pathologically (see, for instance, Cencini 2005: Ch. 8).

This pathological capital accumulation gives rise to (involuntary) unemployment when firms decide to reduce their production level in order to increase their profit rates, since the latter are reduced by capital overaccumulation (see Cencini and Rossi 2015: Ch. 7). In spite of the logical identity between nominal income (global demand) and produced output (global supply), supply is higher than demand in real terms on the goods market, when wage earners receive an income that is the result of an emission of empty money: although nominally identical, demand and supply are really different on the market for produced goods and services, since demand is lower than supply by the whole amount of empty money issued by banks in the amortization of accumulated capital. Therefore the firm sector reduces the output level, thereby creating (involuntary) unemployment, which is thus indeed the result of a monetary–structural disorder rather than of agents' behaviour (as argued by post-Keynesian economists).

Eventually, capital overaccumulation and the related phenomena of inflation as well as unemployment induce a financial crisis across the domestic economy. Contrary to both orthodox and heterodox economics, in fact, such a crisis does not result simply from the agents' behaviour, but from a structural–monetary disorder that Schmitt identified through a conceptually rigorous and logically sound macroeconomic analysis, departing from a variety of firmly-held beliefs – which indeed he showed to be fully wrong on analytical grounds.

Elaborating on this, Schmitt and his scholars have then extended their investigations to the international economy, considering in particular the international monetary regime, based on a few so-called 'key currencies'. In this regard, Schmitt (1973) opened the way to a novel, and far-reaching, analysis of the current international monetary architecture, providing a crystal-clear argument supporting a structural reform of that architecture, to make sure that all payments between countries are final – instead of being just promised as in the current "non-system" for international payments (Williamson 1977: 73). As we noted already, this reform proposal elaborates on the spirit of the Keynes Plan, avoiding the shortcomings of the latter as regards both the emission of a supranational currency – the bancor in Keynes's Plan – and the final payment of international transactions (Rossi 2006a, 2007b, 2009a). The Schmitt plan has then been developed in the framework of a regional monetary union, namely the euro area, to show the merits of a common (rather than a single) currency for a variety of still heterogeneous member countries (see among others Schmitt 1988a and Rossi 2004a, 2004b). Cencini (2001b) has notably proposed a series of international payment systems structured into separate layers at regional level, all of which are interconnected at the world level through an international clearing bank.

During the last twenty years of his life, Schmitt worked intensively, and rather exclusively, on an issue that remains fully unnoticed beyond the Schmitt school, namely, the duplication of countries' external debts (see Schmitt 2012c, 2014). This issue is also the most difficult to understand in monetary macroeconomics, because of the confusion that pervades the economics profession between a country's debt and public debt, that is to say, the debt of the general government sector. As the euro-area crisis has shown, the large majority of economists consider this crisis to be a 'sovereign debt' crisis, although they use this expression to indicate a crisis originated by public debt. In fact, as Schmitt argued extensively, sovereign debt is the debt of the country as a whole, which owes to the rest of the world a net amount of income even though this country's residents already have, collectively, a debt to some non-residents (to wit, their foreign creditors). There is indeed a difference between a country (defined as the set of its residents) and the sum of the economic agents residing in it: the former exists as a result of the existence of its own national currency. Through a series of logical proofs, which Schmitt (2012c, 2014) provides at length considering different perspectives, he is able to show that the payment of a resident's foreign debt elicits an equivalent sovereign debt – for the country as a whole – which is totally unjustified on logical grounds and burdens this country in a pathological way.

Schmitt has not only clearly identified and explained the sovereign debt problem: he has also provided a reform strategy that each indebted country may put into practice to avert the formation of this debt and to earn, in each period, a net income corresponding to that it spends on its net imports. This issue should therefore be of some interest to heterodox scholars investigating external debt servicing and so-called 'global imbalances' at world level. Further, and more importantly, the Schmitt analysis of sovereign debt crises should be closely considered by those government officials (in so-called 'peripheral' countries within the euro area) that are in charge of public finance. Rather than imposing a series of unnecessary – and largely counterproductive – austerity policies, these officials should carefully study the analysis of sovereign debt developed by

180　*Sergio Rossi*

Schmitt, to elaborate on the reform strategy Schmitt (2012c, 2014) proposed, in order to present a valid alternative to fiscal austerity, which cannot but aggravate the euro-area crisis instead of resolving it. A particularly strong interest in the Schmitt reform strategy should exist in Greece, which, as Cencini (2015) points out with regard to the 2003–13 period, would have allowed its government to earn more than 250 billion US dollars, to invest in the Greek economy in the interests of its own residents (rather than to inflate the international financial bubble).

Conclusion

As the chapters forming this volume have shown, the legacy of Bernard Schmitt's work is relevant and worth considering by all those who strive to understand the major issues that remain unsolved in our economic systems at both national and international level. It is, in particular, the task of heterodox economists to elaborate on a valid alternative to the mainstream approach to these issues, to contribute to the collective task of providing an economic policy framework that is sound on analytical grounds, in order to make sure it gives rise to the appropriate policy stance for the solution of these issues in the common interest of all stakeholders. The stakes are high but it is the economists' responsibility to rethink their profession anew, in light of the failures that the global economic crisis – which erupted in 2008 and whose negative consequences are still hampering the world at the time of writing – has revealed to all those able and willing to see them honestly.

Let us hope that the untiring efforts Bernard Schmitt made during his entire scientific career to understand and explain some of the most problematic issues in economics will be honoured by the current generation of economists. This would contribute to making the 'dismal science' a truly scientific approach to the working of our economic systems and the essential understanding of inflation, involuntary unemployment, financial crises, and sovereign debt problems. It would indeed be time to go beyond sterile discussions and a reciprocal ignorance between orthodox and heterodox economists to address the issues that pertain to economic analysis with a perspective to solve them, rather than aiming at increasing the number of the economists' publications *per se* without any positive effect across the economy and society at large – both of which are indeed instrumental for the well-being of everybody, including the economists themselves, and must be taken care of with a long-term perspective.

Bibliography

Arrow, K.J. (1951), *Social Choice and Individual Values*, New York: Wiley and Sons.

Bailly, J.-L. (2003), "On the macroeconomic foundations of the wage–price relationship", in L.-P. Rochon and S. Rossi (eds), *Modern Theories of Money: The Nature and Role of Money in Capitalist Economies*, Cheltenham, UK and Northampton, MA, USA: Edward Elgar, pp. 360–383.

Baranzini, M. (ed.) (1982), *Advances in Economic Theory*, Oxford, UK: Basil Blackwell.

Baranzini, M. and R. Scazzieri (eds) (1986), *Foundations of Economics: Structure of Inquiry and Economic Theory*, Oxford, UK: Basil Blackwell.

Baranzini, M. and A. Cencini (eds) (1987), *Contributi di analisi economica*, Bellinzona, Switzerland: Casagrande.

Barrère, A. (1979), *Déséquilibres économiques et contre-révolution keynésienne*, Paris: Economica.

Barrère, A. (ed.) (1985), *Keynes aujourd'hui: théories et politiques*, Paris: Economica.

Barrère, A. (ed.) (1988), *The Foundation of Keynesian Analysis*, London: Macmillan.

Beretta, E. (2013), *Il concetto di "nazione" nella macroeconomia monetaria internazionale: implicazioni attuali e prospettive future*, Lugano, Switzerland: University of Lugano, Ph.D. dissertation.

Beretta, E. (2014), "Der übersehene (und weitaus gefährlichere) Überschuldungstrend der Eurozone: doch keine Entwarnung in Sicht", *Orientierungen zur Wirtschafts- und Gesellschaftspolitik*, 139, pp. 52–55.

Borchert, M. (2001), *Außenwirtschaftslehre: Theorie und Politik*, Wiesbaden, Germany: Gabler Verlag.

Bradford, W. and G.C. Harcourt (1997), "Units and definitions", in G.C. Harcourt and P.A. Riach (eds), *A 'Second Edition' of The General Theory*, London and New York: Routledge, vol. I, pp. 107–131.

Bradley, X. (2003), "Involuntary unemployment and investment", in L.-P. Rochon and S. Rossi (eds), *Modern Theories of Money: The Nature and Role of Money in Capitalist Economies*, Cheltenham, UK and Northampton, MA, USA: Edward Elgar, pp. 384–408.

Bradley, X., J.-J. Friboulet and C. Gnos (1996), "From Keynes's to the modern analysis of inflation", in A. Cencini and M. Baranzini (eds), *Inflation and Unemployment: Contributions to a New Macroeconomic Approach*, London and New York: Routledge, pp. 107–134.

Bund der Steuerzahler Deutschland e.V. (2015), "Home", available at www.steuerzahler. de/Home/1692b637/index.html (accessed 24 May 2016).

182 Bibliography

Cencini, A. (1982), "The logical indeterminacy of relative prices", in M. Baranzini (ed.), *Advances in Economic Theory*, Oxford, UK and New York: Basil Blackwell and St. Martin's Press, pp. 126–136.

Cencini, A. (1984), *Time and the Macroeconomic Analysis of Income*, London and New York: Pinter Publishers and St. Martin's Press.

Cencini, A. (1988), *Money, Income and Time: A Quantum-Theoretical Approach*, London and New York: Pinter Publishers.

Cencini, A. (1995), *Monetary Theory, National and International*, London and New York: Routledge.

Cencini, A. (1996), "Inflation and deflation: the two faces of the same reality", in A. Cencini and M. Baranzini (eds), *Inflation and Unemployment: Contributions to a New Macroeconomic Approach*, London and New York: Routledge, pp. 17–60.

Cencini, A. (1997a), *Monetary Theory, National and International*, London and New York: Routledge.

Cencini, A. (1997b), "Review of A. Graziani's *La teoria monetaria della produzione*", *Structural Change and Economic Dynamics*, 8 (2), pp. 272–277.

Cencini, A. (2001a), *Monetary Macroeconomics: A New Approach*, London and New York: Routledge.

Cencini, A. (2001b), "What future for the international and the European monetary systems?", *Research Laboratory in Monetary Economics Working Paper*, no. 2.

Cencini, A. (2003), "IS–LM: a final rejection", in L.-P. Rochon and S. Rossi (eds), *Modern Theories of Money: The Nature and Role of Money in Capitalist Economies*, Cheltenham, UK and Northampton, MA, USA: Edward Elgar, pp. 295–321.

Cencini, A. (2005), *Macroeconomic Foundations of Macroeconomics*, London and New York: Routledge.

Cencini, A. (2008), *Elementi di macroeconomia monetaria*, Padua, Italy: CEDAM.

Cencini, A. (2010), "For a new system of international payments", *Banks and Bank Systems*, 5 (1), pp. 47–58.

Cencini, A. (2012), "Toward a macroeconomic approach to macroeconomics", in C. Gnos and S. Rossi (eds), *Modern Monetary Macroeconomics: A New Paradigm for Economic Policy*, Cheltenham, UK and Northampton, MA, USA: Edward Elgar, pp. 39–68.

Cencini, A. (2015), "The sovereign debt crisis: diagnosis and remedy. The case of Greece", University of Lugano, Switzerland, mimeo.

Cencini, A. and B. Schmitt (1976), *La pensée de Karl Marx: critique et synthèse*, Vol. I *La valeur*, Albeuve, Switzerland: Castella.

Cencini, A. and B. Schmitt (1977), *La pensée de Karl Marx: critique et synthèse*, Vol. II *La plus-value*, Albeuve, Switzerland: Castella.

Cencini, A. and B. Schmitt (1991), *External Debt Servicing: A Vicious Circle*, London and New York: Pinter Publishers.

Cencini, A. and B. Schmitt (1992), "Per la creazione di uno spazio monetario europeo garante della sovranità di ogni singolo paese", in R. Chopard (ed.), *Europa '93! E la piazza finanziaria svizzera?*, Lugano, Switzerland: Centro di Studi Bancari and Meta Edizioni, pp. 99–136.

Cencini, A. and M. Baranzini (eds) (1996), *Inflation and Unemployment: Contributions to a New Macroeconomic Approach*, London and New York: Routledge.

Cencini, A. and S. Rossi (2015), *Economic and Financial Crises: A New Macroeconomic Analysis*, Basingstoke, UK and New York: Palgrave Macmillan.

Cencini, A., M. Corti, R. Crivelli and B. Schmitt (1987), "Dossier economia ed epistemologia", *Bloc Notes*, 15–16, pp. 45–130.

Bibliography 183

Defoe, D. (1719/1920), *Robinson Crusoe*, New York: Charles Scribner's Sons.

Deleplace, G. and E.J. Nell (eds) (1996), *Money in Motion: The Post Keynesian and Circulation Approaches*, Basingstoke, UK and New York: Macmillan and St. Martin's Press.

Devillebichot, G. (1969), "Note sur les travaux de Bernard Schmitt", *Revue d'économie politique*, 79 (3), pp. 693–702.

Devillebichot, G. (1979), "Pour sortir enfin d'un régime inepte de « paiements » internationaux: le plan Bernard Schmitt", *Revue d'économie politique*, 89 (5), pp. 623–636.

Dieterlen, P. (1964), *L'idéologie économique*, Paris: Cujas.

Elliott, G.A. (1936), "Transfer of means-of-payment and the terms of international trade", *Canadian Journal of Economics and Political Science / Revue canadienne d'économie et de science politique*, 2 (4), pp. 481–492.

Eurostat (2015), "General government gross debt - annual data", available at http://ec.europa.eu/eurostat/tgm/refreshTableAction.do?tab=table&plugin=1&pcode=teina225&language=en (accessed 24 May 2016).

Feldstein, M. (2000), "Europe can't handle the euro", *Wall Street Journal*, 8 February, available at www.nber.org/feldstein/wj020800.html (accessed 24 May 2016).

Fieleke, N.S. (1996), "Unilateral international transfers: unrequited and generally unheeded", *New England Economic Review*, November/December, pp. 27–37.

Fischer, S. (2004), "Capital account liberalization and the role of the IMF", in *IMF Essays from a Time of Crisis: The International Financial System, Stabilization, and Development*, Cambridge, MA, USA and London: The MIT Press, pp. 117–133.

Fisher, I. (1906), *The Nature of Capital and Income*, London: Macmillan.

Galano III, A. (1994), "International Monetary Fund response to the Brazilian debt crisis: whether the effects of conditionality have undermined Brazil's national sovereignty?", *Pace International Law Review*, 6 (2), pp. 323–351.

Gnos, C. (1998), "The Keynesian identity of income and output", in P. Fontaine and A. Jolink (eds), *Historical Perspectives on Macroeconomics: Sixty Years After the General Theory*, London and New York: Routledge, pp. 40–48.

Gnos, C. (2003), "Circuit theory as an explanation of the complex real world", in L.-P. Rochon and S. Rossi (eds), *Modern Theories of Money: The Nature and Role of Money in Capitalist Economies*, Cheltenham, UK and Northampton, MA, USA: Edward Elgar, pp. 322–338.

Gnos, C. (2006), "French circuit theory", in P. Arestis and M. Sawyer (eds), *A Handbook of Alternative Monetary Economics*, Cheltenham, UK and Northampton, MA, USA: Edward Elgar, pp. 87–104.

Gnos, C. and B. Schmitt (1990), "Le circuit: réalité exhaustive", *Economies et sociétés*, 24 (2), pp. 63–74.

Gnos, C. and S. Rossi (eds) (2012), *Modern Monetary Macroeconomics: A New Paradigm for Economic Policy*, Cheltenham, UK and Northampton, MA, USA: Edward Elgar.

Graeber, D. (2011), *Debt: The First 5,000 Years*, New York: First Melville House.

Graziani, A. (1990), "The theory of the monetary circuit", *Economies et sociétés*, 24 (6), pp. 7–36.

Graziani, A. (2003), *The Monetary Theory of Production*, Cambridge, UK: Cambridge University Press.

Graziani, A. and M. Messori (eds) (1988), *Moneta e produzione*, Turin, Italy: Einaudi.

Hayek, F.A. (1931/1967), *Prices and Production*, New York: Augustus M. Kelly.

Hicks, J. (1967), *Critical Essays in Monetary Theory*, Oxford, UK: Clarendon Press.

184   Bibliography

Horsefield, J.K. (ed.) (1969), "Joint Statement by Experts on the Establishment of an International Monetary Fund, April 1944", *The International Monetary Fund 1945–1965: Twenty Years of International Monetary Cooperation*, Washington, DC: International Monetary Fund, pp. 128–135.

Hume, D. (1742), *Essays, Moral, Political, and Literary*, available online at www.econlib.org/library/LFBooks/Hume/hmMPL26.html (accessed 24 May 2016).

International Monetary Fund (2003), *Balance of Payments Statistics. Part 1: Country Tables. Yearbook 2003*, Washington, DC: International Monetary Fund.

International Monetary Fund (2009), *Balance of Payments and International Investment Position Manual – Sixth Edition (BPM6)*, Washington, DC: International Monetary Fund.

Irvine, C. (2009), "Goldman Sachs boss: 'bankers do God's work'", *The Telegraph*, 8 November, available at www.telegraph.co.uk/finance/newsbysector/banksandfinance/6524972/Goldman-Sachs-boss-bankers-do-Gods-work.html (accessed 24 May 2016).

Kalecki, M. and E.F. Schumacher (1943), "International clearing and long-term lending", *Bulletin of the Oxford University Institute of Statistics*, 5 (5), pp. 29–33.

Kenen, P.B. (1969), "The theory of optimum currency areas: an eclectic view", in R.A. Mundell and A.K. Swoboda (eds), *Monetary Problems of the International Economy*, Chicago, USA: University of Chicago Press, pp. 41–60.

Kester, A.Y. (2001), *International Reserves and Foreign Currency Liquidity: Guidelines for a Data Template*, Washington, DC: International Monetary Fund.

Keynes, J.M. (1929), "The German transfer problem", *Economic Journal*, 39 (153), pp. 1–7.

Keynes, J.M. (1930/1971), *A Treatise on Money*, Vol. I: *The Pure Theory of Money*, London and Basingstoke, UK: Macmillan.

Keynes, J.M. (1930/1983), *A Treatise on Money*, Vol. II: *The Applied Theory of Money*, London and Basingstoke, UK: Macmillan.

Keynes, J.M. (1933/1973), "A monetary theory of production", in G. Clausing (ed.), *Der Stand und die nächste Zukunft der Konjunkturforschung: Festschrift für Arthur Spiethoff*, Munich: Duncker and Humblot, pp. 123–125. Reprinted in *The Collected Writings of John Maynard Keynes*, London and New York: Macmillan and Cambridge University Press, vol. XIII, pp. 408–411.

Keynes, J.M. (1936), *The General Theory of Employment, Interest and Money*, London: Macmillan.

Keynes, J.M. (1971), *The Economic Consequences of the Peace*, in *The Collected Writings of John Maynard Keynes*, vol. II, ed. by D.E. Moggridge, London and New York: Macmillan and Cambridge University Press.

Keynes, J.M. (1978a), *Activities 1922–1932: The End of Reparations*, in *The Collected Writings of John Maynard Keynes*, vol. XVIII, ed. by D.E. Moggridge, London and New York: Macmillan and Cambridge University Press.

Keynes, J.M. (1978b), *Activities 1939–1945: Internal War Finance*, in *The Collected Writings of John Maynard Keynes*, vol. XXII, ed. by D.E. Moggridge, London and New York: Macmillan and Cambridge University Press.

Keynes, J.M. (1980), *The Collected Writings of John Maynard Keynes*, vol. XXV, *Activities 1940–1944. Shaping the Post-War World: the Clearing Union*, ed. by D.E. Moggridge, London and New York: Macmillan and Cambridge University Press.

Krugman, P. (2011), "One size fits one, redux (wonkish)", *New York Times*, 15 June, available at http://krugman.blogs.nytimes.com/2011/06/15/one-size-fits-one-redux-wonkish/?_r=0 (accessed 24 May 2016).

Bibliography   185

Lavoie, M. (1984), "Un modèle post-Keynésien d'économie monétaire fondé sur la théorie du circuit", *Économies et sociétés*, 59 (1), pp. 233–258.

Lee, J. and P.M. Crowley (2009), "Evaluating the stresses from ECB monetary policy in the euro area", *Bank of Finland Discussion Paper*, No. 11.

Machlup, F. (1963), "Reform of the international monetary system", in H.G. Grubel (ed.), *World Monetary Reform: Plans and Issues*, Stanford, CA, USA and London: Stanford University Press and Oxford University Press, pp. 253–260.

Machlup, F. (2003), *International Monetary Economics*, London: Routledge.

Martel, R.J. (1996), "Heterogeneity, aggregation, and a meaningful macroeconomics", in D. Colander (ed.), *Beyond Microfoundations: Post Walrasian Macroeconomics*, Cambridge, UK: Cambridge University Press, pp. 127–144.

Marx, K. (1847/1965), *The Poverty of Philosophy*, available online at www.marxists.org/archive/marx/works/download/pdf/Poverty-Philosophy.pdf (accessed 24 May 2016).

Marx, K. (1858/1972), *Fragment de la version primitive de la «Contribution à la critique de l'économie politique»*, in *Contribution à la critique de l'économie politique*, Paris: Éditions Sociales, pp. 176–255.

Minsky, H.P. (1986), *Stabilizing an Unstable Economy*, New Haven, CT, USA and London: Yale University Press.

Mirowski, P. (1991), *More Heat than Light: Economics as Social Physics, Physics as Nature's Economics*, Cambridge, UK: Cambridge University Press.

Morrison, R.J. (1992), "Gulf war reparations: Iraq, OPEC, and the transfer problem", *American Journal of Economics and Sociology*, 51 (4), pp. 385–399.

Ohlin, B. (1929a), "The reparation problem: transfer difficulties, real and imagined", *Economic Journal*, 39 (154), pp. 172–178.

Ohlin, B. (1929b), "Mr Keynes' views on the transfer problem: a rejoinder", *Economic Journal*, 39 (155), pp. 400–404.

Padoa-Schioppa, T. (2004), *The Euro and Its Central Bank: Getting United after the Union*, Cambridge, MA, USA: The MIT Press.

Parguez, A. (1975), *Monnaie et macroeconomie*, Paris: Economica.

Patinkin, D. (1965), *Money, Interest and Prices*, New York: Harper & Row, second edition.

Petit Robert (1979), *Dictionnaire*, Paris: Société du Nouveau Littré.

Piffaretti, N.F. (2000), *Monnaie électronique, monnaie et intermédiation bancaire*, Ph.D. dissertation, Fribourg, Switzerland: University of Fribourg.

Piffaretti, N.F. (2009), "Reshaping the international monetary architecture: lessons from the Keynes Plan", *Review of Banks and Bank Systems*, 4 (1), pp. 45–54.

Piffaretti, N.F. (2010), "Financing for retirement and the 2007–2009 unwinding of the financial sector", *European Journal of Economic and Social Systems*, 23 (1), pp. 81–96.

Piffaretti, N.F. and S. Rossi (2012), "An institutional approach to balancing international monetary relations: the case for a US–China settlement facility", *International Journal of Humanities and Social Sciences*, 2 (17), pp. 1–11.

Poulon, F. (ed.) (1985), *Les écrits de Keynes*, Paris: Dunod.

Ricardo, D. (1816/1951), *Proposals for an Economical and Secure Currency*, in P. Sraffa and M.H. Dobb (eds), *The Works and Correspondence of David Ricardo*, Vol. IV: *Pamphlets and Papers 1815–1823*, Cambridge, UK: Cambridge University Press, pp. 43–141.

Ricardo, D. (1821/1951), *On the Principles of Political Economy and Taxation*, in P. Sraffa and M.H. Dobb (eds), *The Works and Correspondence of David Ricardo*, Vol. I, Cambridge, UK: Cambridge University Press.

186   *Bibliography*

Ricardo, D. (1823/1951), "Absolute value and exchangeable value", in P. Sraffa and M.H. Dobb (eds), *The Works and Correspondence of David Ricardo*, Vol. IV: *Pamphlets and Papers 1815–1823*, Cambridge, UK: Cambridge University Press, pp. 357–412.

Ricardo, D. (1985), *Scritti monetari*, Rome: Istituto della Enciclopedia Italiana.

Robinson, J. (1937), *Introduction to the Theory of Employment*, London: Macmillan.

Rochon, L.-P. (1999), *Credit, Money and Production: An Alternative Post-Keynesian Approach*, Cheltenham, UK and Northampton, MA, USA: Edward Elgar.

Rochon, L.-P. and S. Rossi (eds) (2003), *Modern Theories of Money: The Nature and Role of Money in Capitalist Economies*, Cheltenham, UK and Northampton, MA, USA: Edward Elgar.

Rochon, L.-P. and S. Rossi (2013), "Endogenous money: the evolutionary versus revolutionary views", *Review of Keynesian Economics*, 1 (2), pp. 210–229.

Rodrik, D. (1988), "The welfare economics of debt service", *National Bureau of Economic Research Working Paper*, No. 2655.

Rossi, S. (1997), *Modalités d'institution et de fonctionnement d'une banque centrale supranationale: le cas de la Banque Centrale Européenne*, Paris: Peter Lang.

Rossi, S. (1998), "Endogenous money and banking activity: some notes on the workings of modern payment systems", *Studi economici*, 53 (3), pp. 23–56.

Rossi, S. (2001), *Money and Inflation: A New Macroeconomic Analysis*, Cheltenham, UK and Northampton, MA, USA: Edward Elgar.

Rossi, S. (2003), "Money and banking in a monetary theory of production", in L.-P. Rochon and S. Rossi (eds), *Modern Theories of Money: The Nature and Role of Money in Capitalist Economies*, Cheltenham, UK and Northampton, MA, USA: Edward Elgar, pp. 339–350.

Rossi, S. (2004a), "Monetary integration strategies and perspectives of new EU countries", *International Review of Applied Economics*, 18 (4), pp. 443–469.

Rossi, S. (2004b), "The enlargement of the euro area: what lessons can be learned from EMU?", *Journal of Asian Economics*, 14 (6), pp. 947–970.

Rossi, S. (2006a), "Cross-border transactions and exchange rate stability", in L.-P. Rochon and S. Rossi (eds), *Monetary and Exchange Rate Systems: A Global View of Financial Crises*, Cheltenham, UK and Northampton, MA, USA: Edward Elgar, pp. 191–209.

Rossi, S. (2006b), "The theory of money emissions", in P. Arestis and M. Sawyer (eds), *A Handbook of Alternative Monetary Economics*, Cheltenham, UK and Northampton, MA, USA: Edward Elgar, pp. 121–138.

Rossi, S. (2007a), "International capital flows within the European Monetary Union: increasing economic divergence between the centre and the periphery", *Intervention: European Journal of Economics and Economic Policies*, 4 (2), pp. 309–329.

Rossi, S. (2007b), "The monetary-policy relevance of an international settlement institution: the Keynes plan 60 years later", in A. Giacomin and M.C. Marcuzzo (eds), *Money and Markets: A Doctrinal Approach*, London and New York: Routledge, pp. 96–114.

Rossi, S. (2007c), *Money and Payments in Theory and Practice*, London and New York: Routledge.

Rossi, S. (2008a), "Endogenous and exogenous money and credit", in P.A. O'Hara (ed.), *International Encyclopedia of Public Policy, Volume 2: Economic Policy*, Perth, Australia: GPERU, pp. 188–198.

Rossi, S. (2008b), "Money, credit, and income distribution: a monetary circuit analysis", in P. Bini and G. Tusset (eds), *Theory and Practice of Economic Policy: Tradition and Change*, Milan, Italy: Franco Angeli, pp. 283–305.

Rossi, S. (2009a), "International payment finality requires a supranational central-bank money: reforming the international monetary architecture in the spirit of Keynes", *China–USA Business Review*, 8 (11), pp. 1–20.

Rossi, S. (2009b), "Monetary circuit theory and money emissions", in J.-F. Ponsot and S. Rossi (eds), *The Political Economy of Monetary Circuits: Tradition and Change in Post-Keynesian Economics*, Basingstoke, UK and New York: Palgrave Macmillan, pp. 36–55.

Rossi, S. (2010), "The 2007–2009 financial crisis: an endogenous-money view", *Studi e Note di Economia*, 15 (3), pp. 413–430.

Rossi, S. (2011a), "Can it happen again? Structural policies to avert further systemic crises", *International Journal of Political Economy*, 40 (2), pp. 61–78.

Rossi, S. (2011b), "Macro and financial economics need a quantum leap", *International Journal of Pluralism and Economics Education*, 2 (3), pp. 306–317.

Rossi, S. (2012), "The monetary–structural origin of TARGET2 imbalances across Euroland", in C. Gnos and S. Rossi (eds), *Modern Monetary Macroeconomics: A New Paradigm for Economic Policy*, Cheltenham, UK and Northampton, MA, USA: Edward Elgar, pp. 221–238.

Rossi, S. (2013), "Financialisation and monetary union in Europe: the monetary–structural causes of the euro-area crisis", *Cambridge Journal of Regions, Economy and Society*, 6 (3), pp. 381–400.

Rossi, S. (2015a), "The euro-area crisis: structural origins and possible exit strategies", in A. Bitzenis, N. Karagiannis and J. Marangos (eds), *Europe in Crisis: Problems, Challenges, and Alternative Perspectives*, Basingstoke, UK and New York: Palgrave Macmillan, pp. 143–154.

Rossi, S. (2015b), "Un nouvel ordre monétaire national et international", in Stiftung Zukunkftsrat (ed.), *Haushalten & Wirtschaften II: Leitideen für eine zukunftsfähige Wirtschafts- und Geldordnung*, Glarus and Chur, Switzerland: Edition Rüegger, pp. 278–281.

Rossi, S. and B. Dafflon (2012), "Repairing the original sin of the European Monetary Union", *International Journal of Monetary Economics and Finance*, 5 (2), pp. 102–123.

Rueff, J. (1963), "Gold exchange standard a danger to the West", in H.G. Grubel (ed.), *World Monetary Reform: Plans and Issues*, Stanford, CA, USA and London: Stanford University Press and Oxford University Press, pp. 320–328.

Samuelson, P.A. (1966), *The Collected Writings of Paul A. Samuelson*, Cambridge, MA, USA and London: The MIT Press.

Schmitt, B. (1959), "L'équilibre de la monnaie", *Revue d'économie politique*, 69 (6), pp. 921–950.

Schmitt, B. (1960), *La formation du pouvoir d'achat*, Paris: Sirey.

Schmitt, B. (1966a), *Monnaie, salaires et profits*, Paris: Presses Universitaires de France.

Schmitt, B. (1966b), "La monnaie au centre de la répartition", *Revue d'économie politique*, 76 (1), pp. 92–114.

Schmitt, B. (1971a), *L'analyse macroéconomique des revenus*, Paris: Dalloz.

Schmitt, B. (1971b), "Le problème de l'intégration de la monnaie", *Revue suisse d'économie politique et de statistique*, 107 (1), pp. 203–222.

Schmitt, B. (1972a), *Macroeconomic Theory: A Fundamental Revision*, Albeuve, Switzerland: Castella.

Schmitt, B. (1972b), "Vers une nouvelle théorie macro-économique?", *Revue d'économie politique*, 82 (1), pp. 139–152.

188 Bibliography

Schmitt, B. (1973), *New Proposals for World Monetary Reform*, Albeuve, Switzerland: Castella.

Schmitt, B. (1975a), *Théorie unitaire de la monnaie, nationale et internationale*, Albeuve, Switzerland: Castella.

Schmitt, B. (1975b), *Génération de la monnaie des monnaies européennes*, Albeuve, Switzerland: Castella.

Schmitt, B. (1977a), *La monnaie européenne*, Paris: Presses Universitaires de France.

Schmitt, B. (1977b), *L'or, le dollar et la monnaie supranationale*, Paris: Calmann-Lévy.

Schmitt, B. (1978a), *Teoria unitária da moeda*, São Paulo, Brazil: Editora da Universidade de São Paulo.

Schmitt, B. (1978b), *Die Theorie des Kreditgeldes*, Stuttgart, Germany: Gustav Fisher.

Schmitt, B. (1982), "Time as quantum", in M. Baranzini (ed.), *Advances in Economic Theory*, Oxford, UK and New York: Basil Blackwell and St. Martin's Press, pp. 115–125.

Schmitt, B. (1984a), *Inflation, chômage et malformations du capital: macroéconomie quantique*, Paris and Albeuve, Switzerland: Economica and Castella.

Schmitt, B. (1984b), *La France souveraine de sa monnaie*, Paris and Albeuve, Switzerland: Economica and Castella.

Schmitt, B. (1984c), *Les pays au régime du FMI. Le vice caché du système actuel des paiements internationaux*, Albeuve, Switzerland: Castella.

Schmitt, B. (1985a), "Introduzione agli scritti monetari di David Ricardo", in D. Ricardo, *Scritti monetari*, Rome: Istituto della Enciclopedia Italiana, pp. 3–85.

Schmitt, B. (1985b), "L'identité de l'offre et de la demande globales dans le temps", in A. Barrère (ed.), *Keynes aujourd'hui: théories et politiques*, Paris: Economica, pp. 171–194.

Schmitt, B. (1985c), "Un nouvel ordre monétaire international: le plan Keynes", in F. Poulon (ed.), *Les écrits de Keynes*, Paris: Dunod, pp. 195–209.

Schmitt, B. (1986), "The process of formation of economics in relation to other sciences", in M. Baranzini and R. Scazzieri (eds), *Foundations of Economics: Structures of Inquiry and Economic Theory*, Oxford, UK and New York: Basil Blackwell and St. Martin's Press, pp. 103–132.

Schmitt, B. (1987a), "Le plan Keynes: vers la monnaie internationale purement véhiculaire", in M. Zerbato (ed.), *Keynésianisme et sortie de crise*, Paris: Dunod, pp. 192–211.

Schmitt, B. (1987b), "Lo sviluppo interrotto o la crisi del capitalismo", *Fondamenti*, 8, pp. 75–105.

Schmitt, B. (1987c), "Comparaison du système et du non-système des paiements internationaux dans le cas du commerce extérieur équilibré", in M. Baranzini and A. Cencini (eds), *Contributi di analisi economica*, Bellinzona, Switzerland: Casagrande, pp. 231–249.

Schmitt, B. (1987d), "Endettement des pays: produit de l'étalon change-or", in R. Barre, A. Dunkel, G. Gaudard, A. Lamfalussy, J. L'Huillier, H. Mercillon, B. Schmitt and R. Triffin, *Les déséquilibres monétaires et financiers internationaux*, Fribourg, Switzerland: Editions Universitaires, pp. 107–174.

Schmitt, B. (1987e), "Per un'analisi epistemologica comparativa della scienza economica", *Bloc Notes*, 15–16, pp. 115–130.

Schmitt, B. (1988a), *L'ECU et les souverainetés nationales en Europe*, Paris: Dunod.

Schmitt, B. (1988b), "The identity of aggregate supply and demand in time", in A. Barrère (ed.), *The Foundation of Keynesian Analysis*, London: Macmillan, pp. 169–193.

Bibliography 189

Schmitt, B. (1988c), "Circuito monetario e moneta bancaria", in A. Graziani and M. Messori (eds), *Moneta e produzione*, Turin, Italy: Einaudi, pp. 5–43.

Schmitt, B. (1988d), "External debt: eternal debt", paper presented at the conference on "The Future of the International Monetary System" at Glendon College, Toronto, Canada: York University, March, unpublished.

Schmitt, B. (1989a), "La France appauvrie par le service da sa dette extérieure", *Economies et sociétés*, 23 (8), pp. 91–100.

Schmitt, B. (1989b), "A monetary reform", paper presented at the Gerzensee Swiss National Bank Seminar, 3 March, unpublished.

Schmitt, B. (1990), *El ECU y las soberanías monetarias en Europa*, Madrid: Editorial Paraninfo.

Schmitt, B. (1993), *Teoria unitaria della moneta, nazionale e internazionale*, Naples, Italy: Liguori.

Schmitt, B. (1993–1994), *Notes sur la théorie de l'intérêt*, Fribourg, Switzerland: University of Fribourg, mimeo.

Schmitt, B. (1994–1995), *Projet de manuscrit sur la dette extérieure*, Fribourg, Switzerland: University of Fribourg, mimeo.

Schmitt, B. (1995–1996), *Cours de théorie monétaire*, Fribourg, Switzerland: University of Fribourg, mimeo.

Schmitt, B. (1996a), "Unemployment: is there a principal cause?", in A. Cencini and M. Baranzini (eds), *Inflation and Unemployment: Contributions to a New Macroeconomic Approach*, London and New York: Routledge, pp. 75–105.

Schmitt, B. (1996b), "A new paradigm for the determination of money prices", in G. Deleplace and E.J. Nell (eds), *Money in Motion: The Post Keynesian and Circulation Approaches*, Basingstoke, UK and New York: Macmillan and St. Martin's Press, pp. 104–138.

Schmitt, B. (1996c), "Monnaie et création monétaire", in *Encyclopaedia Universalis*, Paris: Encyclopaedia Universalis, pp. 693–699.

Schmitt, B. (1996d), *Cours de théorie monétaire*, Fribourg, Switzerland: University of Fribourg, mimeo.

Schmitt, B. (1996e), *[untitled]*, Fribourg, Switzerland: University of Fribourg, mimeo.

Schmitt, B. (1996f), *[untitled]*, Fribourg, Switzerland: University of Fribourg, mimeo.

Schmitt, B. (1997), *Note à l'attention des étudiants*, Fribourg, Switzerland: University of Fribourg, mimeo.

Schmitt, B. (1998a), *Le chômage est son éradication*, Fribourg, Switzerland: University of Fribourg, mimeo.

Schmitt, B. (1998b), *Annexe au cours écrit*, Fribourg, Switzerland: University of Fribourg, mimeo.

Schmitt, B. (1999a), *Critique fondamentale de la pensée néoclassique*, Fribourg, Switzerland: University of Fribourg, mimeo.

Schmitt, B. (1999b), *Preuve analytique de l'inanité de la pensée néoclassique*, Fribourg, Switzerland: University of Fribourg, mimeo.

Schmitt, B. (1999c), *En marge du cours: quelques considérations sur les nombres en économie, dans la pensée néoclassique et au-delà*, Fribourg, Switzerland: University of Fribourg, mimeo.

Schmitt, B. (1999d), *[untitled]*, Fribourg, Switzerland: University of Fribourg, mimeo.

Schmitt, B. (1999e), *L'intérêt étant excepté, toutes les dépenses effectuées entre un pays et le reste du monde sont égales de part et d'autre*, Fribourg, Switzerland: University of Fribourg, mimeo.

190 Bibliography

Schmitt, B. (1999f), *Les intérêts dus par les résidents des pays en voie de développement à des résidents des pays riches sont payés deux fois, à savoir une première fois par les résidents concernés et une deuxième fois par une ponction dans les réserves officielles des PVD*, Fribourg, Switzerland: University of Fribourg, mimeo.

Schmitt, B. (2000a), "The double charge of external debt servicing", *Research Laboratory in Monetary Economics Working Paper*, No. 1.

Schmitt, B. (2000b), "Why the net interest on external debt weighs double on LDCs", *Research Laboratory in Monetary Economics Working Paper*, No. 3.

Schmitt, B. (2000c), *Monnaie et prix: les « achats-ventes »*, Fribourg, Switzerland: University of Fribourg, mimeo.

Schmitt, B. (2003), "Le paiement des intérêts par les PVD est *double*; les statistiques de la Banque mondiale ainsi que l'analyse le prouvent", Lugano, Switzerland: University of Lugano, mimeo.

Schmitt, B. (2004), "Between nations, the interest multiplier is equal to 2", *Research Laboratory in Monetary Economics Working Paper*, No. 12.

Schmitt, B. (2005), *Théorème de l'intérêt: le double poids des intérêts afférents aux dettes extérieures*, Lugano, Switzerland: Reaearch Laboratory in Monetary Economics, mimeo.

Schmitt, B. (2006), "Lugano, mars 2006", Lugano, Switzerland: University of Lugano, mimeo.

Schmitt, B. (2007), *Le thèorème de l'intérêt*, Lugano, Switzerland: Research Laboratory in Monetary Economics, mimeo.

Schmitt, B. (2012a), "Relative prices are undermined by a mathematical error", in C. Gnos and S. Rossi (eds), *Modern Monetary Macroeconomics: A New Paradigm for Economic Policy*, Cheltenham, UK and Northampton, MA, USA: Edward Elgar, pp. 19–38.

Schmitt, B. (2012b), "Money, effective demand, and profits", in C. Gnos and S. Rossi (eds), *Modern Monetary Macroeconomics: A New Paradigm for Economic Policy*, Cheltenham, UK and Northampton, MA, USA: Edward Elgar, pp. 71–99.

Schmitt, B. (2012c), "Sovereign debt and interest payments", in C. Gnos and S. Rossi (eds), *Modern Monetary Macroeconomics: A New Paradigm for Economic Policy*, Cheltenham, UK and Northampton, MA, USA: Edward Elgar, pp. 239–260.

Schmitt, B. (2014), "The formation of sovereign debt: diagnosis and remedy", available at http://papers.ssrn.com/sol3/papers.cfm?abstract_id=2513679 (accessed 24 May 2016).

Schmitt, B. and A. Cencini (1982), "Wages and profits in a theory of emissions", in M. Baranzini (ed.), *Advances in Economic Theory*, Oxford, UK and New York: Basil Blackwell and St. Martin's Press, pp. 137–146.

Schmitt, B. and C. De Gottardi (2003), "An internal critique of general equilibrium theory", in L.-P. Rochon and S. Rossi (eds), *Modern Theories of Money: The Nature and Role of Money in Capitalist Economies*, Cheltenham, UK and Northampton, MA, USA: Edward Elgar, pp. 265–294.

Schmitt, B. and S. Greppi (1996), "The national economy studied as a whole: aspects of circular flow analysis in the German language", in G. Deleplace and E.J. Nell (eds), *Money in Motion: The Post Keynesian and Circulation Approaches*, Basingstoke and New York: Macmillan and St. Martin's Press, pp. 341–364.

Schumacher, E.F. (1943), "Multilateral clearing", *Economica*, 10 (38), pp. 150–165.

Seccareccia, M. (1996), "Post Keynesian fundism and monetary circulation", in G. Deleplace and E. Nell (eds), *Money in Motion: The Post Keynesian and Circulation Approaches*, London and New York: Macmillan and St Martin's Press, pp. 400–416.

Servet, J.-M. (1988), "La monnaie contre l'Etat ou la fable du troc", in *Droit et monnaie: Etat et espace monétaire transnational*, Paris: Litec, pp. 49–62.

Servet, J.-M. (2012), *Les monnaies du lien*, Lyon, France: Presses Universitaires de Lyon.

Smith, A. (1776/1904), *An Inquiry into the Nature and Causes of the Wealth of Nations*, London: Methuen & Co.

Smith, A. (1776/1970), *An Inquiry into the Nature and Causes of the Wealth of Nations*, Harmondsworth, UK: Penguin.

Staley, E. (1935), *War and the Private Investor: a Study in the Relations of International Politics and International Private Investment*, Garden City, NY, USA: Doubleday, Doran & Company.

Verdon, M. (1996), *Keynes and the 'Classics': A Study in Language, Epistemology and Mistaken Identities*, London and New York: Routledge.

Walras, L. (1926), *Éléments d'économie politique pure*, in W. Jaffé (ed.) (1954), *Elements of Pure Economics*, London: George Allen & Unwin.

Werner, P. (1971), *Vers l'union monétaire européenne*, Lausanne, Switzerland: Centre de recherches européennes.

Williams, J.H. (1922), "German foreign trade and the reparation payments", *Quarterly Journal of Economics*, 36 (3), pp. 482–503.

Williams, J.H. (1930), "Reparations and the flow of capital", *American Economic Review*, 20 (1), pp. 73–79.

Williamson, J. (1977), *The Failure of World Monetary Reform, 1971–74*, New York: New York University Press.

World Bank (2015a), "External debt stocks, total (DOD, current US$)", available at http://data.worldbank.org/indicator/DT.DOD.DECT.CD (accessed 24 May 2016).

World Bank (2015b), "Gross external debt position", available at http://data.worldbank.org/data-catalog/quarterly-external-debt-statistics-ssds (accessed 24 May 2016).

World Bank (2015c), "Interest payments on external debt, total (INT, current US$)", available at http://data.worldbank.org/indicator/DT.INT.DECT.CD (accessed 24 May 2016).

World Bank (2015d), "Total reserves (includes gold, current US$)", available at http://data.worldbank.org/indicator/FI.RES.TOTL.CD (accessed 24 May 2016).

Wray, L.R. (1990), *Money and Credit in Capitalist Economies: The Endogenous Money Approach*, Cheltenham, UK and Northampton, MA, USA: Edward Elgar.

Wray, L.R. (2010), "Money", *Levy Economics Institute of Bard College Working Paper*, no. 647, Annandale-on-Hudson, New York, NY: Levy Economics Institute of Bard College.

Zerbato, M. (ed.) (1987), *Keynésianisme et sortie de crise*, Paris: Dunod.

Index

absolute exchange 33–49; absolute exchange of the isolated worker 34–8; European monetary union 138, 140; exchange on the producer services market 42–4; exchange on the product market 44–8; nature and role of money 25; overview xx, 33–4, 48–9; as a principle of economics 39–48; Schmitt and heterodox economics 12, 174, 175, 176

accumulation process *see* capital accumulation

amortization *see* capital amortization

amortization-goods 76, 77, 78, 79, 81, 82, 99

L'analyse macroéconomique des revenus (Schmitt) 6, 27

Arrow, K.J. 48

austerity 179–80

Bailly, J.-L. 173

balance of payments: European monetary union 135, 137; international monetary relations 122, 123, 125; net interest payments on external debt 110, 116, 117, 119, 121; Schmitt research and legacy 10, 16, 19; sovereign debt crisis 150, 155, 158

banking reform 85–101; department of emissions and department of saving 89–93; distinction between money and income 86; distinction between saving and fixed-capital departments 98–101; equality between sales and purchases 87–8; fundamental analytic principles 86–9; fundamental principles of

normative analysis 89–101; investment and reforming payments 61–2; macroeconomic identity of supply and demand 86–7; macroeconomic saving and investment 88–9; overview xxii–xxiii, 85, 101; structure of a fixed-capital department 93–8

bank money xxii, 2, 7, 8, 25, 44, 47, 86, 115

Bank of England 61

banks: absolute and relative exchange 43, 44, 45, 47; capitalism 69–75; European monetary union 138, 139, 142; *La formation du pouvoir d'achat* 24–7, 29; inflation and unemployment 56, 57, 61, 178; macroeconomic analysis of unemployment 65, 69–75, 82–3; nature and role of money 24–7; Schmitt research and legacy 4, 5, 8, 9, 14

Baranzini, M. 11

Barrère, A. 25

barter 33, 39, 44, 140

Beretta, E. 105, 120, 121

Blankfein, L.C. 136

Böhm-Bawerk, E. von 81

Borchert, M. 113

Bradford, W. 175

Bradley, X. 173

Brazil 113–14

Bretton Woods conference 125, 140, 177

budgetary problem 106

Bund der Steuerzahler Deutschland e.V. 120

Bundesbank 142

Bureau *see* Sovereign Bureau

Index

capital: inflation and unemployment
xx–xxi, 55, 57; macroeconomic
analysis of unemployment 66–9, 74–7,
79, 80, 83; national banking reform
xxii, 97; Schmitt research and legacy
12, 14, 15, 175
capital account (balance of payments) 116,
119
capital accumulation: accumulation
process 51–6; amortization process
57–9, 60; inflation and unemployment
xx–xxi, 50, 51–6, 57–9, 60, 178;
national banking reform 100, 101
capital amortization: accumulation process
51, 52, 55; amortization of fixed capital
75–7; amortization process 56–62;
inflation and unemployment xxi, 51,
52, 55, 56–62, 63, 178; macroeconomic
analysis of unemployment 64, 75–7;
national banking reform 99, 101;
Schmitt research and legacy 15, 178
capital gains 52, 60
capitalism 11, 51, 69–75, 80, 82, 83
capital over-accumulation 51, 52, 55,
57–9, 60, 178
capital-time 14, 93, 97
Cencini, A.: absolute exchange 49;
European monetary union 137, 141;
*External Debt Servicing: A Vicious
Circle* 11, 18, 108; international
monetary relations 126, 127, 128, 129,
131; national banking reform 93; net
interest payments on external debt 18,
108, 119, 120; *La pensée de Karl Marx*
10, 11, 30; Schmitt and heterodox
economics 173, 174, 175, 176, 177,
178, 179, 180; sovereign debt crisis
144–57
central bank 47, 115, 139, 140, 142, 143
Centre National de la Recherche
Scientifique (CNRS) xvii
China 131
circuit of incomes xx, 12, 52–6, 62, 88
circuit of money 5, 7–9, 25, 26, 88, 128
circuit of profits xx, 54–5, 56, 59
clearing system 122–5, 127, 133, 177, 179
CNRS *see* Centre National de la Recherche
Scientifique
commercial banks 4, 61, 89

commercial exports/imports 110, 111, 117,
118, 150
commodity money 30, 136
common currency xxv, 135, 139, 140, 142,
177, 179
conceptual definitions 1
consumption: absolute exchange and
relative exchange 33–43, 45, 48–9;
inflation and unemployment 53, 54, 60;
nature and role of money xix, 23, 24;
production–consumption relation 36–8,
42, 44, 45; saving and investment 88;
Schmitt and heterodox economics 174,
176; Schmitt research and legacy 2, 3,
6, 12, 13
consumption-goods 77, 79, 82, 99, 100
'cost-push' inflation 178
creation-destruction 36, 37, 48, 65
credit 115, 138, 140
Crowley, P.M. 142
currencies xxv, 16, 115, 135, 138–43,
166–70, 177–9
current account (balance of payments) 19,
108, 110–11, 114, 116, 119, 121

Dafflon, B. 138, 141
Dawes Committee 106
debt 4, 8 *see also* external debt
debt clock (*Schuldenuhr*) 120
deflation xxii, 6, 9, 12, 15, 52, 87, 125
Defoe, D. 34, 35, 37
De Gottardi, C. 17, 173
demand: global demand 6–7, 9, 15, 75, 87,
89, 128, 178; inflation and
unemployment 178; international
monetary relations 126, 127;
Keynesian multiplier 28, 29; national
banking reform 86–7, 89; Schmitt
research and legacy 6, 7, 9, 15, 17, 18,
31
'demand-pull' inflation 178
depersonalized firm xxi, 15, 95–9, 101,
178
developing countries *see* Least Developed
Countries
Dieterlen, P. 35
disembodied firm xxi, 15, 95–9, 101, 178
distributed profit 73, 76
distribution 66

194 *Index*

dividends 26, 54, 55, 56, 62, 98
division of labour xx, 39, 41, 42, 46
dollar standard 11, 123, 140, 176
domestic economy: absolute exchange
and relative exchange 33–49; *La
formation du pouvoir d'achat* 23–32;
inflation and unemployment 50–63;
macroeconomic analysis of
unemployment 64–84; national
banking reform 85–101; overview
xviii–xxiii, 177–8
domestic payments: international monetary
relations xxiv, 133; national banking
reform 85, 88, 93, 96, 98, 100–1;
Schmitt research and legacy 14, 178;
sovereign debt crisis 146, 148, 160,
162–4
double charge: first formal proof 147–51;
international monetary relations 133;
net interest payments on external debt
107, 108; reason double charge has
gone unnoticed 154–6; Schmitt and
heterodox economics 179; second
formal proof 151–2; solution to the
sovereign debt crisis 160–2, 164;
sovereign debt crisis 146, 147–51,
152–6, 169–70; third formal proof
152–4
double-entry bookkeeping: European
monetary union 137, 138, 139;
international monetary relations 125,
126; national banking reform 86, 87,
89; net interest payments on external
debt 19, 115, 118, 121
dual production 15, 59, 63

e-banking 115
ECB *see* European Central Bank
economic agents 7–8, 31, 38–40, 48, 57,
85–7, 89, 115
Economic and Monetary Union (EMU)
141, 142
economic growth 57, 93
'economic miracle' 59
economics *see* heterodox economics;
macroeconomics
economic value 4, 8, 25, 98
effective demand xix, 3, 6, 29, 126
efficiency 66, 69, 74, 122–3, 128

electronic money 109
Elliott, G.A. 121
emissions xx–xxi, 12–15, 17, 34–8, 40, 43,
44, 69, 89–93, 126, 133
employment 69, 169, 170, 171
empty debt 114, 121
empty emissions ('empty money') 15, 56,
63, 73, 178
EMU (Economic and Monetary Union)
141, 142 *see also* European monetary
union
endogenous money 34, 174, 177
"L'équilibre de la monnaie" (Schmitt) 1
EU *see* European Union
euro 11, 131, 135, 141, 142
euro-area crisis: European monetary
union xxiv–xxv, 135–8, 141–3; net
interest payments on external debt
108; Schmitt and heterodox economics
177, 179, 180; sovereign debt crisis
144
European Central Bank (ECB) xxv, 136,
137, 162
European Commission 162
European Monetary Fund 11
European monetary union 135–43;
crisis-prone monetary architecture of
the euro area 141–3; new theory of
money and monetary union 138–41;
overview xxiv–xxv, 135–6, 143; radical
critique of money and monetary union
136–8; Schmitt and heterodox
economics 176–7, 179
European Union (EU) 11, 131, 135, 144,
177
Eurostat 120
exchange *see* absolute exchange; relative
exchange
exchange economy xviii, xix, 132, 140,
174, 176
exchange rates 16, 135, 138, 141, 142
exogenous money 36, 174
exploitation theory 41
exports: international monetary relations
124, 128; net interest payments on
external debt 19, 110–13, 116, 117,
118; sovereign debt crisis 145–7,
149–53, 155, 156, 168, 169; sovereign
debt crisis solution 158–65, 167

external debt 105–21; definition 144, 145; international monetary relations 131; net interest payments on external debt 105–21; overview xxiii, 105, 120–1; pathology of net interest on external debt 116–20; reparation and (net) interest payments 105–8; Schmitt research and legacy 16, 18–20, 179; secondary burden 108–16; sovereign debt crisis xxv, xxvi, 144, 145, 148, 152–4, 156–7; sovereign debt crisis solution 158–9, 162, 164, 165–8

External Debt Servicing: A Vicious Circle (Cencini and Schmitt) 11, 18, 108

fable of barter 39
factor market 175
factors of production 24, 56, 58, 66–8, 175
Fedwire 121
Feldstein, M. 142
Fieleke, N.S. 121
financial account (balance of payments) 19, 110, 116, 119
financial bubble 20, 145, 147, 162, 180
financial imports/exports 110, 111, 117, 118, 150
financial market 59–60, 63, 69, 81, 100–1, 127
financial wages 26
firms: absolute exchange 40, 43; as intermediaries 57–8; Keynesian multiplier 29; Schmitt research and legacy 2, 3, 5, 9
fiscal austerity 179–80
fiscal policy 141
Fischer, S. 141
Fisher, I. 36–8
fixed capital: amortization of fixed capital 75–7; distinction between saving and fixed-capital departments 98–101; inflation and unemployment 55, 57, 59, 63; macroeconomic analysis of unemployment xxi, xxii, 75–7; national banking reform 88, 93–101; Schmitt research and legacy 14, 15; structure of a fixed-capital department 93–8
foreign currency (inflows/outflows): net interest payments on external debt 106, 112, 113, 116, 117, 118;

Schmitt research and legacy 19, 20; sovereign debt crisis 159, 166–7, 168, 169, 170
foreign debt 108, 145–8, 153–6, 161–4, 168, 179
foreign exchange reserves xxiii, 111, 113–15, 118–20, 138, 148
La formation du pouvoir d'achat (Schmitt) 23–32; fundamental revision of macroeconomic theory 27–9; historical perspective 23–32; nature and role of money 23–7; overview xviii, 23, 31–2; reference to the history of monetary theory 29–31; Schmitt research and legacy 1–3, 4
The formation of sovereign debt: diagnosis and remedy (Schmitt) xviii
France 16, 129
La France souveraine de sa monnaie (Schmitt) 16
Friboulet, J.-J. 173
full employment 69, 76, 81, 82
Funk–Schacht Plan 123

Galano III, A. 114
GDP *see* Gross Domestic Product
general equilibrium model 3, 18, 54, 174
General Theory (Keynes) xvii, xviii–xix, 1, 7, 23, 29
Génération de la monnaie des monnaies européennes (Schmitt) 10, 11
Germany: European monetary union xxv, 136, 141–2; international monetary relations 122, 123, 129–30; net interest payments on external debt xxiii, 105–7, 120; reparation payments xxiii, 105–8, 116, 120–1, 122, 129–30; sovereign debt crisis 170
Glass–Steagall Act 61
global demand and supply 6–7, 9, 15, 75, 87, 89, 128, 178
Gnos, C. 25, 49, 173
gold 11, 118
'golden rule' 9, 89
goods market 54, 55
Graeber, D. 39
Graziani, A. 25, 46
Greece 142, 145, 180
Greppi, S. 173

196   Index

Gross Domestic Product (GDP) 59, 112, 121, 138
gross profits 51, 59, 60
growth 51, 57, 59, 83, 93, 138

Harcourt, G.C. 175
Hayek, F.A. 35
heterodox economics: overview xxvii, 173–4, 180; Schmitt and heterodox economics 173–80; Schmitt on conceptual and methodological grounds 174–7; Schmitt on real-world economic issues 177–80
Hicks, J. 46, 137
Horsefield, J.K. 125, 131
"How to Pay for the War" memorandum (Keynes) 122
Hume, D. 43

imports: international monetary relations 124, 128; net interest payments on external debt 19–20, 110–13, 116–18, 179; sovereign debt crisis 145–51, 152–7, 168, 169, 172; sovereign debt crisis solution 158–64, 165–8; surplus imports no longer create external debt 165–8
impossibility theorem 48
income: absolute exchange and relative exchange xx, 36, 40, 42–8; circuit of incomes xx, 12, 52–6, 62, 88; definition 139, 168; European monetary union 139; formation and spending of income 23–7; *La formation du pouvoir d'achat* 23–9, 31–2; fundamental revision of macroeconomic theory 27–9; inflation and unemployment xx, 52–6, 62, 63; international monetary relations 127; macroeconomic analysis of unemployment xxi, 65–9, 72–4, 81, 83, 84; money and income 65–9, 86; national banking reform xxii, 86, 88–93, 97; net interest payments on external debt 112; reference to the history of monetary theory 29–31; Schmitt and heterodox economics 176; Schmitt research and legacy xix, 2, 3, 5–7, 9, 12–15; sovereign debt crisis 168, 171

inertia 73
inflation 50–63; accumulation process 51–6; amortization process 56–62; definition 177; international monetary relations 126; national banking reform xxii, xxiii, 85, 87, 88, 100; over-accumulation and inflation 57–9; overview xx–xxi, 50, 62; Schmitt and heterodox economics 177–8, 180; Schmitt research and legacy 6, 9, 12, 15, 16, 173; sovereign debt crisis 171; and unemployment 50–63
Inflation, chômage et malformations du capital (Schmitt) xviii, xxii, 5, 11–16, 29, 62
Inland Revenue 159
interest xxiii, 18, 19, 61, 80–2, 120–1, 140, 142
interest-goods 71, 72, 74, 75, 79, 80
interest profit 70, 71, 75, 83
international clearing union 123–4, 125, 177, 179
international economy: European monetary union 135–43; Keynes, Schumacher and international monetary relations 122–34; net interest payments on external debt 105–21; overview xxiii–xxvii, 176, 178–9; Schmitt and heterodox economics 173–80; sovereign debt crisis 144–57; sovereign debt crisis solution 158–72
international euro xxv, 135
International Investment Position (IIP) 111–12
International Monetary Fund 109, 112, 117, 125, 143, 162
international monetary relations 122–34; international system of payments for the global village 130–2; overview xxiii–xxiv, 10, 122–3, 133–4, 178–9; proposal for a new system of international payments 123–5; Schmitt's advances 125–7; special set of financial relations 127–30
international payments: international monetary relations xxiii, xxiv, 123–5, 129, 130–2, 133; international system of payments for the global village

130–2; proposal for a new system of international payments 123–5; Schmitt and heterodox economics 176, 179; Schmitt research and legacy 7, 10, 11, 16, 19, 20; sovereign debt crisis xxvi, 146, 154, 157, 165

invested profit: inflation 178; macroeconomic analysis of unemployment 70, 71, 73, 75, 83, 84; national banking reform 95, 96, 98, 100, 101

investment: definition 55–6; inflation and unemployment 51, 55–6, 57, 61–2; Keynesian multiplier 27; national banking reform 88–9, 97; and saving 88–9; Schmitt research and legacy xix, 2, 3, 7, 14

investment banks 61

investment-goods 73, 75–8, 81, 82, 99

involuntary unemployment 51, 52, 60–1, 88, 178, 180

Irvine, C. 136

Italy 145

Joint Committee of the Nuffield College Reconstruction Survey 122

"Joint Statement by Experts on the Establishment of the International Monetary Fund, April 1944" 125, 131

Kalecki, M. 122

Kenen, P.B. 141

Kester, A.Y. 115

key currencies 16, 140, 178

Keynesian multiplier 3, 6, 7, 27

Keynes, J.M.: absolute exchange and relative exchange xix, 33, 40; European monetary union 139, 140; *La formation du pouvoir d'achat* 23, 24, 27, 28, 29, 30, 31; *General Theory* xvii, xviii–xix, 1, 7, 23, 29; "How to Pay for the War" memorandum 122; international monetary relations xxiii–xxiv, 122, 123, 125–7, 129, 130, 133; macroeconomic analysis of unemployment 67, 81; money and purchasing power xviii–xix; net interest payments on external debt xxiii, 105, 106; saving and investment 88; Schmitt

and heterodox economics 175, 177; Schmitt research and legacy 1, 2, 3, 4, 6, 14, 16; *Treatise on Money* 1, 7, 29, 126, 129

Keynes–Ohlin–Rueff debate xxiii, 105, 120

Keynes Plan xxiv, 124, 126, 131, 132, 133, 140, 179

Krugman, P. 142

labour: absolute exchange and relative exchange 35–8, 39, 43; formation and spending of income 24; inflation and unemployment 53, 55; macroeconomic analysis of unemployment 64, 66–9, 74, 75, 83; national banking reform 97, 98; Schmitt research and legacy 4, 6, 175

labour theory of value 11, 30

Latin America 113–14

Lavoie, M. 25

Lavoisier's law 38, 65

Least Developed Countries (LDCs) xxiii, 19, 105, 107–8, 119–20, 128, 141, 144

Lee, J. 142

Leihzins 81

loanable funds 83, 91

loan disbursements 113, 114, 118, 119

loans: inflation and unemployment 55, 61; macroeconomic analysis of unemployment 69–73, 75, 83; national banking reform 89, 100; nature and role of money 27; net interest payments on external debt 107, 110, 118; sovereign debt crisis 145–8, 150–6, 172; sovereign debt crisis solution 161, 163, 164, 166, 167

Maastricht criteria 141

Machlup, F. 113, 143

macroeconomic analysis of unemployment 64–84; amortization of fixed capital 75–7; banks and capitalism 69–75; explanation of unemployment 77–82; money and income 65–9; overview xxi–xxii, 64; reform to defeat unemployment 82–4

macroeconomics: absolute exchange and relative exchange 33, 43, 48;

198 *Index*

fundamental revision of macroeconomic theory 27–9; international monetary relations 122, 125, 126; macroeconomic identity of supply and demand 86–7; net interest payments on external debt 115; Schmitt research and legacy 6, 7, 176; sovereign debt crisis 158, 159

Macroeconomic Theory: A Fundamental Revision (Schmitt) 7, 27

malformation of capital xx, 51, 56, 62

manufacturing 53, 82

Martel, R.J. 176

Marx, K. 11, 30, 41, 44, 49, 67, 80, 178

mathematical modelling 7, 18, 39

methodological individualism xx, 33

microeconomics 33, 39, 158–9, 176

migration 132

Minsky, H.P. 38

Mirowski, P. 49

monetary circuit 5, 7–9, 25, 26, 88, 128

monetary economy of exchange 140

monetary emissions xx, 17, 125, 126, 133

monetary policy 86, 141

monetary rate of interest 81, 82

monetary theory xix, 29–31, 138

monetary union *see* European monetary union

money: absolute exchange and relative exchange xx, 33, 34, 36–8, 40–8; as asset–liability xxv, 7–10, 38, 78, 86, 135, 139; circuit of incomes xx, 12, 52–6, 62, 88; circuit of money 5, 7–9, 25, 26, 88, 128; European monetary union 135, 136–8, 143; *La formation du pouvoir d'achat* xviii–xix, 23–7, 28, 29–31, 32; history of monetary theory 29–31; international monetary relations 123, 126; lack of physicality of modern money 115; macroeconomic analysis of unemployment 64, 65–9, 78, 79; money and income 65–9, 86; national banking reform xxii, 86, 87, 88, 99; nature and role of money 23–7; net interest payments on external debt 109, 114, 115; new theory of money and monetary union 138–41; Schmitt and heterodox economics 174, 175;

Schmitt research and legacy 1–6, 7–9, 11, 12, 15, 16–17; as unit of account 2, 25, 30

La monnaie européenne (Schmitt) 10, 11

Monnaie, salaires et profits (Schmitt) xviii, 3–6, 31

Morrison, R.J. 106

multilateral clearing 123, 127, 133

national banking reform 85–101; department of emissions and department of saving 89–93; distinction between money and income 86; distinction between saving and fixed-capital departments 98–101; equality between sales and purchases 87–8; fundamental analytic principles 86–9; fundamental principles of normative analysis 89–101; investment and reforming payments 61–2; macroeconomic identity of supply and demand 86–7; macroeconomic saving and investment 88–9; overview xxii–xxiii, 85, 101; structure of a fixed-capital department 93–8

national central banks 47, 115, 139, 140, 142, 143

National Clearing Fund 127

national income: absolute exchange and relative exchange 38, 44, 48; definition 168; *La formation du pouvoir d'achat* 24, 28, 30, 32; international monetary relations 126; macroeconomic identity of supply and demand 87; Schmitt research and legacy xix, 5, 6; sovereign debt crisis 168

national production 74, 87, 125, 168, 170–1

natural rate of interest 80, 81, 82

negative money 43, 46

neoclassical economics 3, 7, 17–18, 30–1, 136–7, 140, 174

net imports 154, 156–7, 161–3, 166, 168, 169, 172, 179

net interest payments on external debt 105–21; overview xxiii, 105, 120–1; pathology affecting (net) interest on external debt 116–20; reparation and (net) interest payments 105–8; Schmitt

research and legacy 18, 19; secondary burden 108–16
net profits 51, 59, 60
"A new paradigm for the determination of money prices" (Schmitt) 17
New Proposals for World Monetary Reform (Schmitt) 7, 142
nominal definitions 1
nominal money 5, 17, 25
nominal wages 5, 6
normative analysis: department of emissions and department of saving 89–93; distinction between saving and fixed-capital departments 98–101; fundamental principles 89–101; international monetary relations 131; national banking reform xxii, 85, 88; structure of a fixed-capital department 93–8
numéraire 31, 40

Ohlin, B. 129
L'or, le dollar et la monnaie supranationale (Schmitt) 10, 11
output: absolute exchange and relative exchange xx, 35, 37, 40–1, 43; national banking reform 99; national production 74, 87, 125, 168, 170–1; Schmitt and heterodox economics 175; Schmitt research and legacy 1, 3, 5, 6, 12
over-accumulation of capital 51, 52, 55, 57–9, 60, 178
over-indebtedness 55, 59–61

Padoa-Schioppa, T. 141
Parguez, A. 25
Patinkin, D. 31
Les pays au régime du FMI (Schmitt) 16, 144
La pensée de Karl Marx, critique et synthèse (Cencini and Schmitt) 10, 11, 30
physical productivity 66–9, 75, 98
Piffaretti, N.F. 123, 129, 131, 132
Portugal 145
positive analysis 87, 88, 131
pound sterling 123
poverty 122–3

prices 3, 13, 14, 17–18, 28
private internal/external debt 109
"The process of formation of economics in relation to other sciences" (Schmitt) 17
producing services market 54, 55, 56, 68, 69, 79
production: absolute exchange and relative exchange 33–41, 42–4, 45, 48–9; definition 62; inflation and unemployment 53, 54, 55, 60, 62, 178; international monetary relations 126; macroeconomic identity of supply and demand 86–7; national production 74, 87, 125, 168, 170–1; new theory of money and monetary union 139; physical and value productivity 66; Schmitt and heterodox economics 174, 175, 176, 178; Schmitt research and legacy 2, 3, 6, 12, 13; sovereign debt crisis 170–1
production–consumption relation 36–8, 42, 44, 45
productivity 66–9, 75, 100, 129, 141
product markets 44–8, 68
profit: circuit of profits xx, 54–5, 56, 59; inflation and unemployment xx, 51, 54–5, 58–62, 178; macroeconomic analysis of unemployment xxi, xxii, 64–9, 70–3, 76, 80, 83–4; national banking reform xxii, 88, 94–100; nature and role of money 26; profits cannot exceed wages 70–3; Schmitt and heterodox economics 175, 178; Schmitt research and legacy 3, 5, 6, 11, 13, 14, 15
profit-goods 71, 74–5, 78, 80
Projet de manuscript sur la dette extérieure (Schmitt) 18
public debt xxv, 109, 120, 121, 144, 179
purchasing power: absolute exchange and relative exchange 41, 46; European monetary union 135, 136, 137, 139, 140; *La formation du pouvoir d'achat* 24, 25, 27, 28, 30–2; inflation 59, 177; international monetary relations 128, 129, 130; macroeconomic analysis of unemployment 68, 72, 73, 83; macroeconomic identity of supply and demand 87; overview xviii–xix;

200 *Index*

Schmitt research and legacy 2, 3, 4, 5, 17, 177; sovereign debt crisis 171

quantum macroeconomics: absolute exchange and relative exchange 33, 34, 48; *La formation du pouvoir d'achat* 29, 31–2; international monetary relations 127, 129, 130, 133; national banking reform xxii, 86, 88; net interest payments on external debt 107, 108; Schmitt research and legacy xvii. 14–17, 173
quantum time 11–14, 29, 35, 53–4

real balance effect 31
real emissions 12–13, 34–8, 40, 43
real-exchange economy xix, 33
real income 72, 73, 168, 169
real money 7, 17, 25, 29, 43, 73
reform: net interest payments on external debt 179, 180; Schmitt and heterodox economics 176, 179; sovereign debt crisis 157, 168–72; *see also* national banking reform
relative exchange: absolute exchange and relative exchange xix, xx, 33; absolute exchange as a principle of economics 40, 44, 46, 47; absolute exchange of the isolated worker 36; nature and role of money 25; Schmitt and heterodox economics 175, 177
relative prices 3, 17–18, 31, 46, 174
"Relative prices are undermined by a mathematical error" (Schmitt) 17
reparation payments xxiii, 105–8, 116, 120–1, 122, 129–30
reproduction of capital 76–7
Ricardo, D. xix, 16, 17, 30, 49, 61, 67, 133, 136
Robertson, D. xvii
Robinson Crusoe (Defoe) 34–8
Robinson, J. 44
Rochon, L.-P. 25, 174
Rodrik, D. 113
Rossi, S.: European monetary union 137, 138, 140, 141; international monetary relations 131; Schmitt and heterodox economics 173, 174, 177, 178, 179
Rueff, J. 130, 138, 140, 176

sales and purchases 87–8, 89, 149–50, 161, 170
Samuelson, P.A. xix, 7
satisfaction 34, 35, 36, 37, 38, 42, 48
saving: department of emissions and the department of saving 89–93; distinction between saving and fixed-capital departments 98–101; national banking reform 88–93, 98–101; saving and investment 88–9; Schmitt research and legacy xix, 7, 14
Say's law xix, 8, 28, 38
Schmitt, B.: absolute exchange and relative exchange xx, 33–8, 41–4, 46, 48, 49; *L'analyse macroéconomique des revenus* 6, 27; background xvii; "L'équilibre de la monnaie" 1; European monetary union xxiv–xxv, 135, 136–41, 142, 143; on external debt 18–20; *External Debt Servicing: A Vicious Circle* 11, 18, 108; formation and spending of income 23–7; *La formation du pouvoir d'achat* xviii, 1–3, 4, 23–32; *The formation of sovereign debt: diagnosis and remedy* xviii; *La France souveraine de sa monnaie* 16; fundamental revision of macroeconomic theory 27–9; *Génération de la monnaie des monnaies européennes* 10, 11; and heterodox economics xxvii, 173–80; inflation and unemployment xx–xxi, 50, 51, 53–5, 57, 61–3; *Inflation, chômage et malformations du capital* xviii, xxii, 5, 11–16, 29, 62; "An internal critique of general equilibrium theory" 17; international monetary relations xxiv, 125–7, 128–34; *L'or, le dollar et la monnaie supranationale* 10, 11; macroeconomic analysis of unemployment xxi–xxii, 64–84; *Macroeconomic Theory: A Fundamental Revision* 7, 27; main achievements since mid-1980s 16–20; *Modern Monetary Macroeconomics* (Gnos and Rossi) 108–9; *La monnaie européenne* 10, 11; *Monnaie, salaires et profits* xviii, 3–6, 31; national banking reform xxii–xxiii, 85–7, 89,

93, 96–100; nature and role of money xviii–xix; net interest payments on external debt xxiii, 105, 107–9, 111, 112, 114–16, 119, 120; "A new paradigm for the determination of money prices" 17; *New Proposals for World Monetary Reform* 7, 142; *Les pays au regime du FMI* 16, 144; *La pensée de Karl Marx, critique et synthèse* 10, 11, 30; "The process of formation of economics in relation to other sciences" 17; *Projet de manuscript sur la dette extérieure* 18; reference to the history of monetary theory 29–31; on relative prices 17–18; "Relative prices are undermined by a mathematical error" 17; research from 1959 to 1966 1–6; research from 1966 to 1984 6–11; research in 1984 11–16; research work and scientific legacy xvii, xviii, 1–20; solution to the sovereign debt crisis 158–72; "Sovereign debt and interest payments" 19; sovereign debt crisis xxv–xxvii, 144, 145, 147–57; *Le théorème de l'intérêt* 19; *Théorie unitaire de la monnaie, nationale et internationale* xviii, 7–10, 87; "Time as quantum" 11; "Vers une nouvelle théorie macro-économique?" 7; "Wages and profits in a theory of emissions" 11

Schumacher, E.F. xxiii–xxiv, 122, 123–4, 125, 127, 132, 133

Seccareccia, M. 25

secondary burden xxiii, 108–16, 118

Servet, J.-M. 39

single currency xxv, 135, 138–43, 179

Smith, A. 25, 30, 34, 39, 44, 67

Sovereign Bureau xxvii, 148, 159, 160, 162, 163, 165–8

"Sovereign debt and interest payments" (Schmitt) 19

sovereign debt crisis 144–57; definition of sovereign debt 109, 144; external debt and net imports 156–7; first formal proof of the double charge 147–51; overview xxv–xxvii, 144; reason double charge has gone unnoticed 154–6; Schmitt research and legacy 16,

19–20, 179, 180; second formal proof of pathological nature of sovereign debts 151–2; solution to the sovereign debt crisis 158–72; sovereign debt 144–7; third formal proof of duplication of external debts 152–4

sovereign debt crisis solution 158–72; certainty that gains are net and final 161–5; main leading ideas of the reform 159–68; new presentation of the reform 168–72; overview 158–9; surplus imports and external debt 165–8

Spain 142, 145

Special Drawing Rights (SDR) 118, 131

Sraffa, P. xvii

Staley, E. 106

sterling 123

supply: *La formation du pouvoir d'achat* 28, 29, 31; global supply 6–7, 9, 15, 75, 87, 89, 128, 178; inflation and unemployment 178; international monetary relations 126; macroeconomic identity of supply and demand 86–7; Schmitt research and legacy 6, 7, 9, 15, 17, 18

supranational currency 8, 11, 179

surplus value 11, 67

TARGET2 system xxv, 121, 135, 136, 137

Le théorème de l'intérêt (Schmitt) 19

Théorie unitaire de la monnaie, nationale et internationale (Schmitt) xviii, 7–10, 87

"Time as quantum" (Schmitt) 11

time quantum 11–14, 29, 35, 53–4

transfer problem 106

Treatise on Money (Keynes) 1, 7, 29, 126, 129

Treaty of Versailles 106

Troika 162, 167, 170

unemployment: accumulation process 51–6; amortization of fixed capital 75–7; amortization process 56–62; banks and capitalism 69–75; European monetary union 138, 141; explanation of unemployment 77–82; inflation and unemployment 50–63; international monetary relations 122, 126;

202   *Index*

investment and reforming payments 61–2; Keynesian multiplier 28, 29; macroeconomic analysis 64–84; money and income 65–9; national banking reform xxii, xxiii, 85, 88, 100; over-indebtedness and unemployment 59–61; overview xx–xxii, 50, 62, 64; reform to defeat unemployment 82–4; Schmitt and heterodox economics 15, 177, 178, 180; sovereign debt crisis xxvii, 148, 169, 170, 171
United Kingdom 124
United States 124, 125, 131
US dollar 11, 123, 140, 176

value: absolute exchange and relative exchange 34, 36, 41; history of monetary theory 30, 31; macroeconomic analysis of unemployment 82; national banking reform 98; nature and role of money 25; Schmitt research and legacy 11, 13, 14, 175
value productivity 66, 68, 69, 75
Verdon, M. 136
"Vers une nouvelle théorie macro-économique?" (Schmitt) 7

wage-goods xxi, 71–2, 75–6, 78–9, 82, 99–100
wages: absolute exchange and relative exchange 40–5, 48; *La formation du pouvoir d'achat* 24, 25–6, 31; inflation and unemployment 54–5, 57, 58, 59, 61; international monetary relations 127; macroeconomic analysis of unemployment xxi, 64–8, 69–71, 72–6, 78, 79, 82; national banking reform 86, 87, 90–6, 99, 100; Schmitt and heterodox economics 174, 175; Schmitt research and legacy 4–6, 12–14
"Wages and profits in a theory of emissions" (Schmitt) 11
Walras, L. 17, 18, 31, 67, 174
war reparations xxiii, 105–8, 116, 120–1, 122, 129–30
Werner, P. 138
Wicksell, K. 80, 81
Williams, J.H. 106, 107
Williamson, J. 140, 176, 179
World Bank 114, 120, 143
World War I 106, 122
World War II 61, 106, 122, 124, 133
Wray, L.R. 38, 42